Home Education and Constitutional Liberties

JOHN W. WHITEHEAD
WENDELL R. BIRD

Home Education and Constitutional Liberties

*The Historical and Constitutional Arguments
in Support of Home Instruction*

Second Edition, Revised

THE RUTHERFORD INSTITUTE REPORT: VOLUME 2

CROSSWAY BOOKS • WESTCHESTER, ILLINOIS
A DIVISION OF GOOD NEWS PUBLISHERS

Note: This book is not intended to be, and does not constitute, the
giving of legal advice. Particular court decisions may not apply to
particular factual situations, or may not be legally binding in
particular jurisdictions. The existence of many unfavorable
decisions indicates that reliance should not be placed on the
favorable decisions as necessarily dispositive or assuring victory.
This book is not intended to substitute for individual reliance on
privately retained legal counsel.

Contents

Preface   7

Part I: Parental Liberty and the Educational Dilemma

1. The Dilemma in Education   13

2. The Overlooked History of Home Education   23

3. Parental Liberty and Education   28

   *Part II: Freedoms of Religion and Privacy and
          Other Basic Liberties*

4. The Freedom of Religion   37

5. The Freedom of Speech and Belief   49

6. The Right to Privacy and Other
   Constitutional Liberties   53

   *Part III: Compulsory Education Statutes and
          Their Requirements*

7. Statutes Requiring "Public or Private Schools"
   or Requiring "Equivalent Education"   63

8. Teacher Certification Requirements   72

Part IV: Compelling State Interests and
Least Burdensome Means

9. Alleged Compelling State Interests   83
10. The Least Burdensome Means   96
11. The Educational Merit of Home Education   101

Part V: Superseded and Erroneous Court Decisions

12. Superseded Court Decisions   107
13. Erroneous Court Decisions   113

Conclusion

14. Practical Suggestions for Home Education   123
15. Freedom in Education   129
    Reading List   *131*
    Organizations and Curricula   *133*
    The Authors   *145*

Preface

Families should be encouraged to take a larger—not smaller—role in the education of the young. Parents willing to teach their own children at home should be aided by the schools, not regarded as freaks or lawbreakers. And parents should have more, not less, influence on the schools.

Alvin Toffler
The Third Wave

There is a growing movement of parents to educate their children independently of the public and private school settings. Referred to as "home education," "home instruction," "home schooling," "deschooling," or "unschooling," this educational alternative has proliferated in recent years.

In the following pages, this important subject is discussed in both its historical and constitutional aspects. The historical perspective reveals that home education was once a primary form of education in America. In fact, many of America's great leaders, writers, and educators have been products of home education.

The constitutional perspective stresses several fundamental constitutional rights that protect home instruction. Concomitant with the rise in home education has been the increase in legal confrontation between parents and authorities enforcing (or misapplying) state compulsory education laws. This has raised many important constitutional issues such as the liberty of parents to educate their children at home and, among others, the freedom of speech and belief, the freedom of religion, as well as the right to privacy.*

In what follows, it must not be forgotten that home education is vitally important because it concerns our country's basic institution—the family. Because home education touches the very core of our nation's life, it should, as Alvin Toffler advocates in *The Third Wave,* be encouraged and nurtured, not maligned or attacked.

The authors personally support conventional nonpublic education rather than home education for their children; thus, they are not biased in favor of home education by their own family decisions. However, they recognize the importance of the constitutional rights in-

*On behalf of the Rutherford Institute, the authors have prepared an exhaustive legal brief (120 pages), with thorough appendix (160 pages), that provides a technical legal defense of home education. They filed such briefs with the Georgia Supreme Court in the case of *Roemhild v State* and with the North Carolina Supreme Court in *Delconte v State.* Both of those state supreme courts ruled in favor of home instruction on statutory grounds, and in doing so relied on the cases and arguments presented in the Rutherford briefs (which were not generally raised in the other parties' briefs). The authors have filed similar briefs in the Minnesota Supreme Court, the Arkansas Court of Appeals, and other courts.

The Rutherford Institute will file this brief in similar cases. For more information write: The Rutherford Institute, P.O. Box 510, Manassas, Virginia 22110.

The authors gratefully thank David J. Myers of University of Chicago Law School for his editorial assistance.

volved, and the ramifications for the family raised, in the state's frequent assertion of control over home education and ultimately over the child.

The future of valuable constitutional rights, and possibly even the family itself, may depend on how we deal with home education in the coming years. Certainly, little could be more important.

John W. Whitehead
Manassas, Virginia

Wendell R. Bird
Atlanta, Georgia

PART ONE

Parental Liberty
and
the Educational Dilemma

The decline in public education has placed many parents in an educational dilemma. Many have selected home education, often only to be challenged by state authorities.

In Part One of this book, the educational dilemma is analyzed. The historical perspective that supports home education as a valid educational alternative is discussed. Finally, the right to parental liberty is discussed in its historical and constitutional context.

1

The Dilemma in Education

A child educated only at school is an uneducated child.

George Santayana

American schools are in trouble. In fact, the problems of schooling are of such crippling proportions that many schools may not survive. It is possible that our entire public education system is nearing collapse.[1]

News Report on Educational Study

So reads the frank opening passage to an extensive report on public education prepared by John I. Goodlad, dean of the UCLA Graduate School of Education.

The Degeneration of Public Education

Another study, conducted by the National Commission on Excellence in Education, likewise highlights the academic decline in public education:

[T]he educational foundations of our society are presently being eroded by a rising tide of mediocrity that

13

threatens our very future as a Nation and a people. . . . If an unfriendly foreign power had attempted to impose on America the mediocre educational performance that exists today, we might well have viewed it as an act of war. As it stands, we have allowed this to happen to ourselves. We have even squandered the gains in student achievement made in the wake of the Sputnik challenge. Moreover, we have dismantled essential support systems which helped make those gains possible. We have, in effect, been committing an act of unthinking, unilateral educational disarmament.[2]

These recent studies, among others, reveal that the public educational system is on a serious backslide. The consequence has been a drastic deterioration of student academic performance, reflected in the sharp drop in the number of high-achieving students. For example, in 1972 only 3.5 percent of those public school students who took the Scholastic Aptitude Test (SAT) scored 700 on the mathematical section; a mere 1.7 percent scored that high on the verbal portion.[3]

SAT scores, however, have understated the deterioration. One study indicates:

In a check on itself, the Educational Testing Service, which administers the SATs, included the 1963 and 1973 test questions in some of its 1976 tests. After studying the results, an advisory panel reached the little-publicized conclusion that the tests had become easier over the years; the students had scored at a level as much as ten points higher on the 1973 questions than they did on those from 1963.[4]

This study cancels the significance of the news that SAT scores increased slightly in one recent year, temporarily arresting the consistent decline over two decades.

Moreover, in the past two decades our nation's public school children have not even been taking the courses needed to prepare them for effective living in a technologically oriented world. According to the National Commission on Excellence in Education study, public school children in the United States fall short of those in other industrialized countries by nineteen measures of academic achievement. Their reading, computational, and "higher-order" skills such as logic and the ability to draw inferences have declined rapidly—along with their scores on the SAT, science achievement tests, and other standardized examinations. As one analysis of the study notes:

> One of the most shocking findings is that only one-fifth of the 17-year-olds in public education can write a persuasive essay; only one-third can solve a mathematical problem requiring several steps; and 13 percent, by the simplest tests of reading, writing and comprehension, are functionally illiterate. (That figure may be as high as 40 percent among minority students.)[5]

While recent steps may improve the quality of public education in a few areas, the overall situation is one of serious and continued decline.

It is striking, according to historical revisionist Samuel L. Blumenfeld, that literacy was much higher in pre-1835 American society[6]—that is, *before* the advent of public education in this country. The present low literacy rate is even more startling when coupled with the realization that in 1980-81 the United States spent 6.8 percent of its gross national product on education (twice as much as in 1949-50). This amounts to approximately $200 million more than is spent by any other nation in the world.[7] Moreover, apart from national defense, public education now represents the largest single tax-based system of cash flow in this country. Public education is, therefore, a vast public investment that now yields a dangerously low return.

Faced with these problems in public education, many parents have instead selected private education. Likewise, a significant number of parents have chosen home education for their children. In recent years, these educational alternatives generally have proven more effective than the public schools in terms of educational output.

The Alternative of Home Education

It must not be forgotten that children have *always* been instructed within the family by their parents. Historian R. J. Rushdoony comments:

> [T]he family is man's first and basic school. Parents have very extensively educated their child before the child ever sets foot inside a school. Moreover, every mother regularly performs the most difficult of all educational tasks, one which no school performs. The mother takes a small child, incapable of speaking or understanding a word in any language, and, in a very short time, teaches it the mother tongue. This is a

difficult and painstaking task, but it comes simply and naturally in the family as an expression of the mother's love and the child's response to that love. At every stage of the child's life, the educational function of the home is the basic educational power in the life of the child.[8]

Therefore, whereas public education involves open-ended group instruction (or mass teaching), home education is the structured, individual instruction of a child (or children) by parents in basic living skills as well as in traditional and additional courses of academic study. Generally, home instruction is from a specific religious or philosophical viewpoint.

Home education thus embodies the tutorial method of instruction that numerous studies have found superior to traditional classroom instruction. In fact, the statistical analysis of nearly eighty separate studies indicates that a pupil taught individually achieves about thirty percentile ranks higher on standardized tests than a pupil taught in a standard class of twenty-five students.[9]

Home education has been advocated by numerous scholarly sources, one of which concludes:

> A recent national study of home schools confirmed among its other findings that youngsters educated at home achieve higher than national averages in standardized measures.[10]

Many popular studies have also strongly supported home schooling.[11] Therefore, the educational effectiveness of home schools has been adequately demonstrated by the existing and available studies,[12] as well as by the evidence presented in some recent court cases.[13]

Several news stories and interviews in the early 1980s discussed Grant Colfax, who went directly from eleven years of home education in California to Harvard College (as did President John Quincy Adams). In the 1970s, John and Eugene Meyer similarly went directly from twelve years of home education to Yale College. The state of Alaska has always used home instruction to educate a number of children in remote areas.

Even if that educational effectiveness had not been demonstrated and the constitutional rights described in the following chapters did not exist, however, it would yet be shortsighted as a matter of policy to restrict home education in view of recent personal computer technology that promises to raise home instruction potentially to the state of the art.[14] This is especially true in view of the significant and long-term decline of the quality of public education.

The Extensiveness of Home Education

The number of families involved in home education is difficult to determine. Researcher John Naisbitt estimates, in the best-seller *Megatrends,* that the figure may be as high as one million.[15]

There is no definite figure on home instruction because many families do not want to be studied or counted. Fearing prosecution and harassment from state authorities, a large but uncertain number of parents simply hide their children.

The Permissibility of Home Education

This is unfortunate since, as the evidence shows, home education in no way violates the state's presumed objective to develop students into effective, responsible citizens. To deny or excessively restrict home instruction as an educational option is to deny many students the opportunity to reach their highest academic potential, because the public schools often leave children underchallenged and ill-prepared in even the most basic verbal and mathematical skills. In addition, restricting parental liberty in educating children at home chokes the diversity and pluralism on which our country was founded and for which many individuals have given their lives.[16] As Dr. Donald Erickson, former Professor of Education at the University of Chicago, writes:

> [S]tate regulation of nonpublic schools must encourage diverse approaches to the achievement of goals. . . . The biggest danger is not that a few schools will depart from the orthodox, but the methodologies will become sacrosanct and compulsory, like the Copernican view of the solar system, before the evidence is in. . . . [S]tate regulation of nonpublic schools must encourage the pursuit of pluralistic goals.[17]

A recent law journal article stated that "[m]ost states today expressly or impliedly allow the option of home education to fulfill the compulsory education statutes."[18] Several states have recently enacted statutes expressly authorizing home education.[19] However, a minority of states prohibits or prohibitively regulates home instruction.

Author Alvin Toffler, in the quotation at the beginning of this book, similarly concludes that "[p]arents willing to teach their own children at home should be aided by the schools, not regarded as lawbreakers."

In light of the proven effectiveness of home instruction, as well as its historical and constitutional foundations, there is every reason to apply to it the individual freedom stressed by the United States Supreme Court in *Wisconsin v. Yoder.*[20] In that case the Court struck down a compulsory attendance law as applied to the Amish for two challenged years of high school instruction, saying:

> We must not forget that in the Middle Ages important values of the civilization of the Western world were preserved by members of religious orders who isolated themselves from all worldly influences against great obstacles. There can be no assumption that today's majority is "right" and the Amish and others like them are "wrong." A way of life that is odd or even erratic but interferes with no rights or interests of others is not to be condemned because it is different.[21]

Notes

1. *Another Study Says Schools Are in Peril,* Washington Post, July 20, 1983, at A2.
2. National Commission on Excellence in Education, *A Nation at Risk: The Imperative for Education Reform* (1982), *reprinted in* 129 Congressional Record S 6059, S 6060 (daily ed. May 5, 1983).
3. Brimelow, *What To Do About America's Schools,* Fortune, Sept. 19, 1983, at 60.
4. *Id.* at 60, 61.
5. Emmett, *American Education: The Dead End of the 80s,* Personal Computing, Aug. 1983, at 96, 97.

6. *See generally* Samuel L. Blumenfeld, *Is Public Education Necessary?* (Old Greenwich, Conn.: Devon-Adair, 1981).

7. Brimelow, *supra* note 3, at 62.

8. Rousas J. Rushdoony, *Law and Liberty* 79 (Nutley, N.J.: Craig Press, 1971).

9. *See generally* Gene Glass & Mary Lee Smith, *Meta-Analysis of Research on the Relationship of Class Size and Achievement* (San Francisco: Far Liest Laboratory for Educational Research and Development, 1979); Mary Lee Smith & Gene Glass, *Relationship of Class Size to Classroom Processes, Teacher Satisfaction, and Pupil Effect: A Meta-Analysis* (1979) (in subsequent study, individual tutoring had positive effects on student attitudes and motivations); Cohen & Philby, *The Class Size / Achievement Issue: New Evidence and a Research Plan*, 60 Phil Delta Kappan 492 (1979); Smith & Glass, *The Effect of Class Size on What Happens in Classrooms*, Education Digest, March 1980, at 16.

10. Moore, *Research and Common Sense: Therapies for Our Homes and Schools*, 84 Teachers College Record (Columbia University) 355, 372-74 (1982). *See also* Raymond Moore & Dorothy Moore, *School Can Wait* 27-48, 205-20 (Provo, Utah: Brigham Young University Press, 1979); Holt, *Schools and Home Schoolers: A Fruitful Partnership*, 64 Phi Delta Kappan 391 (1983).

11. *See generally* John Holt, *Teach Your Own* (New York: Delacorte, 1981); John Holt, *The Underachieving School* (New York: Pitman, 1969); John Holt, *Instead of Education* (New York: Dutton, 1976); John Holt, *How Children Fail* (New York: Pitman, 1967); Ivan Illich, *Deschooling Society* (New York: Harper & Row, 1971); Everett Reimer, *School Is Dead* (Garden City, N.Y.: Doubleday, 1971); Vernon Smith, *Alternative Schools* (Bloomington, Ind.: Phi Delta Kappa Educational Foundation, 1974).

12. A recent study of more than 1,000 high schools nationwide, sponsored by the United States Department of Education and entitled *Public and Private Schools*, supports the claim that private education (which would include home education) is superior in educational effectiveness to public education. As University of Chicago sociologist James Coleman, author of the study, comments: "When family background factors that predict achievement are controlled, students in both Catholic and other private schools are shown to achieve at a higher level than students in public schools." King, *Home Schooling: Up from Underground*, Reason, Apr. 1983, at 22, 25. *See generally* James S. Coleman, Thomas Hoffer & Sally Kilgore, *High School Achievement* (New York: Basic Books, 1982).

13. *E.g., State v. Nobel*, No. S791-0114-A (Mich. Dist. Ct., Allegan County, Jan. 9, 1980).

14. *See generally* Alvin Toffler, *The Third Wave* (New York: Morrow, 1980); Alvin Toffler, *Learning for Tomorrow: The Role of the Future in Education* (New York: Random House, 1974); *Video Merger of Home and School Is Envisioned*, Education Week, June 23, 1982, at 4.

15. John Naisbitt, *Megatrends: Ten New Directions Transforming Our Lives* 144 (New York: Warner Books, 1982).

16. *E.g., Bright v. Isenbarger*, 314 F. Supp. 1382, 1391 (N.D. Ind. 1970), *aff'd*, 445 F. 2d 412 (7th Cir. 1971); *see West Virginia State Board of Education v. Barnette*, 319 U.S. 624, 641-42 (1943).

17. Donald Erickson, *Freedom's Two Educational Imperatives: A Proposal,* in Public Controls for Nonpublic Schools 159, 160, 165 (D. Erickson ed., Chicago: Univ. of Chicago Press, 1969).
18. Beshoner, *Home Education in America: Parental Rights Reasserted,* 49 Univ. of Missouri (Kansas City) Law Review 191, 194 (1981).
19. *E.g.,* Ga. H.B. 327 (1984); Mont. S.B. 331 (1983); Miss. H.B. 4 (1982); Col. H.B. 1346 (1983); La. H.B. 1782 (1980).
20. *Wisconsin v. Yoder,* 406 U.S. 205 (1972).
21. *Id.* at 223-24.

2

The Overlooked History of Home Education

The child is not the mere creature of the state; those who nurture him and direct his destiny have the right, coupled with the high duty, to recognize and prepare him for additional obligations.

Pierce v. Society of Sisters (1925)

America began its remarkable history without public education—with the exception of some local common schools in New England. The United States Constitution does not even mention education. From the beginning of this country, education was an area of concern left to parents through home education and private organizations (often churches) in the states. At that time, education was almost exclusively private, although it was sometimes financially aided by the state. Parent-directed home education, then, has roots deep in America's history.

Home Education in Colonial America

Home education was a major form, if not the predominant form, of education in colonial America and in the

23

early years after the adoption of the Constitution. As one legal commentator notes:

> Historically, the education of children in the United States was a matter of parental discretion. Decisions to educate or not to educate, and the substance of that education—method and curriculum—were made by the parents as a right.[1]

Home education was successful. John Adams observed in 1765 that "a native in America, especially of New England, who cannot read and write is as rare a Phenomenon as a Comet."[2] The Dupont study in 1800 noted that literacy was universal in early America.[3]

Therefore, the recent renaissance of home education "is actually the closing of a circle, a return to the philosophy which prevailed in an earlier America. . . . In New England, the rest of the colonies, and states admitted later which had no comparable 'education' statutes, the responsibility for the child's education was left solely up to the parents."[4] For example, in the Plymouth Colony, "most of the heads of families were not only fully competent to teach their own sons and daughters, but found it no severe hardship to give their time to the training of the few whose parents had either died or were needy."[5]

Home Education of Early Leaders and Intellectuals

Many of America's most illustrious leaders were educated wholly or substantially through home education. Nine presidents were primarily taught through home education, including George Washington,[6] James Madison,[7] John Quincy Adams,[8] and Franklin D. Roosevelt.[9] In fact, John Quincy Adams never attended a formal school until he entered Harvard at the age of fourteen. President Abraham Lincoln likewise received all of his education, except one year, through home instruction,[10] and President Woodrow Wilson received most of his precollege instruction through home education.[11]

Most illustrious women in colonial and early republic years were taught through home education, such as Abigail Adams,[12] Mercy Warren,[13] and Martha Washington.[14] Moreover, the brilliant black author Phyllis Wheatley was educated at home.[15]

Generals George Patton[16] and Douglas MacArthur,[17] authors Mark Twain,[18] Agatha Christie,[19] and Pearl S. Buck,[20] as well as intellectuals John Stuart Mill[21] and George Bernard Shaw,[22] were primarily trained through home instruction. Similarly, industrialist Andrew Carnegie,[23] philosopher Benjamin Franklin,[24] orator Patrick Henry,[25] and inventor Thomas Edison[26] were similarly schooled primarily through home education.

It is interesting that Thomas Edison was expelled from public school at age ten.[27] A public schoolteacher told his mother that Thomas was "addled." Edison attributed his success to the instruction and encouragement given him by his mother.[28]

The product of home education was near-universal literacy, as recognized by Daniel Webster[29] in the nineteenth century, as well as John Adams, and Dupont. Unfortunately, as discussed in Chapter 1, the literacy rate has sharply declined with the advent of modern public education.

Notes

1. Tobak & Zirkel, *Home Instruction: An Analysis of the Statutes and Case Law*, 8 Univ. of Dayton Law Review 13, 14 (1982).
2. *Diary and Autobiography of John Adams* (L. Butterfield ed., Cambridge, Mass.: Harvard University Press, 1961).
3. Pierre Samuel Dupont de Nemours, *National Education in the United States of America* (Newark, Del.: University of Delaware Press, 1923).
4. Beshoner, *Home Education in America: Parental Rights Reasserted*, 49 Univ. of Missouri (Kansas City) Law Review 9, 191 (1981).
5. William T. Davis, *History of the Town of Plymouth* 52 (Philadelphia: J. W. Lewis & Co., 1885).
6. John C. Fitzpatrick, *George Washington Himself* 19 (Indianapolis: Bobbs-Merrill Co., 1933).
7. *James Madison 1751-1836*, at 1 (Ian Elliot ed., Dobbs Ferry, N.Y.: Oceana Pubs., 1969).
8. 1 *Memoirs of John Quincy Adams* 7 (Charles Francis Adams ed., Philadelphia: J. B. Lippincott, 1874).
9. 1 *F.D.R.: His Personal Letters* 5 (Elliot Roosevelt ed., New York: Duell, Sloan & Pearce, 1947).
10. Benjamin P. Thomas, *Abraham Lincoln: A Biography* 7, 8, 12 (New York: Alfred A. Knopf, 1952); Albert J. Beveridge, *Abraham Lincoln* 63 (New York: Houghton-Mifflin Co., 1928).
11. Ray S. Baker, *Woodrow Wilson: Life and Letters* 37 (Garden City, N.Y.: Doubleday, Page & Co., 1927).
12. Charles W. Akers, *Abigail Adams: An American Woman* 8 (Boston: Little, Brown & Co., 1980).
13. Alice Brown, *Mercy Warren* 23 (New York: Charles Scribner's Sons, 1903).
14. Alice Curtis Desmond, *Martha Washington: Our First Lady* 7 (New York: Dodd, Mead & Co., 1963).
15. G. Herbert Renfro, *Life and Works of Phillis Wheatley* 11, 12 (Freeport, N.Y.: Books for Libraries Press, 1972); Benjamin Brawley, *The Negro in Literature and Art in the United States* 17, 18 (New York: Duffield & Co., 1939).
16. Harry H. Semmes, *Portrait of Patton* 4, 5 (New York: Appleton Century Crofts, 1955).
17. 1 D. Clayton James, *The Years of MacArthur* 53 (Boston: Houghton Mifflin & Co., 1970).
18. DeLancey Ferguson, *Mark Twain: Man and Legend* 21, 24, 29 (New York: Bobbs-Merrill & Co., 1943).
19. Agatha Christie, *Agatha Christie: An Autobiography* 13, 14 (New York: Dodd, Mead & Co., 1977).
20. Paul A. Doyle, *Pearl S. Buck* 24 (New York: Twayne Publishers, 1965).
21. Michael St. John Packe, *The Life of John Stuart Mill* 19, 20 (London: Secker & Warburg, 1954).
22. Hesketh Pearson, *George Bernard Shaw: A Full-Length Portrait* 11 (New York: Harper & Bros., 1942).
23. 1 Burton J. Hendrick, *The Life of Andrew Carnegie* 21 (Garden City, N.Y.: Doubleday, Doran & Co., 1932).

The Overlooked History of Home Education

24. 1 John Bigelow, *The Life of Benjamin Franklin, Written by Himself* 99 (Philadelphia: J. B. Lippincott, 1916).
25. Robert Douthat Meade, *Patrick Henry: Patriot in the Making* 51 (Philadelphia: J. B. Lippincott, 1957).
26. Matthew Josephson, *Edison* 21 (New York: McGraw-Hill, 1959).
27. *Id.* at 20-23.
28. King, *Home Schooling: Up From Underground*, Reason, Apr. 1983, at 26.
29. 1 *The Works of Daniel Webster* 125 (Boston: C. C. Little & J. Brown Co., 1851).

3

Parental Liberty and Education

[T]his case involves the fundamental interest of parents, as contrasted with that of the State, to guide the religious future and education of their children. The history and culture of Western civilization reflect a strong tradition of parental concern for the nurture and upbringing of their children. This primary role of the parents in the upbringing of their children is now established beyond debate as an enduring American tradition.

Wisconsin v. Yoder (1972)

Early court decisions universally acknowledged the parental liberty of family self-determination and therefore the parents' authority in selecting the child's education. In the 1700s Sir William Blackstone, the greatest legal authority of that century, stated in his famous *Commentaries* that parents had total authority over their children's education under the common law.[1] This carried over well into the 1800s. As one legal writer has acknowledged: "The case law shows a stubborn adherence to the common law doctrine of the parental right to provide a child's education. . . . Early court decisions elevated parental rights in this area above *any* possible interest of the state; the parents' right to educate their own children was equated with a democratic freedom."[2] This was also true of the early 1900s.

The Constitutional Basis

For example, in 1925, the United States Supreme Court, in *Pierce v. Society of Sisters,* overturned a state law requiring public school education, on the basis of the parental liberty over education. The challenged statute effectively forbade parental selection of religious schools, other private schools, or home education. In response to this law, the Supreme Court held:

> [T]he Act of 1922 unreasonably interferes with the liberty of parents and guardians to direct the upbringing and education of children under their control. . . . The fundamental theory of liberty upon which all governments in this Union repose excludes any general power of the State to standardize its children by forcing them to accept instruction from public teachers only. The child is not the mere creature of the State; those who nurture him and direct his destiny have the right, coupled with the high duty, to recognize and prepare him for additional obligations.[3]

Similarly in 1927, in *Farrington v. Tokushige,* the Court overturned a slightly less direct state attack on nonpublic education by prohibitive regulation, again on the basis of parental liberty.[4] The Court noted that the "parent has the right to direct the education of his own child without unreasonable restrictions."[5] Furthermore, the Court said:

> Enforcement of the Act probably would destroy most, if not all, of [the private schools]; and, certainly, it would deprive parents of their opportunity to procure for their children instruction which they think important and we can not say is harmful.[6]

As recently as 1972, the United States Supreme Court has explicitly upheld parental liberty over children's education. In *Wisconsin v. Yoder*, the Court overturned a compulsory education statute because it abridged both the free exercise of religion of parents and children and the parental liberty toward children.[7] The Court stated:

> Thus, a State's interest in universal education, however highly we rank it, is not totally free from a balancing process when it impinges on fundamental rights and interests, such as those specifically protected by the Free Exercise Clause of the First Amendment, and the traditional interest of parents with respect to the religious upbringing of their children so long as they, in the words of *Pierce*, "prepare [them] for additional obligations." . . . [T]his case involves the fundamental interest of parents, as contrasted with that of the State, to guide the religious future and education of their children.[8]

Yoder involved a religious education *in place of public schools*—and vocational home instruction in the two years between eighth grade and age sixteen.

The *Yoder* decision was a clear reaffirmation by the

Supreme Court of its older holding in *Pierce v. Society of Sisters* with its emphasis on parental liberty. As the Court said in *Yoder:*

> However read, the Court's holding in *Pierce* stands as a charter of the rights of parents to direct the religious upbringing of their children.[9]

Without question, the *Pierce* decision is "generally accepted as currently effective" constitutional precedent.[10]

A "Fundamental Right"

Parental liberty, it must be emphasized, is not just an ordinary constitutional right, but is recognized as a fundamental constitutional right. The Supreme Court in *Yoder* expressly held:

> [T]his case involves the *fundamental interest* of parents, as contrasted with that of the State, to guide the religious future and *education of their children.* The history and culture of Western civilization reflect a strong tradition of parental concern for the nurture and upbringing of their children. This primary role of the parents in the upbringing of their children is now established beyond debate as an enduring American tradition. If not the first, perhaps the most significant statements of the Court in this area are found in *Pierce v. Society of Sisters.*[11]

The Ohio Supreme Court in 1976 similarly stated:

> Thus, it has long been recognized that the right of a parent to guide the education, including the religious

education, of his or her children is indeed a *"fundamental right."*[12]

The significance of the right of parental liberty being classified as "fundamental" is that, when parents and state conflict, the state *must* demonstrate that its interest is a compelling interest in order to override the constitutional right or rights involved.

In fact, any question of First Amendment freedoms (such as religious exercise, speech and belief, privacy, and parental liberty) is viewed by courts within a three-step process. First, there must be a First Amendment right involved that conflicts with a governmental program or requirement. Second, the state must have burdened the exercise of that right. And third, there must not be any compelling state interest, or if there is, the state must not have satisfied that interest by the least burdensome means possible, justifying that burden.[13]

The compelling state interest test is discussed in detail in Chapter 9. In light of the decline in the state's own educational system, the state cannot demonstrate any compelling state interest, except in very limited circumstances, that properly could override the fundamental right of parental liberty over the child's education.

Home Education Cases
There are various cases specifically dealing with parental liberty and home instruction. Most of these cases affirm this basic constitutional right.

For example, in *Commonwealth v. Roberts*[14] the Massachusetts Supreme Court acknowledged and upheld the parental liberty of parents to instruct their children at home. The court noted that the purpose of the compulsory education statute was that "all the children shall be educated, not that they shall be educated in any particular way."[15]

Similarly, in *Trustees of Schools v. State*[16] another court also recognized the parental liberty over the child's education:

> [T]he policy of our law has ever been to recognize . . . that the [parent's] natural affections and superior opportunities of knowing the physical and mental capabilities and future prospects of his child will insure the adoption of that course which will most effectively promote the child's welfare.[17]

As recent as 1983, in *Calhoun County Department of Education v. Page*,[18] a South Carolina court upheld parental liberty in a home school situation. The state court involved held that the parents' right to teach their children in a home school "is a basic constitutional 'liberty' guaranteed by the U.S. Constitution and the Fourteenth Amendment of the U.S. Constitution."[19]

Notes

1. 1 William Blackstone, *Commentaries on the Laws of England* *450-53 (London: T. Cadell & W. Davies, 1809).
2. Beshoner, *Home Education in America: Parental Rights Reasserted*, 49 Univ. of Missouri (Kansas City) Law Review 191, 192 (1981). *See also Trustees of School v State*, 87 Ill. 303, 308 (1887); *Rulison v Post*, 79 Ill. 567, 573 (1875); *State v Peterman*, 32 Ind. App. 665, 70 N.E. 50 (1904); *Commonwealth v Roberts*, 159 Mass. 372, 374, 34 N.E. 402, 403 (1893); *State ex rel. Sheibley v School District*, 31 Neb. 552, 48 N.W. 393 (1891); *Calhoun County Department of Education v Page*, No. 83DR966 (S.C. Fam. Ct., Calhoun County, June 28, 1983), *appeal dismissed*, No. 83-CP-40-0830 (S.C. Sup. Ct. Feb. 3, 1984).

3. 268 U.S. 510, 534-35 (1925). *See also Meyer v. Nebraska,* 262 U.S. 390, 399 (1923).
4. 273 U.S. 284 (1927).
5. *Id.* at 298.
6. *Id.*
7. 406 U.S. 205 (1972).
8. *Id.* at 214.
9. *Id.* at 232.
10. Thomas Emerson, *The System of Freedom of Expression* 600 (New York: Random House, 1970); Arons, *The Separation of School and State: Pierce Reconsidered,* 46 Harvard Educational Review 76, 96 (1976); Stocklin-Enright, *The Constitutionality of Home Education: The Role of the Parent, the State and the Child,* 18 Willamette Law Review 563, 568-69 (1982).
11. 406 U.S. at 232.
12. *State v. Whisner,* 47 Ohio St. 2d 181, 213-14, 351 N.E. 2d 750, 769 (1976). *Accord, e.g., In re Peirce,* 122 N.H. 762, 768, 451 A. 2d 363, 367 (1982) (concurring opinion); *Perchemlides v. Frizzle,* No. 16641, slip op. at 6 (Mass. Super. Ct., Hampshire County, Nov. 13, 1978); *Calhoun County Department of Education v. Page,* No. 83DR966, slip op. at 7 (S.C. Fam. Ct., Calhoun County, June 28, 1983), *appeal dismissed,* No. 83-CP-40-0830 (S.C. Sup. Ct. Feb. 3, 1984).
13. *Wisconsin v. Yoder,* 406 U.S. 205, 211, 215 (1972); *Sherbert v. Verner,* 374 U.S. 396, 399, 405-06 (1963).
14. 159 Mass. 372, 34 N.E. 402 (1893).
15. 159 Mass. 372, 34 N.E. at 403.
16. 87 Ill. 303 (1887).
17. *Id.* at 308. *Accord, Rulison v. Post,* 79 Ill. 567, 573 (1875). In *State ex rel. Sheibley v. School District,* 31 Neb. 552, 48 N.W. 393 (1891), the court similarly referred to the parental liberty over education. *See also State v. Peterman,* 32 Ind. App. 665, 70 N.E. 550 (1904).
18. No. 83DR966 (S.C. Fam. Ct., Calhoun County, June 28, 1983), *appeal dismissed,* No. 83-CP-40-0830 (S.C. Sup. Ct. Feb. 3, 1984).
19. *Id.,* slip op. at 7.

PART TWO

Freedoms of Religion and Privacy and Other Basic Liberties

A great number of parents choose home education because of their religious beliefs. When challenged by state authorities, their First Amendment right to free exercise of religion is then at stake. Part Two discusses this valuable right as well as the freedoms of speech and belief, the right to privacy, and liberties protected by the Ninth Amendment to the United States Constitution.

4

The Freedom of Religion

Congress shall make no law respecting an establishment of religion, or prohibiting the free exercise
thereof. . . .

First Amendment to the
United States Constitution

Many parents who teach their children at home do
so because of strongly held religious beliefs. These beliefs center around parental responsibility over children
and, often, a biblical basis for education.

Religious Exercise in Home Education

Those individuals who pursue home education on religious grounds generally do so because they hold a religious belief that education must be Bible-centered. As
Dr. R. J. Rushdoony, a historian and Bible scholar, explains:

> With faith in the God of Scripture, a thorough Chris-
> tian education, and the development of its meaning
> for every area of life, is *mandatory*. . . .
> If the Bible is what it declares itself to be, then it

is the most basic book in education. All knowledge must be organized in terms of the God of Scripture as the creator and interpreter of all reality.[1]

This religious belief that the Bible should pervade the curriculum is generally accompanied by a religious belief that education should be controlled by parents, either directly or indirectly through religious schools that they select, in order to impart religious truths and values. Such individuals basically view children as gifts bestowed by the Creator (with a corresponding duty to the Creator properly to care for and nurture the children). One educator has noted:

> The Bible-believing Christian needs to be reminded repeatedly that responsibility for education lies primarily with the parents and secondly with the church. Neither the school nor the state has the right, under God, to usurp this responsibility.[2]

These individuals see the family in biblical terms as, among other things, an educational institution. The prime beneficiaries of the educational function of the family are children. As such, parents are given the responsibility by the Bible of carefully instructing their children. Some of the basic Bible verses relied upon are:

> And these words, which I command thee this day, shall be in thine heart: And thou shalt teach them diligently unto thy children, and shalt talk of them when thou sittest in thine house, and when thou walkest by the way, and when thou liest down, and when thou risest up.[3]

Train up a child in the way he should go: and when he is old, he will not depart from it.[4]

And, ye fathers, provoke not your children to wrath: but bring them up in the nurture and admonition of the Lord.[5]

The first actual mention of teaching in the Bible in any form is found in Genesis where, speaking of Abraham, it is said: "For I know him, that he will command his children and his household after him, and they shall keep the way of the Lord to do justice and judgment."[6] This verse and the others cited state that the foundation of all teaching must be the Bible, and that the primary focus of teaching, from a Christian standpoint, must be moral and spiritual, rather than secularistic or cultural.

This, in effect, means that every academic subject must be approached and taught from a moral and spiritual viewpoint. Many religious parents believe this objective can best be accomplished through home education. This, they believe, is their moral responsibility and the essence of religious education.

The United States Supreme Court itself has noted the pervasively religious nature of religious education in the various cases dealing with religious schools. The Court has said:

The very purpose of many of those schools is to provide an integrated secular and religious education; the teaching process is, to a large extent, devoted to the inculcation of religious values and belief. . . . "[T]he secular education those schools provide goes hand in hand with the religious mission that is the only reason for the schools' existence. Within the institution, the two are inextricably intertwined."[7]

The same is true of home education conducted from a religious viewpoint.

Moreover, the Supreme Court has expressly ruled that a sincere religious conviction need not be a formal denominational doctrine or a universally-shared sectarian belief for it to be fully protected as religious exercise under the First Amendment. The Court has held:

> [T]he guarantee of free exercise is not limited to beliefs which are shared by all of the members of a religious sect. Particularly in this sensitive area, it is not within the judicial function and judicial competence to inquire whether the petitioner or his fellow worker more correctly perceived the commands of their common faith.[8]

Therefore, even if most individuals within most religious groups do not apprehend a religious imperative for home education, home education is nevertheless protected religious exercise. Also, if it is a sincere religious belief, "it is," as the Supreme Court has held, "no business of courts to say that what is a religious practice or activity for one group is not religious under the protection of the First Amendment."[9]

Wisconsin v. Yoder

A leading decision on free exercise of religion is the United States Supreme Court decision in *Wisconsin v. Yoder*.[10] In that case, the Amish challenged a compulsory education statute, which required school attendance after eighth grade through age sixteen, as an abridgment of free exercise of religion. The Amish instead practiced a religious way of life that required unstructured vocational education *at home* in the years after eighth grade through age sixteen.

The court emphasized that "the values and programs of the modern secondary school are in sharp conflict with the fundamental mode of life mandated by the Amish religion," and consequently found a violation of their free exercise of religion:

> The conclusion is inescapable that secondary schooling, by exposing Amish children to worldly influences in terms of attitudes, goals, and values contrary to beliefs, and by substantially interfering with the religious development of the Amish child and his integration into the way of life of the Amish faith community at the crucial adolescent stage of development, contravenes the basic religious tenets and practice of the Amish faith, both as to the parent and the child.[11]

Although the Supreme Court found this a burden on free exercise of religion, the state argued that its alleged compelling interest in education should override the burden on religious liberty. The Court disagreed:

> Thus, a State's interest in universal education, however highly we rank it, is not totally free from a balancing process when it impinges on fundamental rights and interests, such as those specifically protected by the Free Exercise Clause of the First Amendment, and the traditional interest of parents with respect to the religious upbringing of their children. . . .[12]

The Court also denied that the state's interest was served by a least burdensome means.[13] The constitutional test is that, if the state does prove a compelling interest, then the state must also demonstrate that it is using the method of satisfying that interest that least burdens the First Amendment rights of the individuals involved. These issues are discussed in detail in Part Four.

The Court also rejected the state's argument that " 'actions,' even though religiously grounded, are outside the protection of the First Amendment" or are not fully protected by that Amendment, stating:

> [T]here are areas of conduct protected by the Free Exercise Clause of the First Amendment and thus beyond the power of the State to control, even under regulations of general applicability. . . . This case therefore, does not become easier because respondents were convicted for their "actions" in refusing to send their children to the public high school; *in this context belief and action cannot be neatly confined in logic-tight compartments.*[14]

The Supreme Court similarly rejected the state's argument that the compulsory education law could not violate First Amendment rights because "Wisconsin's requirement for school attendance to age 16 applies uniformly to all citizens of the State and does not, on its face, discriminate against religions or a particular religion."[15] The Court replied:

> A regulation neutral on its face may, in its application, nonetheless offend the constitutional requirement for governmental neutrality if it unduly burdens the free exercise of religion.[16]

The *Yoder* rationale has *not* been limited solely to the Amish. In numerous cases it has been extended to other religious faiths.[17] Thus, *Wisconsin v. Yoder* provides a durable constitutional base for protecting the First Amendment rights of non-Amish parents who, out of religious conviction, choose to educate their children at home from their religious viewpoint.

Nonestablishment of Religion

The First Amendment, besides guaranteeing the free exercise of religion, also prohibits the state from establishing a religion. This provision has been construed by the United States as:

(1) Prohibiting *excessive entanglement* between government and religion;

(2) Voiding governmental action which has the *primary effect* of either advancing or inhibiting religion; and,

(3) Rendering unconstitutional any law or state action that does not have a demonstrable secular *purpose.*[18]

When home education is undertaken for religious reasons, burdensome regulation can produce excessive entanglement with religion, just as burdensome regulation of institutional religious schools produces excessive entanglement with religion. In fact, there have been a number of court decisions finding excessive entanglement in attempted governmental interference with religious schools.[19] There is no reason why a different result would obtain in the home instruction situation.

For home education impelled by religious reasons, any prohibition against or prohibitive regulation of such home education would constitute "showing hostility to religion," which would be a primary effect violative of the establishment clause.[20] As previously noted, any governmental action that would have the primary effect of inhibiting or showing hostility toward religion is prohibited by the First Amendment (just as governmental action that has the primary effect of subsidizing or advancing religion is prohibited).

This would mean that a state compulsory education law would be unconstitutional as applied if it rendered illegal home education or burdensomely regulated home instruction. Those parents who conduct home education for religious reasons would be inhibited in their religious exercise. This type of governmental activity is what the Supreme Court has called "callous indifference," if not "hostility," toward religion, both of which are unconstitutional.[21]

Home Education Decisions

Several recent court decisions have acknowledged that the constitutional right to home education is guaranteed as free exercise of religion. Consequently these courts have recognized a constitutionally-required exception to compulsory attendance statutes that did not permit home education.

For instance, in *State v. Nobel*,[22] a 1980 case, a Michigan district court sustained the religious exercise right to home education and dismissed charges under a compulsory education statute. The court held:

Mrs. Nobel received a Bachelor of Arts degree from Calvin College in elementary education. Mrs. Nobel has had several years of teaching experience prior to September 1, 1978, and while she has never applied for a teacher's certificate, did receive a provisional teaching certificate pursuant to her degree in elementary education by the time of her graduation.

Mrs. Nobel refuses to obtain the teaching certificate because of her religious beliefs. Mrs. Nobel testified that her daily life was governed by her understanding of the word of God as contained in the Bible and it is her firmly held religious belief that parents are responsible for the education and religious training of their children and that the parents must not delegate that role and authority to the government or any State . . . that for her to accept State certification would, according to her religious beliefs, be placing her responsibilities for education of her children in a position subservient to that of the State in violation of her religious beliefs.

Testimony of Mrs. Nobel at trial indicated that her religious beliefs would prevent her from sending her children to the public schools because public school education directly conflicts with her belief in God and her interpretation of the teachings of the Bible and her religious beliefs in general.

Mrs. Nobel further testified that she could not send her children to any certified private school in the area because they too failed to met her standards of religious training and education.

Pursuant to her religious beliefs, Mrs. Nobel began a program of home education which consisted of the same basic subject material as is taught in the public schools. Defendants['] exhibit #1 indicates the schedules of the children for 180 days of the school year. No evidence was offered or shown to indicate that this curriculum was deficient in any way.

The Nobels have a documented and sincere religious belief[,] and this Court won't and no Court should interfere with the free exercise of a religious belief on the facts of this case.[23]

In another recent case, *Delconte v. State,* a trial court in North Carolina similarly recognized that home education was protected by freedom of religious exercise (and the state's Supreme Court affirmed the decision on other grounds). The trial court stated:

They interpret the Bible as commanding, at the risk of God's displeasure, that parents teach and train their children in the ways of life. Their refusal to send their children to public schools or to a private church school is based on sincere religious grounds.

If the "Hallelujah School" were not entitled to recognition as a "qualified school" the enforcement of North Carolina's compulsory attendance law upon the plaintiff would violate the plaintiff's right under the Free Exercise Clause of the First Amendment.

There are other cases upholding the constitutionality of home education on free exercise of religion grounds.[24] For example, a 1983 decision, *State v. Tollefsrud,*[25] specifically recognized home instruction as protected religious exercise.

Obviously, religious as well as nonreligious parents should have access to the full range of educational alternatives for their children. If, pursuant to religious belief and exercise, home education is the alternative chosen, then that choice is protected by the First Amendment.

Notes

1. Rousas John Rushdoony, *The Philosophy of the Christian Curriculum* 104 (Vallecito, Cal.: Ross House Pubs., 1981).
2. Henry M. Morris, *Education for the Real World* 182 (San Diego: Creation-Life Pubs., 1977). *Accord, State v. Whisner*, 47 Ohio St. 2d 181, 200, 351 N.E. 2d 750, 762 (1976); Philosophy Committee of Bob Jones University, *The Christian Philosophy of Education* 5 (1978).
3. *Deuteronomy* 6:6, 7.
4. *Proverbs* 22:6. This principle is further confirmed in the New Testament: "And that from a child thou has known the holy scriptures, which are able to make thee wise unto salvation through faith which is in Christ Jesus." 2 *Timothy* 3:15.
5. *Ephesians* 6:4.
6. *Genesis* 18:19.
7. *Meek v. Pittenger*, 421 U.S. 349, 366 (1975). *Accord, e.g., Hunt v. McNair*, 413 U.S. 734, 743 (1973); *Lemon v. Kurtzman*, 403 U.S. 602, 616 (1971); *Bangor Baptist Church v. Maine*, 576 F. Supp. 1299 (D. Me. 1983).
8. *Thomas v. Review Board*, 450 U.S. 707, 715-16 (1981).
9. *Fowler v. Rhode Island*, 345 U.S. 67, 69-70 (1953).
10. 406 U.S. 205 (1972).
11. *Id.* at 217-18.
12. *Id.* at 214.
13. *Id.*
14. *Id.* at 219-20. *Accord, e.g., Wooley v. Maynard*, 430 U.S. 705 (1977); *West Virginia State Board of Education v. Barnette*, 319 U.S. 624 (1943).
15. 406 U.S. at 220.
16. *Id.*
17. *See, e.g., State ex rel. Nagle v. Olin*, 64 Ohio St. 2d 341, 415 N.E. 2d 279 (1980); *State v. Whisner*, 47 Ohio St. 2d 181, 351 N.E. 2d 750 (1976); *State v. Tollefsrud*, No. K8222, slip op. at 3 (Minn. County Ct., Houston County, Feb. 9, 1983) (home education case); *State v. Nobel*, No. S791-0114-A, slip op. at 11 (Mich. Dist. Ct., Allegan County, Jan. 9, 1980) (home education case); Lines, *Private Education Alternatives and State Regulation*, 12 Journal of Law & Education 189, 201-02 (1983).
18. *See, e.g., Roemer v. Maryland Board of Public Works*, 426 U.S. 736, 748 (1976); *Meek v. Pittenger*, 421 U.S. 349, 358 (1975).
19. *See, e.g., NLRB v. Catholic Bishop*, 440 U.S. 490, 502 (1979) (establishment clause generally); *New York v. Cathedral Academy*, 434 U.S. 125, 132-33 (1977); *Surinach v. Pesquera de Busquets*, 604 F.2d 73, 75-76 (1st Cir. 1979); *McCormick v. Hirsch*, 460 F. Supp. 1337, 1350, 1357 (M.D. Pa. 1978); *Hinton v. Kentucky State Board of Education*, No. 88314 (Ky. Cir. Ct. Oct. 4, 1978), *aff'd sub. nom. Kentucky State Board for Secondary & Elementary Education v. Rudasill*, 589 S.W.2d 877 (Ky. 1979), *cert. denied*, 446 U.S. 938 (1980).
20. *School District of Abington Township v. Schempp*, 374 U.S. 203, 225 (1963). *Accord, Everson v. Board of Education*, 330 U.S. 1, 18 (1947) (government may not be "adversary" of religion or "handicap" religion); *Walz v. Tax Commission*, 397 U.S. 664, 669 (1970) (no "governmental interference with religion"); *Zorach v. Clauson*, 343 U.S. 306, 314 (1952) (no "callous indifference to religious groups"); *United States v. Branigan*, 299 F. Supp. 225, 231 (S.D.N.Y. 1969) (no "hostility toward religion").

21. *Zorach v Clauson*, 343 U.S. 306, 314 (1952).
22. No. S791-0114-A (Mich. Dist. Ct., Allegan County, Jan. 9, 1980).
23. *Id.*, slip op. at 2-3, 12.
24. In *People v Levisen*, 404 Ill. 574, 90 N.E.2d 213 (1950), the Levisens instructed their seven-year-old daughter at home because of religious beliefs as Seventh-day Adventists, and the Illinois Supreme Court recognized the freedom of religion involved. 404 Ill. at 575-76, 90 N.E. 2d at 214. In *Wright v State*, 21 Okla. Crim. 430, 209 P. 179 (1922), the parents had a religious belief in undertaking and managing the child's education at home, and the court acknowledged that. *Accord, Zorach v Clauson*, 303 N.Y. 161, 100 N.E. 2d 463, 468 (1951), *aff'd*, 343 U.S. 306 (1952); *In re Foster*, 69 Misc. 2d 400, 330 N.Y.S. 2d 8, 12 (1972); *State v Lundsten*, Nos. 7220 & 7221, slip op. at 12 (Minn. County Ct., Beltrami County, May 20, 1980).
25. *State v Tollefsrud*, No. K8222 (Minn. County Court, Houston County, Feb. 9, 1983).

5

The Freedom of Speech
and Belief

The Constitution says that Congress (and the States)
may not abridge the right to free speech. This provision means what it says.
*Tinker v. Des Moines Independent Community
School District* (1969)

The fundamental parental right to teach one's own
child at home is not based solely on religious liberty, but
is also grounded in several other constitutional protec-
tions. These rights merge to provide strong constitutional arguments in favor of home instruction.

First Amendment Freedoms of Speech and Belief
The First Amendment protection for freedom of speech
includes freedom of belief and thought.[1] Freedom of
belief includes the right to hold and implement a parent's philosophy and ideology.

The Supreme Court recently upheld the "right of
freedom of thought" in *Wooley v. Maynard*.[2] That case
involved the refusal of a Jehovah's Witness to display a

state motto on his automobile license plate. The court stated:

> We begin with the proposition that the right of freedom of thought protected by the First Amendment against state action includes both the right to speak freely and the right to refrain from speaking at all. A system which secures the right to proselytize religious, political, and ideological causes must also guarantee the concomitant right to decline to foster such concepts. The right to speak and the right to refrain from speaking are complementary components of the broader concept of "individual freedom of mind."[3]

Freedom of speech and belief is the basis for some parents' choice of home education. As a legal article in the *University of Missouri (Kansas City) Law Review* notes:

> The notion that home education is a desirable and legal alternative is one that is rapidly gaining reputable followers. While in the past parents frequently based their decision on religious considerations, this increasingly is no longer the case. In support of the parental right to educate children at home is the argument that conscientious and informed parents are the most aware of the children's needs and are best qualified to integrate learning materials with their family's own philosophy and values. . . . Critics in the field of education argue that schools have flattened cultural diversity and personal individuality in setting up strict programs of learning which are identical on each grade level throughout the nation. These critics view the present system of mass education as promoting conformity, anti-intellectualism, passivity, alien-

ation, classism and hierarchy. . . . Contributing to the dissatisfaction of parents are declining scores on the Scholastic Aptitude Tests (SAT), little or no assigned homework, inflated grades, automatic promotion, below-level textbooks and objective, rather than essay, examinations.[4]

"Freedom of mind" is assured only when a system allows individual and group privacy and ideological self-determination. Even assuming that the state has a compelling interest in education, it should be careful not to interfere with freedom of thought and belief. The constitutional violation is complete when there exists even a *possibility* that the state might, by its disallowance of the home education alternative, hinder the private thoughts or beliefs of parents and children.

Philosophic Grounds for Home Education
There are numerous parents who, on nonreligious free speech and belief grounds, teach their children at home. Both author Alvin Toffler, in his best-seller *The Third Wave,* and educator John Holt, in his books, provide nonreligious ideological encouragement for home education.[5]

A 1981 court decision, *In re Falk,*[6] takes the nonreligious position of free speech and belief as the reason for upholding a home education program. In fact, the Falks' basis for selecting home education was *philosophical* opposition to the group learning experience common to modern public education.[7]

In a 1978 decision that received nationwide attention, *Perchemlides v. Frizzle,*[8] the parents selected home instruction for philosophical reasons. The Massachusetts superior court in that case upheld the right of "nonreligious as well as religious parents . . . to choose from the full range of educational alternatives for their children."[9]

With the powerful impact of education on students' ideologies and values, protected freedom of speech and belief is involved in parents' opposition to public education and in their selection of home education for impartation of parental beliefs.

Notes

1. *Abood v. Detroit Board of Education*, 431 U.S. 209, 235-36 (1977); *Torcaso v. Watkins*, 367 U.S. 488, 498 (1961).
2. 430 U.S. 705 (1977).
3. *Id.* at 714 (quoting *West Virginia State Board of Education v. Barnette*, 319 U.S. 624, 637 (1943)).
4. Beshoner, *Home Education in America: Parental Rights Reasserted*, 49 Univ. of Missouri (Kansas City) Law Review 191, 193 (1981).
5. Alvin Toffler, *The Third Wave* 386 (New York: Morrow, 1980). *See generally* John Holt, *Instead of Education* (New York: Dutton, 1976); John Holt, *The Underachieving School* (1969); John Holt, *How Children Fail* (New York: Pitman, 1967). *Accord*, Ivan Illich, *Deschooling Society* (New York: Harper & Row, 1971); Everett Reimer, *School Is Dead* (Garden City, N.Y.: Doubleday, 1971); Vernon Smith, *Alternative Schools* (Bloomington, Ind.: Phi Delta Kappa Educational Foundation, 1974).
6. 110 Misc. 2d 104, 441 N.Y.S. 2d 785 (Fam. Ct. 1981).
7. 110 Misc. 2d 104, 441 N.Y.S. 2d at 786-87. Likewise, in *In re Skipwith*, 14 Misc. 2d 325, 180 N.Y.S. 2d 852 (Dom. Rels. Ct. 1958), the parents' basis for home education again was philosophical objections to the quality and content of nearby public schools. 180 N.Y.S.2d at 855. Although not a home education case, in *Santa Fe Community Schools v. New Mexico Board of Education*, 85 N.M. 783, 518 P.2d 272 (1974), the unapproved school involved was a progressive school affiliated with a commune, exercising freedom of speech and belief. 518 P.2d at 274.
8. No. 16641 (Mass. Super. Ct., Hampshire County, Nov. 13, 1978).
9. *Id.*, slip op. at 9.

6

The Right to Privacy and
Other Constitutional Liberties

[T]he right of privacy... protects the right to choose
alternative forms of education.

Perchemlides v. Frizzle (1978)

Constitutional Right to Privacy

In *Stanley v. Georgia*,[1] the United States Supreme Court
recognized the right to be free from unwarranted governmental intrusions into one's privacy.[2] The right to
privacy, or what has been called the "right to be let
alone,"[3] may not be infringed by the state absent a compelling interest.

The Supreme Court has likewise held that the constitutional right to privacy includes "matters relating to
marriage, procreation, conception, family relationships
and *child rearing and education*."[4] In fact, the right to
privacy, along with free exercise of religion and freedom
of speech, is the constitutional basis of the parental liberty discussed in Chapter 3.

Parents, as we have seen, possess the right to educate their children at home as a vital part of the freedom
of speech and belief guaranteed by the First Amend-

ment. In this respect, nearly a century ago Professors Warren and (later Justice) Brandeis commented that the right to privacy does not depend on the nature of expression.[5]

In the leading case of *Perchemlides v. Frizzle*,[6] a court explicitly recognized within the right of privacy the right of all parents "to choose from the full range of educational alternatives for their children."[7] The parents in that case had undertaken home education because they disagreed with values inculcated by public schools, and believed that they could impart both a superior education and a more acceptable philosophy at home. The Massachusetts superior court sustained their right to home education under the constitutional right to privacy. The court said:

> [T]he right to privacy, which protects the right to choose alternative forms of education, grows out of constitutional guarantees in addition to those contained in the First Amendment. Nonreligious as well as religious parents have the right to choose from the full range of educational alternatives for their children. There will remain little privacy in the "right to privacy" if the state is permitted to inquire into the motives behind the parents' decisions regarding the education of their children. As plaintiffs here point out, the plaintiffs in *Pierce* included a secular military academy, and the holding in that case did not mention religious beliefs or the free exercise clause of the First Amendment.[8]

Ninth Amendment Rights

The Ninth Amendment to the United States Constitution provides:

> The enumeration in the Constitution of certain rights shall not be construed to deny or disparage others retained by the people.[9]

This provision for "rights retained by the people" has been construed by the courts as granting certain substantive rights. For example, the courts have upheld parental rights over the care, custody, and nurture of their children;[10] the right to privacy;[11] the right to travel and abide in any state;[12] and parents' liberty toward their children.[13] The trend in the courts, then, is to recognize more and more rights within the protection of the Ninth Amendment.[14]

For example, in *Perchemlides,* the court involved recognized the Ninth Amendment's significance for the parents' constitutional interest in the child's education. The court stated:

> The plaintiffs have a right under G.L.c76, §1 to home education for their child, and this right bears constitutional protection, not by specific constitutional delineation but through its inclusion in the penumbra of certain protected constitutional rights, most notably those guaranteed by the Ninth Amendment.[15]

Due Process Rights

The due process clause of the Fourteenth Amendment prohibits laws or regulations that are impermissibly vague or that involve impermissible administrative discretion.

The due process restriction on vague laws was summarized by the United States Supreme Court in *Grayned v. City of Rockford.*[16]

It is a basic principle of due process that an enactment is void for vagueness if its prohibitions are not clearly defined. Vague laws offend several important values. First, because we assume that man is free to steer between lawful and unlawful conduct, we insist that laws give the person of ordinary intelligence a reasonable *opportunity to know what is prohibited,* so that he may act accordingly. Vague laws may trap the innocent by not providing fair warning. Second, if arbitrary and discriminatory enforcement is to be prevented, laws must provide *explicit standards* for those who apply them. A vague law impermissibly delegates basic policy matters to policemen, judges and juries for resolution on an *ad hoc* and subjective basis, with the attendant dangers of arbitrary and discriminatory application.[17]

This has important implications for compulsory education statutes, which typically require attendance at "public or private schools" or require "equivalent" education to public education. These vagueness strictures under the due process clause apply with particular force to compulsory education laws because the sanctions are typically criminal penalties.[18]

First, compulsory education statutes with no definition of "private school," "equivalency," or like terms are impermissibly vague in the first sense. Such undefined terms do not afford the person of ordinary intelligence a reasonable opportunity to know what is prohibited.

This first aspect of the vagueness rule was the basis for the 1983 decisions of the Wisconsin and Georgia Supreme Courts that dismissed criminal actions under the compulsory education statutes against parents involved in home education.[19] The Wisconsin court struck down the law because of its vagueness since it did not define the term "private school." The court held:

> The State Superintendent of Public Instruction, reading the statutes, court decisions, and dictionary definition of school together, proposed in an amicus brief that the phrase "private school" be defined as follows:
> "[A] private school is a facility offering the various grade levels available in the public schools, and commonly understood by the public to be a 'school.' . . . Thus, a private school is an educational institution. . . ."
> We are not convinced that these definitions are the only ones a citizen, an administrator, or a court using dictionary definitions, court decisions and the statutes could deduce. In any event, the *legislature or its delegated agent should define the phrase "private school";* citizens or the court should not have to guess at its meaning. . . .
> We hold that sec. 118.15(1)(a) is *void for vagueness* insofar as it fails to define "private school." We reverse the judgment and remand the cause to the circuit court to dismiss the complaint.[20]

Note that the court rejected the proposed definition of a private school as solely an "institution," and stated that the legislature rather than a judge should define the term.

The other aspect of the vagueness rule, that "laws must provide explicit standards for those who apply them" in order to avoid "arbitrary and discriminatory enforcement," overlaps a parallel First Amendment rule. In *Cantwell v. Connecticut*,[21] the United States Supreme Court struck down a licensing law for literature sales. The Court specifically noted that the law's need for a governmental determination, without precise standards to prevent arbitrary official action, constituted a prior restraint on the exercise of First Amendment rights.[22]

Second, compulsory education statutes violate the due process clause by vagueness in this second sense, when they lack precise definitions of "private school," "equivalency," or like terms, and thereby leave that determination in the unchecked discretion of public school officials.[23]

Obviously, compulsory education statutes are best interpreted to permit home education. Such an interpretation is reflected in the majority of decisions and the most recent court decisions, as discussed in Chapter 7.

Thus, the basic freedoms guaranteed by our Constitution apply to parents who choose the home education alternative. If such parents are challenged by state authorities, and these rights are properly construed, there is no compelling interest sufficient to override such substantial liberties.

Notes

1. 394 U.S. 557 (1969).
2. *Id.* at 564. *Cf. Griswold v. Connecticut*, 381 U.S. 479, 482 (1965) (recognizing a personal right to acquire information for private use). *See generally* Dixon, *The Griswold Penumbra: Constitutional Charter for an Expanded Law of Privacy?*, 64 Michigan Law Review 197, 213 (1965).
3. Warren & Brandeis, *The Right to Privacy*, 4 Harvard Law Review 193 (1890).
4. *Paul v. Davis*, 424 U.S. 693, 713 (1976); *Carey v. Population Services International*, 431 U.S. 678, 691-96 (1977) (plurality opinion); *Runyon v.*

McCrary, 427 U.S. 160, 178 n. 15 (1976); *Griswold v. Connecticut,* 381 U.S. 479, 482-83 (1965); *Duchesne v. Sugarman,* 566 F. 2d 817, 824-25 (2d Cir. 1977).

5. Warren & Brandeis, *supra* note 3, at 193.
6. No. 16641 (Mass. Super. Ct., Hampshire County, Nov. 13, 1978).
7. *Id.,* slip op. at 9.
8. *Id.*
9. U.S. Constitution amendment IX.
10. *Doe v. Irwin,* 441 F. Supp. 1247 (D.C. Mich.), *rev'd on other grounds,* 615 F. 2d 1162 (6th Cir. 1980), *cert. denied,* 449 U.S. 829 (1980).
11. *Galella v. Onassis,* 487 F. 2d 986 (2d Cir. 1973).
12. *Town of Pompey v. Parker,* 385 N.Y.S. 2d 959, 53 App. Div. 2d 125 (1976).
13. *In re J.P.,* 648 P. 2d 1364 (Utah 1982).
14. Caplan, *The History and Meaning of the Ninth Amendment,* 69 Va. Law Review 223 (1983).
15. Slip op. at 27.
16. 408 U.S. 104 (1972).
17. *Id.* at 108-09. *Accord, Papachristou v. City of Jacksonville,* 405 U.S. 156, 162 (1972).
18. *E.g., Grayned v. City of Rockford,* 408 U.S. 104, 108 (1972); *Papachristou v. City of Jacksonville,* 405 U.S. at 162.
19. *State v. Popanz,* 112 Wis. 2d 166, 176-177, 332 N.W. 2d 750, 756 (1983); *Roemhild v. State,* 251 Ga. 519, 308 S.E. 2d 154 (1983).
20. 112 Wis. 2d 166, 332 N.W. 2d at 755, 756 (emphasis supplied).
21. 310 U.S. 296 (1940).
22. *Id.* at 306-07. *Accord, Kunz v. New York,* 340 U.S. 290, 294-95 (1951); *Jones v. Opelika,* 319 U.S. 103 (1943), *adopting,* 316 U.S. at 611 (dissenting opinion).
23. *E.g., Calhoun County Department of Education v. Page,* No. 83DR966, slip op. at 3 (S.C. Fam. Ct., Calhoun County, June 28, 1983), *appeal dismissed,* No. 83-CP-40-0830 (S.C. Sup. Ct. Feb. 3, 1984).

PART THREE

Compulsory Education Statutes
and Their Requirements

*There are three general categories of compulsory educa-
tion statutes: (1) those that refer to "public or private education" without any reference to home education; (2) those that
refer to public education and "equivalent" or "approved" or
"other" nonpublic education; and (3) those that explicitly authorize "home education."*

*The following chapters in Part Three discuss court deci-
sions permitting home instruction under statutes not providing
explicitly for home education, and under statutes providing for
equivalent or approved or similar instruction. The final chapter in Part Three discusses why any statutory requirement for
teacher certification is unconstitutional.*

7

Statutes Requiring "Public or Private Schools" or Requiring "Equivalent Education"

The state may not set standards that are so difficult to satisfy that they effectively eviscerate the home education alternative.

Perchemlides v. Frizzle (1978)

This chapter discusses compulsory education statutes (1) that refer to "public or private education" without making any reference to home education, and (2) that imply an exception for home instruction by allowing for "equivalent" instruction (or some other such terms as "comparable," "otherwise," or "elsewhere").

Laws Allowing "Public or Private Schools" Only

Any statutory prohibition against home education should be presumed unconstitutional, as several court decisions have held or assumed.[1] If a statute may be construed to preserve its constitutionality, however, it should be so construed.[2] This means, for example, that a statute that mentions only public or private education should be interpreted to include home education within the definition of "private education."[3] If not, the law would be unconstitutional.

Any burdensome regulation of home education is also unconstitutional (just as burdensome regulation of religious schools is unconstitutional).[4] The unconstitutionality of such laws has been clearly enunciated in numerous Supreme Court and other court decisions.[5] It was clearly articulated in *Perchemlides v. Frizzle*,[6] in which the court recognized the unconstitutionality of burdensome regulations on home education:

> The state may not, however, set standards that are so difficult to satisfy that they effectively eviscerate the home education alternative. This is not only prohibited by the constitutional protections extended to the right to a home education, as discussed, but also by the compulsory attendance statute, the goal of which is "that all children shall be educated, but not that they shall be educated in any particular way."[7]

The better line of cases construes those compulsory education statutes that refer only to "public or private schools" to include "home education" within the parameters of the term "private schools." Professors James Tobak and Perry Zirkel write in the *University of Dayton Law Review*:

> In the jurisdictions that expressly require attendance at either public or private schools, the primary question has been whether home instruction qualifies as a private school. The courts have split about equally on this issue. One group of decisions has interpreted

private school narrowly to not include home instruction. The other group has interpreted private school broadly and liberally to include home instruction.[8]

In fact, courts in Illinois, Indiana, North Carolina, South Carolina, and Minnesota, and the attorney general in Michigan—all of which have construed "public or private school" statutes—have explicitly ruled that home education constitutes attendance at a "private school."

In *People v. Levisen,*[9] for instance, the Illinois Supreme Court confronted a free exercise of religion challenge, and ruled that "a school . . . is a place where instruction is imparted to the young, [and] the number of persons being taught does not determine whether the place is a school."[10] The court noted that the "object is that all children shall be educated, not that they shall be educated in any particular manner or place."[11]

· In an earlier case, *State v. Peterman,*[12] an Indiana appeals court similarly held that home education constituted a "private school." The court noted:

> A school, in the ordinary acceptation of its meaning, is a place where instruction is imparted to the young. If a parent employs and brings into his residence a teacher for the purpose of instructing his child or children, then such instruction is given as the law contemplates, the meaning and spirit of the law have been fully complied with. . . . We do not think the number of persons, whether one or many, make a place where instruction is imparted any less or more a school.[13]

Another line of new cases, led by the Georgia Supreme Court[14] and the Wisconsin Supreme Court,[15] has found the phrase "public or private school" in compulsory education statutes to violate the due process clause of the Fourteenth Amendment, because of the failure of the statutes to define a "private school."

Therefore, a compulsory education statute that requires attendance at "public or private schools" is best construed in view of existing precedents to include home education as a "private school." This approach is the legal construction that preserves the constitutionality of such laws. Otherwise, such a requirement should be struck down as contrary to First Amendment rights or to the due process clause of the Fourteenth Amendment.

Laws Requiring Public or "Equivalent" Education

Some state compulsory education laws refer to public education and "equivalent" or "approved" nonpublic education. A clear majority of courts in these states (the newer decisions in general) construes such statutes to permit home education. As Professors Tobak and Zirkel note:

> Although a majority of courts have held home instruction qualifies under the equivalence exemption, a substantial minority, adopting the socialization rationale of *State v. Hoyt*, have concluded home instruction is not, nor could it be, equivalent to the institutional, group learning experience.[16]

The cases that have construed these statutes to the contrary were almost all decided before United States Supreme Court decisions such as *Wisconsin v. Yoder*,[17] that allow for broad interpretation of compulsory education statutes (to include such alternatives as home education).

Unconstitutionality of Equivalency Requirements

Although there is no problem with statutory language such as "otherwise" or "elsewhere," statutory language that *requires* "equivalent" or "comparable" instruction is unconstitutional as the statute is applied to home instruction. As another legal writer concludes:

> If the provision requires literal equivalence to public schools, then it is no real alternative and unless a wider choice is allowed under the "private school" option, it is unconstitutionally restrictive.[18]

The following court decisions support that conclusion.

In 1927 in *Farrington v. Tokushige*,[19] the United States Supreme Court overturned a statute that extensively regulated nonpublic education, and that thereby denied what the Court referred to as "reasonable choice and discretion in respect of teachers, curriculum and textbooks."[20] The Court held:

> The foregoing statement is enough to show that the school Act and the measures adopted thereunder go far beyond mere regulation of privately supported schools where children obtain instruction deemed valuable by their parents and which is not obviously in conflict with any public interest. They give affirmative direction concerning the intimate and essential details of such schools, entrust their control to public officers, and deny both owners and patrons reasonable choice and discretion in respect of teachers, cur-

riculum and textbooks. Enforcement of the Act probably would destroy most, if not all of them; and, certainly, it would deprive parents of fair opportunity to procure for their children instruction which they think important and we can not say is harmful.[21]

No constitutional right to nonpublic education is left if burdensome regulations may be imposed to make nonpublic education essentially identical to public education. Many courts have recognized this problem.

For example, in the 1976 decision of *State v. Whisner,*[22] an Ohio statute was challenged on the grounds that it imposed "minimum standards" that extensively regulated religious schools. The Ohio Supreme Court ruled these standards unconstitutional under the free exercise clause, because they were so pervasive and all-encompassing that total compliance with each and every standard by a nonpublic school would effectively eradicate the distinction between public and nonpublic education.[23]

In *State v. LaBarge,*[24] another 1976 case, the challenged Vermont statute required education at a school where the child "is otherwise being furnished with equivalent education" and where teachers' "qualifications are essentially equivalent to the minimum standards for public school teachers."[25] The Vermont Supreme Court overturned this equivalency requirement as applied to religious schools, holding that "compulsory school attendance, even in an equivalency basis, must yield to First Amendment concerns."[26]

As one commentator has correctly concluded:

Given the considerable protection under the first amendment to both speech and religion, as well as the protection of the due process clause, parents should not be expected to prove that alternative education meets any particular standard.[27]

Nonabsoluteness of Equivalency Requirements

Even if an equivalency requirement were not ruled unconstitutional, it would be proper to construe such statutes to require only general and nonabsolute equivalence so that home education would be permitted. A number of courts have ruled along these lines.

An example is the 1981 case of *In re Falk.*[28] There a New York court determined that the home instruction provided by parents, who were high school graduates with some technical training but with no previous teaching experience, was "substantially equivalent" as required by the compulsory education statute.[29]

In 1976 in *State v. Massa,*[30] a New Jersey court again determined that home education could qualify under the equivalency requirement. This was true primarily because the state had not met its burden of proof of showing nonequivalence. Moreover, the court expressly rejected the earlier legal rule that one aspect of equivalence was "social development" or socialization from group interaction.[31]

Other courts have followed suit and have ruled in favor of home education.[32]

If an equivalency requirement cannot be construed to allow home education, it should be overruled as abridging the due process clause of the Fourteenth

Amendment because of the impermissible vagueness of the term "equivalency" or "comparable education," as discussed above in Chapter 6.

Notes

1. *E.g., Perchemlides v. Frizzle,* No. 16641 (Mass. Super. Ct., Hampshire County, Nov. 13, 1978); *State v. Tollefsrud,* No. K8222 (Minn. County Ct., Houston County, Feb. 9, 1983); *State v. Lundsten,* Nos. 7220 & 7221, slip op. at 13-14 (Minn. County Ct., Beltrami County, May 20, 1980); *State v. Nobel,* No. S791-0114-A, slip op. at 12 (Mich. Dist. Ct., Allegan County, Jan. 9, 1980); *see Wisconsin v. Yoder,* 406 U.S. 205, 213-14, 232 (1972); *Pierce v. Society of Sisters,* 268 U.S. 510, 534-45 (1925); *Meyer v. Nebraska,* 262 U.S. 390, 399 (1923).

2. *E.g., NLRB v. Catholic Bishop,* 440 U.S. 490, 500 (1979) (National Labor Relations Act construed not to apply to religious schools); *St. Martin Evangelical Lutheran Church v. South Dakota,* 451 U.S. 772, 780 (1981) (unemployment compensation tax construed not to apply to religious schools).

3. *E.g., People v. Levisen,* 404 Ill. 574, 576-77, 90 N.E. 2d 213, 215 (1950); *Santa Fe Community Schools v. New Mexico State Board of Education,* 85 N.M. 783, 518 P. 2d 572 (1974).

4. *E.g., Perchemlides v. Frizzle,* slip op. at 11; *State v. Budke,* No. 05009, slip op. at 8 (Minn. Dist. Ct., 7th Dist., Nov. 1, 1983).

5. *E.g., NLRB v. Catholic Bishop,* 440 U.S. 490 (1979); *Farrington v. Tokushige,* 273 U.S. 284, 298 (1927); *Surinach v. Pesquera de Busquets,* 604 F. 2d 73 (1st Cir. 1979); *Bangor Baptist Church v. Maine,* 576 F. Supp. 1299 (D. Me. 1983); *Kentucky State Board for Secondary & Elementary Education v. Rudasill,* 589 S.W. 2d 877 (Ky. 1979), *cert. denied,* 446 U.S. 938 (1980); *City of Concord v. New Testament Baptist Church,* 118 N.H. 56, 382 A. 2d 377 (1978); *State v. Whisner,* 47 Ohio St. 2d 181, 351 N.E. 2d 750 (1976); *State v. LaBarge,* 134 Vt. 276, 357 A. 2d 121 (1976).

6. No. 16641 (Mass. Super. Ct., Hampshire County, Nov. 13, 1978).

7. *Id.,* slip op. at 11.

8. Tobak & Zirkel, *Home Instruction: An Analysis of the Statutes and Case Law,* 8 Univ. of Dayton Law Review 1, 29-30 (1982).

9. 404 Ill. 574, 90 N.E. 2d 313 (1950).

10. *Id.* at 576-77, 90 N.E. 2d at 215.

11. *Id. Accord, Delconte v. State,____* N.C. ____, ____ S.E. 2d ____ (1985); *Commonwealth v. Roberts,* 159 Mass. 372, 374, 34 N.E. 402, 403 (1893).

12. 32 Ind. App. 665, 70 N.E. 550 (1904). *Accord, State v. Tollefsrud,* No. K8222 (Minn. County Ct., Houston County, Feb. 9, 1983); *Calhoun County Department of Education v. Page,* No. 83DR966 (S.C. Fam. Ct., Calhoun County, June 28, 1983), *appeal dismissed,* No. 83-CP-40-0830 (S.C. Sup. Ct. Feb. 3, 1984).

13. *Id.* at 669, 70 N.E. at 551.

14. *Roemhild v. State,* 251 Ga. 569, 308 S.E. 2d 154 (1983).

15. *State v. Popanz,* 112 Wis. 2d 166, 332 N.W. 2d 750, 756 (1983).
16 Tobak & Zirkel, *supra* note 8, at 35.
17. 406 U.S. 205 (1972).
18. Stocklin-Enright, *The Constitutionality of Home Instruction: The Role of the Parent, the State and the Child,* 18 Willamette Law Review 563, 601, 610 (1982).
19. 273 U.S. 284 (1927).
20. *Id.* at 298.
21. *Id. See also* Arons, *The Separation of School and State:* Pierce *Reconsidered,* 46 Harvard Education Review 99, 103 (1976).
22. 47 Ohio St. 2d 181, 351 N.E. 2d 750 (1976).
23. *Id.* at 211-12, 341 N.E. 2d at 768.
24. 134 Vt. 276, 357 A. 2d 121 (1976).
25. *Id.* at 278, 357 A. 2d at 123.
26. *Id.* at 280, 357 A. 2d at 124.
27. Lines, *Private Education Alternatives and State Regulation,* 12 Journal of Law & Education 189 (1983). Another recent law journal article concluded that equivalence requirements are unconstitutional, at least if they are strictly applied:

    > If the provision requires literal equivalence to public schools, then it is no real alternative and unless a wider choice is allowed under the "private school" option, it is unconstitutionally restrictive.

    Stocklin-Enright, *supra* note 18, at 610.
28. 110 Misc. 2d 104, 441 N.Y.S. 2d 785 (Fam. Ct. 1981).
29. *Id.* at 109, 441 N.Y.S. 2d at 789.
30. 95 N.J. Super. 382, 231 A. 2d 252 (1967).
31. *Id.* at 391, 231 A. 2d at 257.
32. In *State v. Vaughn,* 44 N.J. 142, 207 A. 2d 537 (1965), the New Jersey Supreme Court similarly stated that home instruction could qualify under the equivalency requirement. *See* 44 N.J. 142, 207 A. 2d at 540. In *Commonwealth v. Roberts,* 159 Mass. 372, 34 N.E. 402 (1893), the Massachusetts Supreme Judicial Court construed the statutory terms "otherwise instructed for a like period of time in the branches of learning required by law" to permit home instruction. *Id.* at 374, 34 N.E. at 403. In *Perchemlides v. Frizzle,* No. 16641 (Mass. Super. Ct., Hampshire County, Nov. 13, 1978), a recent decision interpreted the compulsory education exemption for children "otherwise instructed in a manner approved in advance by the superintendent" to permit home instruction.

8

Teacher Certification Requirements

For her to accept certification would not make her a better teacher, nor would it make her children learn easier, nor would it provide any additional benefits for her, her children, or the State.

State v. Nobel (1980)

Statutes in only seventeen states mention at all the person (that is, teacher, parents, etc.) who provides instruction. Eleven of these statutes use only such minimal terms as a "competent person," while only six of these statutes require a "certified teacher."[1] Courts have never, to the best of our knowledge, created and imposed any requirement for teacher certification, nor could they in the proper exercise of their jurisdiction.

Virtually every decision upholding home education has involved a noncertified teacher.[2] For example, in *People v. Turner*,[3] a 1950 New York appellate court held that a parent was competent to teach, although not certified by the state. That parent satisfied the requirements of the compulsory education law.

Many court decisions have held that teacher certification requirements are unconstitutional if applied to nonpublic schools with First Amendment grounds for opposing certification requirements.[4] The same rationale should invalidate such certification requirements for home education.

State certification requires completion of a state-approved training program. Many home instructors, as a recent study indicates, contend that such training is largely irrelevant to the highly personalized, one-to-one setting of home learning:

> Public school teachers, they claim, are trained not so much to teach as to measure, classify, and control large groups of students. As evidence, home schoolers frequently note that private schools rarely require state certification of their teachers, yet their students generally score higher on achievement tests than do public school students, who must be taught by state-certified teachers.[5]

Furthermore, the state-approved training typically is in education courses that rarely provide training in content for academic disciplines, but that instead stress training in methodology (but not for the tutorial approach).

Free Exercise of Religion Problems

A teacher certification requirement conflicts with freedom of religious exercise in several ways. First, the primary requirement for a teacher for religious home instruction is theological, in that the teacher must hold certain religious beliefs. As one educator states of religious education:

> The two most important components in the implementation of true Christian education are the curriculum and the faculty. . . .
>
> Although there is certainly a place under the cultural mandate for research and discovery of new truth, the function of *teaching* is indoctrination in truth already known.[6]

Second, teacher certification involves a license or prior approval of a function that many individuals believe on religious grounds that God has already approved.[7] In their view, certification interferes with the sovereignty (or "Lordship") of God by asserting a sovereignty of the state over the religious instructor that God has already approved. This was precisely the argument by Peter and Ruth Nobel in a leading home school case.

In *State v. Nobel*,[8] a Michigan district court found a teacher certification requirement unconstitutional as applied to the Nobels. The Nobels had selected home education pursuant to religious belief. The court held:

> No evidence has been introduced in this case that would demonstrate that the State has a compelling interest in applying teacher certification laws to the Nobels or that the educational interest of the State could not be achieved by a requirement less restrictive on the religious beliefs of the Nobels. An evaluation of the Nobel children has indicated that all five are intelligent and appear to be well-adjusted and normal. Mrs. Nobel has demonstrated and the evidence establishes that she is a qualified teacher excepting for the certification requirement.
>
> . . . For her to accept certification would not

make her a better teacher, nor would it make her children learn easier, nor would it make her children more intelligent, nor would it provide any additional benefits for her, her children, or the State; but it would, indeed, interfere with her freedom to exercise her religious beliefs. . . .

The interest of the State in requiring certification on the facts as contained in this particular case must give way to the free exercise of religious belief.[9]

Other First Amendment Problems

For home education that is undertaken for First Amendment reasons, *any* requirement for teacher certification is unconstitutional. Most courts have ruled accordingly.

For example, in *Farrington v. Tokushige*,[10] a statute was challenged that required certified teachers as well as approved curriculum and textbooks for nonpublic schools. The United States Supreme Court overturned that statute as in violation of the constitutional right of parental liberty. The Court said:

> They give affirmative direction concerning the intimate and essential details of such schools, entrust their control to public officers, and deny both owners and patrons reasonable choice and discretion in respect of teachers, curriculum and text-books. Enforcement of the Act probably would destroy most, if not all, of them; and, certainly, it would deprive parents of fair opportunity to procure for their children instruction which they think important and we cannot say is harmful.[11]

Another example is the case of *Kentucky State Board for Elementary & Secondary Education v. Rudasill*,[12] in which the Kentucky Supreme Court in 1979 struck down a requirement for teacher certification as well as textbook approval for nonpublic schools. The court noted:

> It cannot be said as an absolute that a teacher in a non-public school who is not certified under KRS 161.030(2) will be unable to instruct children to become intelligent citizens. Certainly, the receipt of "a bachelor's degree from a standard college or university" is an indicator of the level of achievement, but it is not a *sine qua non* the absence of which establishes that private and parochial school teachers are unable to teach their students to intelligently exercise the elective franchise.[13]

Similarly, in *State v. LaBarge*,[14] the Vermont Supreme Court overturned a law, as being violative of the First Amendment, which required a nonpublic school to have teachers with "qualifications essentially equivalent to the minimum standards for public school teachers" as well as to furnish "equivalent education" generally.[15] The court said that "compulsory school attendance, even on an equivalency basis, must yield to First Amendment concerns."[16]

The *Willamette Law Review* article on home education ably summarizes the unconstitutionality of a teacher certification requirement:

> Everyday experience and our own personal development informs us that the state teacher certificate is neither an infallible, an adequate nor exclusive assur-

ance of competency to impart or engender skills, information or knowledge. State reliance on teacher certification as a requirement for approval of private schools cannot be justified on the basis of the state's primary interest in the citizen's ability to operate the franchise or the state's secondary interest in surveillance of the parents' discretion over their children's education. It may be a convenient administrative rule to require state certification but it cannot stand as the only way to qualify as an instructor when to do so would cut off otherwise qualified individuals wishing to instruct their own or other children. Much of value is simply not taught (nor teachable) in the teacher training institutions and to that extent is uncertifiable. To attempt to confine to the walls of such institutions the monopoly on teaching the young is to allow the state to go too far and certainly entails a lessening of diversity of exposure for the children.

Those cases upholding state legislature requirements of teacher certification as an absolute for private school approval conflict with parental constitutional rights. They are overly restrictive and give too great a leeway to state interests. They are contrary to United States Supreme Court cases consistently upholding the primacy of the parents' interests in the parent/state relationship. If such Supreme Court decisions mean anything they must mean that the state cannot introduce a regulation, however innocuous and reasonable it may superficially appear, when such regulation has the effect of barring the parents' decision to choose a non-state-sanctioned teacher to educate their child. . . .

Any state which requires teacher certification or its equivalent, as a prerequisite to approval of a private school, or a nonschool alternative, is thereby acting unconstitutionally.[17]

Fourteenth Amendment Problems

In addition to the above constitutional defects of teacher certification requirements, such requirements also violate the due process clause by creating an irrebuttable presumption. The irrebuttable presumption involved is that uncertified parents are not capable of adequately instructing their children.

Statutes creating irrebuttable presumptions "have long been disfavored under the Due Process Clauses of the Fifth and Fourteenth Amendments."[18] For example, in *Stanley v. Illinois*,[19] the United States Supreme Court in 1972 struck down a statute containing an irrebuttable presumption that unmarried fathers were incompetent to raise their children. The court noted that "all unmarried fathers are not in this category; some are wholly suited to have custody of their children."[20] Similarly, the state may not presume that all parents are in the category of not being suited to educate their children.[21]

Burden of Proof Problems

Because compulsory education laws generally carry criminal penalties, the usual rules of criminal law apply to prosecution of parents. In a criminal prosecution the Fourteenth Amendment requires that the state bear the ultimate burden of proving every fact necessary to the crime *beyond a reasonable doubt.*[22] The state, therefore, must carry the burden of proving beyond any reasonable doubt that the parents involved are *not* competent to teach.

The state's burden of proof in home education cases also includes the burden of demonstrating that its requirements are necessitated by a compelling state interest, and that its requirements are the least burdensome means to achieve any such interest. As discussed in Chapters 9 and 10, these are nearly insurmountable burdens to overcome.

Similarly, the state must bear the ultimate burden of proof beyond a reasonable doubt that home education does not meet any equivalency provision and that home education does not constitute a "private school."[23] Most of the decisions emphasize that, even if an element such as "equivalency" is phrased as an exception in the compulsory education statute, the state still must bear the ultimate burden of proof on the point as an essential element of the alleged crime. This means that most of the home education cases to the contrary, which generally are older decisions, are unconstitutional in light of the rule that requires all necessary factors to be resolved beyond a reasonable doubt in criminal cases.

Notes

1. Tobak & Zirkel, *Home Instruction: An Analysis of the Statutes and Case Law,* 8 Univ. of Dayton Law Review 1, 12 (1982).
2. *E.g., State v. Massa,* 95 N.J. Super. 382, 391, 231 A. 2d 252, 257 (1967); *People v. Turner,* 277 App. Div. 317, 319-20, 98 N.Y.S. 2d 886, 888 (1950); *In re Falk,* 110 Misc. 2d 104, 441 N.Y.S. 2d 785, 788 (Fam. Ct. 1981); *Perchemlides v. Frizzle,* No. 16641 (Mass. Super. Ct., Hampshire County, Nov. 13, 1978); *State v. Nobel,* No. S791-0114-A, slip op. at 3 (Mich. Dist. Ct., Allegan County, Jan. 9, 1980).
3. 277 App. Div. 317, 98 N.Y.S. 2d 886 (1950).
4. *E.g., Farrington v. Tokushige,* 273 U.S. 284, 298 (1927); *Bangor Baptist Church v. Maine,* 576 F. Supp. 1299 (D. Me. 1983); *Kentucky State Board for Elementary & Secondary Education v. Rudasill,* 589 S.W. 2d 877, 884 (Ky. 1979), *cert. denied,* 446 U.S. 938 (1980); *State v. LaBarge,* 134 Vt. 276, 357 A. 2d 121, 124 (1976); *see Bell v. Department of Licensing,* 182 Mont. 21, 594 P. 2d 331, 332 (1979).
5. King, *Home Schooling: Up from Underground,* Reason, Apr. 1983, at 25.

6. Henry M. Morris, *Education for the Real World* 163-64 (San Diego: Creation-Life Pubs., 1977). *Accord, Kentucky State Board for Elementary & Secondary Education v Rudasill,* 589 S.W. 2d 877 (Ky. 1979), *cert. denied,* 446 U.S. 938 (1980).

7. *E.g., Bangor Baptist Church v Maine,* 576 F. Supp. 1299 (D. Me. 1983); *State v Nobel,* No. S791-0114-A, slip op. at 2 (Mich. Dist. Ct., Allegan County, Jan. 9, 1980).

8. No. S791-0114-A (Mich. Dist. Ct., Allegan County, Jan. 9, 1980).

9. *Id.,* slip op. at 8, 11, 12.

10. 273 U.S. 284 (1927).

11. *Id.* at 298.

12. 589 S.W. 2d 877 (Ky. 1979), *cert. denied,* 446 U.S. 938 (1980).

13. *Id.* at 884. The lower court decision that was affirmed had overturned teacher certification on the grounds that it violated the First Amendment, and lacked any justification by a compelling state interest served by the least burdensome means, noting that "qualifications for employment of a teacher are first of all religious" and that paper certification was not even rationally related to teacher quality. *Hinton v Kentucky State Board of Education,* No. 88314, slip op. at 3-4, 9-10 (pt. 1) (Ky. Cir. Ct. Oct. 4, 1978).

14. 134 Vt. 276, 357 A. 2d 121 (1976).

15. *Id.* at 278, 357 A. 2d at 123.

16. *Id.* at 280, 357 A. 2d at 124. In *Bell v Department of Licensing,* 182 Mont. 21, 594 P. 2d 331 (1979), the Montana Supreme Court overturned a regulatory requirment for certification of barber college instructors as being unauthorized by the relevant statute. *Id.* at 23, 594 P. 2d at 332.

17. Stocklin-Enright, *The Constitutionality of Home Education: The Role of the Parent, the State and the Child,* 18 Willamette Law Review 563, 606-08 (1982).

18. *E.g., Vlandis v Kline,* 412 U.S. 441 (1973).

19. 405 U.S. 645 (1972).

20. *Id.* at 654.

21. *See generally Vlandis v Kline,* 412 U.S. 441 (1973); *Cleveland Board of Education v LaFleur,* 414 U.S. 643 (1974).

22. *Mullaney v Wilbur,* 421 U.S. 684, 704 (1975); *In re Winship,* 379 U.S. 358, 364 (1970).

23. *E.g., State v Vaughn,* 44 N.J. 142, 146, 207 A. 2d 537, 540 (1965); *Wright v State,* 21 Okla. Crim. 430, 430-31, 209 P. 179, 180 (1922); *In re Monnia,* 638 S.W. 2d 782 (Mo. Ct. App. 1982); *State v Davis,* 598 S.W. 2d 189, 191 (Mo. Ct. App. 1981); *State v Pilkinton,* 310 S.W. 2d 304, 308 (Mo. Ct. App. 1958); *State v Massa,* 95 N.J. Super. 382, 390-91, 231 A. 2d 252, 257 (1967); *Sheppard v State,* 306 P. 2d 346, 353 (Okla. Crim. App. 1957); *State v White,* 325 N.W. 2d 76, 79 n. 3 (Wis. Ct. App. 1982), *overruled on other grounds; State v Popanz,* 112 Wis. 2d 166, 332 N.W. 2d 750 (1983).

PART FOUR

Compelling State Interests and Least Burdensome Means

Part Four analyzes the compelling state interest test that has been developed by the United States Supreme Court, which comes into play whenever a fundamental right is threatened by the state. This test requires that an individual's constitutional rights must prevail unless the state establishes a compelling interest in the narrow requirement at issue and also proves its use of the least burdensome means possible to achieve that state interest.

9

Alleged Compelling State Interests

The state may justify an inroad on religious liberty by showing that it is the least restrictive means of achieving some compelling state interest. However, it is still true that "[t]he essence of law that has been set and written on the subject is that only those interests of the highest order . . . can overbalance legitimate claims to the free exercise of religion."[1]

Thomas v. Review Board (1981)

The United States Supreme Court employs a test under which First Amendment liberties and other fundamental freedoms prevail over a conflicting governmental requirement *unless* the government can demonstrate both (1) that its requirement is necessitated by a compelling state interest and (2) that any such interest is accomplished by the least burdensome means.[2] This compelling interest test applies to freedom of speech and belief, privacy, parental liberty, and other First Amendment liberties and fundamental freedoms, as well as to free exercise of religion.[3]

For example, if the parental liberty of home education is challenged by a state agency, the state must demonstrate that it possesses a compelling interest sufficient to override parental liberty. However, even if it does demonstrate such an interest, the state must also show, as discussed in Chapter 10, that it has served its interest by the least burdensome means possible.

No Compelling Interest in Prohibiting or Prohibitively Regulating Home Education

Historically the state, in home education cases, has argued that it has a compelling state interest in education and that that interest is threatened by home education.[4] However, one legal writer gives the proper perspective:

> The state may be able to require that its populace grow up literate, but it should not be able to mandate a day-by-day, hour-by-hour directive of what a child's education should consist of and where his education should take place. Institutionalized schooling is not the least restrictive means, and it may not even bear a reasonable relation to the state's objective.[5]

The focus, then, must be on any state interest that is *actually* threatened by home instruction, not on the broader interest in education generally.

There are three basic factors that must be taken into account when considering any alleged state interest. First, the absence of any compelling state interest in prohibiting or prohibitively regulating home education is evident in the permissibility of home education in about three-quarters of the fifty states (as well as the total nonregulation of home education in a large number of the states). In fact, several states have recently deregulated and authorized home instruction, including Georgia, Montana, Mississippi, Colorado, Louisiana, and Arizona. Alaska actually has an officially-sponsored program for home education of children in remote villages, and many states officially provide home instruction for children who are seriously ill. There cannot be a compelling state interest in prohibiting or substantially regulating home education when the majority of states permit home education, especially in view of the trend of recent deregulatory statutes, and when some states even officially sponsor home instruction.

Second, the absence of any compelling state interest in prohibiting or prohibitively regulating home education is evident in the failure of the very content and curriculum of public schools that state educational authorities seek to impose on home education. This failure of public schools was recently noted by the National Commission on Excellence in Education. The report concluded:

> Some 23 million American adults are functionally illiterate by the simplest tests of everyday reading, writing, and comprehension.
>
> About 13 percent of all 17-year-olds in the United States can be considered functionally illiterate. . . .
>
> Average achievement of high school students on most standardized tests is now lower than 26 years ago when Sputnik was launched.
>
> The College Board's Scholastic Aptitude Tests (SAT) demonstrate a virtually unbroken decline from 1963 to 1980. Average verbal scores fell over 50

points and average mathematics scores dropped nearly 40 points.

College Board Achievement Tests also reveal consistent declines in recent years in such subjects as physics and English.[6]

There can be no compelling interest in imposing the mediocrity and unacceptable results of public schools on home education.

Third, it is important to recognize the vested interest of public schools in stifling competing educational alternatives. Public schools lose $2,000-$3,000 in revenue from state funds for each student instructed by home education or private schools.[7] Consequently, many public school officials view home education with a jaundiced eye.

On the individual constitutional interest side of the equation, it is worth noting, as did the United States Supreme Court in *Wisconsin v. Yoder,*[8] the importance of "the diversity we profess to admire and encourage,"[9] as well as the pluralism that our educational system itself is supposed to tolerate and encourage. Moreover, as a matter of policy, it would be unwise to restrict home education now that it is on the verge of a technological revolution (home computers, etc.), and when it embodies the best in educational methods (the tutorial method), while providing greater individual choice for pluralistic diversity.

No Subordinating Interest in Compulsory Education
There is no compelling state interest in prohibiting or burdensomely regulating home education. As early as 1925 in the landmark case of *Pierce v. Society of Sisters,*[10]

the United States Supreme Court began a line of decisions protecting parental liberty against any alleged compelling state interest in education. The Court there overturned a prohibition of nonpublic education, and thereby established (before the compelling interest test had been adopted) that the government could not have a compelling interest in prohibiting nonpublic education. The subsequent Supreme Court decision in *Farrington v. Tokushige* effectively established that the state does not have a sufficient interest in prohibitively regulating nonpublic education in its curriculum, teachers, or textbooks.

These cases culminated in the landmark decision of *Wisconsin v. Yoder*.[11] In this case the Supreme Court assessed and rejected the "state's broader contention that its interest in its system of compulsory education is so compelling that even the established religious practices of the Amish must give way."[12] The state's argument was based on two contentions: "that some degree of education is necessary to prepare citizens to participate effectively and intelligently in our open political system," and that it "prepares individuals to be self-reliant and self-sufficient participants in society."[13]

Although the Court agreed with these two general propositions, it scrutinized the narrow state interest involved rather than a broad and general state interest in education. It concluded that there was no compelling state interest in requiring the two challenged years of high school attendance. The Court said:

> In the face of our consistent emphasis on the central values underlying the Religion Clauses in our consti-

tutional scheme of government, we cannot accept a
parens patriae claim of such all-encompassing scope
and with such sweeping potential for broad and un-
foreseeable application as that urged by the State.[14]

While acknowledging the importance of Thomas
Jefferson's argument for "the need for education as a
bulwark of a free people against tyranny," the Court
noted that Jefferson did not have in mind "compulsory
education through any fixed age beyond a basic education," and that "he was reluctant to directly force instruction of children 'in opposition to the will of the
parent.' "[15]

In assessing which state interests in public education are compelling, the United States Supreme Court
has held that the state has no federal constitutional man-
date that requires the state to maintain the public school
system at all. In fact, the Court specifically commented
in another decision:

> Education, of course, is not among the rights afforded
> explicit protection under our Federal Constitution.
> Nor do we find any basis for saying it is implicitly so
> protected. . . .
> We have carefully considered each of the argu-
> ments supportive of the District Court's finding that
> education is a fundamental right or liberty and have
> found those arguments unpersuasive.[16]

This language and that of *Wisconsin v. Yoder* preclude a
finding that the state has the compelling interest in education that is necessary to override the individual inter-

est in the freedoms of religion, belief, privacy, and parental liberty.

Other court decisions involving nonpublic education (generally private religious schools) have concluded that no compelling state interest exists to justify most state regulations.[17] Several home education decisions, as well, have expressly found that no compelling state interest justifies prohibition or burdensome regulation of home education. This was true in the leading case of *State v. Nobel*,[18] where the court involved determined that no compelling state interest justified a teacher certification requirement for home education. This same finding of lack of a compelling state interest has been made in many other home instruction decisions such as *State v. Tollefsrud*,[19] *State v. Lundsten*,[20] and *Delconte v. State*.[21]

No Compelling Interest in Teacher Certification

Teacher certification in nonpublic education is another area where the state lacks any compelling interest. This is evident in the lack of close correlation between certification and teaching quality, the lack of any ground for imposing public school mediocrity (or worse) on nonpublic education, and the perception of most states that a teacher certification requirement for nonpublic education is simply not necessary. Clearly, a certification requirement would effectively prohibit home education by most parents—even by most of those parents who are college graduates with good teaching abilities.

Again, *State v. Nobel*[22] is on point. In that case a court held that no compelling state interest justifies a teacher certification requirement for home education and such a requirement is, therefore, unconstitutional. The court stated:

> No evidence has been introduced in this case that would demonstrate that the State has a compelling interest in applying teacher certification laws to the Nobels or that the educational interest of the State could not be achieved by a requirement less restrictive on the religious beliefs of the Nobels.[25]

One legal commentator notes in a published article:

> Everyday experience and our own personal development inform us that the state teacher certificate is neither an infallible, an adequate nor exclusive assurance of competency to impart or engender skills, information or knowledge. . . . It may be a convenient administrative rule to require state certification but it cannot stand as the only way to qualify as an instructor when to do so would cut off otherwise qualified individuals wishing to instruct their own children. Much of value is simply not taught (or teachable) in the teacher training institutions and to that extent is uncertifiable. To attempt to confine to the walls of such institutions the monopoly on teaching the young is to allow the state to go too far and certainly entails a lessening of diversity of exposure for the children.
>
> Those cases upholding state legislative requirements of teacher certification as an absolute for private school approval conflict with parental constitutional rights.[24]

In particular, the absence of teacher certification requirements in more than 80 percent of the states for home education and private schools underscores the lack of a compelling state interest in requiring teacher certification. Further discussion of certification requirements appears in Chapter 8.

No Interest in Socialization

Many public educators urge that group learning and social contact by children with their age-group peers is essential to the educational process. This has been termed "socialization." There is little doubt that the peer group occupies a vital place in the life of students in public secondary and elementary schools.

In recent years, however, socialization and peer pressure have been critically viewed for their *negative* effects.

One such negative effect is persistent conformity. Conformity to behavior and beliefs of fellow-students is at the least very strong. Sometimes conformity becomes an obsessive drive of public school pupils, and is almost always a harmful rather than positive influence. The Supreme Court recognized this fact in *Wisconsin v. Yoder*[25] by stating that "[f]ormal high school education beyond the eighth grade . . . places Amish children in an environment hostile to Amish beliefs . . . with pressure to conform to the styles, manners, and ways of the peer group."[26] *Yoder* upheld the freedom of religious right and parental liberty to avoid this peer pressure, and rejected the state's arguments.

This, of course, raises another problem. The child's need for group acceptance and social approval influences the development of his values, and this influence is often very negative toward religious convictions. As one important study notes, pressure from peers carries particular influence upon religious convictions because "strong social support is required for the maintenance of a system of religious belief."[27] If, for example, a public school student complies with peer pressure, he may forsake the religious convictions, values, and practices of his parents, conforming instead to those of fellow-students.[28]

A further negative effect of socialization is that the rare nonconforming student who withstands such pressure in public schools is generally, as numerous psychological and sociological studies show, rejected as a deviant or stigmatized in various ways. This can have severe emotional effects on such students when religious beliefs are involved. In fact, one influential study indicates that "doubting religious doctrines is the source of much mental anguish and emotional distress on the part of the adolescent."[29]

These types of negative effects of so-called "socialization" are an important part of what many home educators are attempting to avoid. In fact, the socialization that some public school officials seek to impose is the very thing that many parents seek to avoid for First Amendment reasons. Fortunately, the courts in recent years are beginning to deny any importance to the socialization factor, essentially reasoning that it is not the state's business how well young people fit socially with other young people.

Although some older court decisions prohibited home education because of an alleged state interest in socialization (that is, group learning and social contact), "the modern view is to disregard socialization as not . . . an appropriate standard for home instruction."[30] One reason for this is that the courts are recognizing that socialization is *not* an education factor, but rather a social factor that is not even a legitimate state concern (much less a compelling state interest).[31] The *Yoder* decision of the United States Supreme Court appears to have resolved the issue conclusively by not accepting the state's argument that socialization is a compelling interest, and then by identifying the aspects of socialization that actually violated the First Amendment.

Numerous court decisions have noted that the state interest is only that "all the children shall be educated, not that they shall be educated in any particular way."[32] The state interest, if any, is only in the educational product, not in the means. As will be discussed in Chapters 10 and 11, home education is a constitutionally protected and educationally effective means.

Notes

1. *Thomas v. Review Board*, 450 U.S. 707, 718 (1981). *Accord, Wisconsin v. Yoder*, 406 U.S. 205, 215 (1972); *Sherbert v. Verner*, 374 U.S. 398, 406 (1963).
2. *Wisconsin v. Yoder*, 406 U.S. 205, 235-36 (1972); *Sherbert v. Verner*, 374 U.S. 398, 406 (1963).
3. *E.g., First National Bank v. Bellotti*, 435 U.S. 765, 786 (1978); *NAACP v. Button*, 371 U.S. 415, 439 (1963).
4. *E.g., Fogg v. Board of Education*, 76 N.H. 296, 299, 8 A. 173, 173-74 (1912).
5. Beshoner, *Home Education in America: Parental Rights Reasserted*, 49 Univ. of Missouri (Kansas City) Law Review 191, 204-05 (1981).
6. National Commission on Excellence in Education, *A Nation at Risk* (1983), *reprinted in* 128 Congressional Record S6059, S6060 (daily ed. May 5, 1983).
7. *E.g., Sheridan Road Baptist Church v. Michigan Department of Education*, No.

80-260-26205-AZ, slip op. at 8 (Mich. Cir. Ct., Ingraham County, Dec. 29, 1982), *rev'd on other grounds*, 132 Mich. App. 1, 348 N.W. 2d 263 (1984) (currently on appeal).

8. 406 U.S. 205 (1972).
9. *Id.* at 226.
10. 268 U.S. 510 (1925).
11. 406 U.S. 205 (1972).
12. *Id.* at 221.
13. *Id.*
14. *Id.* at 234.
15. *Id.* at 225-26 n.14. In *State v. Yoder*, 49 Wis. 2d 430, 182 N.W. 2d 539 (1971), which the United States Supreme Court affirmed, the Wisconsin Supreme Court expressly ruled that "compulsory education . . . in itself is not a compelling interest," and that "there is not such a compelling state interest in two years of high school compulsory education as will justify the burden it places upon the appellants' free exercise of their religion." 49 Wis. 2d 430, 182 N.W. 2d at 542, 547.
16. *San Antonio Independent School District v. Rodriguez*, 411 U.S. 1, 35, 37 (1973).
17. *E.g., Surinach v. Pesquera de Busquets*, 604 F.2d 73, 79 (1st Cir. 1979) (financial disclosure requirement); *Kentucky State Board for Elementary & Secondary Education v. Rudasill*, 589 S.W. 2d 877 (Ky. 1979), *cert. denied*, 466 U.S. 938 (1980) (*aff'g* No. 88314, slip op. at 1-3, pt. 2) (Ky. Cir. Ct. Oct. 4, 1978)) (teacher certification requirement and textbook approval requirement); *see also* S. Arons, *Compelling Belief: The Culture of American Schooling* (New York: McGraw-Hill, 1982); Carper, Rendering Unto Caesar: A Perspective on Christian Day Schools, State Regulation, and the First Amendment (Nov. 4, 1982) (unpublished paper presented to American Educational Studies Association); Stocklin-Enright, *The Constitutionality of Home Education: The Role of the Parent, the State and the Child*, 18 Willamette Law Review 563, 607 (1982).
18. No. S791-0114-A (Mich. Dist. Ct., Allegan County, Jan. 9, 1980).
19. No. K8222 (Minn. County Ct., Houston County, Feb. 9, 1983). The court found no compelling interest in prohibiting home education:

It is also suggested by the prosecution that the State's interest in the compulsory school attendance of the Tollefsrud children is paramount to that of the parents and that the children's interests must be recognized.
     This argument was rejected in *Yoder.*

Id., slip op. at 4.
20. Nos. 7220 & 7221, slip op. at 13 (Minn. County Ct., Beltrami County, May 20, 1980).
21. No. 82-CVS-0176, slip op. at 4 (N.C. Super. Ct., Harnett County, Jan. 7, 1983), *aff'd on other grounds*, ____ N.C. ____, ____ S.E. 2d ____ (1985).
22. No. S791-0114-A (Mich. Dist. Ct., Allegan County, Jan. 9, 1980).
23. *Id.*, slip op. at 8.
24. Stocklin-Enright, *supra* note 17, at 606-07. *See also Farrington v. Tokushige*, 273 U.S. 284, 298 (1927); *Kentucky State Board for Elementary & Secondary Education v. Rudasill*, 589 S.W. 2d 877 (Ky. 1979), *cert. denied*, 466 U.S. 938 (1980) (*aff'g* No. 88314 (Ky. Cir. Ct. Oct. 4, 1978)); *State v. LaBarge*,

134 Vt. 276, 357 A. 2d 121 (1976); *State v. Nobel,* No. S791-0114-A (Mich. Dist. Ct., Allegan County, Jan. 9, 1980).
25. 406 U.S. 205 (1972).
26. *Id.* at 211.
27. Brown, *A Study of Religious Belief,* 53 British Journal of Psychology 259, 268 (1962).
28. One study indicates that some students come "to perceive the majority estimates as correct," others believe "that their perceptions are inaccurate," while others "suppress their observations" though aware of the majority's error. Asch, *Effects of Group Pressure Upon the Modification and Distortion of Judgments,* in Group Dynamics Research and Theory 189, 191, 193, 194 (2d ed. D. Cartwright & A. Zander, New York: Harper & Row, 1960).
29. Elizabeth Hurlock, *Child Development* 359 (New York: McGraw-Hill, 1942). Numerous such studies are cited in Bird, *Freedom of Religion and Science Instruction in Public Schools,* 87 Yale L.J. 515, 527, 532-34 (1978).
30. Tobak & Zirkel, *Home Instruction: An Analysis of the Statutes and Case Law,* 8 Univ. of Dayton Law Review 1, 58-59 (1982). *See also State v. Massa,* 95 N.J. Super. 382, 387, 231 A. 2d 252, 255 (1967).
31. *E.g., Perchemlides v. Frizzle,* No. 16641 (Mass. Super. Ct., Hampshire County, Nov. 13, 1978).
32. *E.g., People v. Levisen,* 404 Ill. 574, 575, 90 N.E.2d 213, 215 (1950); *Commonwealth v. Roberts,* 159 Mass. 372, 374, 34 N.E. 402, 403 (1893).

10

The Least Burdensome Means

The state may justify an inroad on religious liberty by showing that it is the least restrictive means of achieving some compelling state interest.

Thomas v. Review Board (1981)

Even if the state can demonstrate a compelling interest threatened by home education, it still must prove that it is satisfying that interest by the least burdensome means possible. In other words, even if the state can demonstrate a compelling interest in regulating nonpublic education, it must yet prove that home instruction is *not* an appropriate means for satisfying the state interest.

Not Criminal Sanctions

The criminal penalties that compulsory education statutes impose are clearly not the least burdensome means for achieving any interest that the state may have in education. To restate this in perspective, well-meaning parents should not be subjected to criminal punishment

96

for attempting to recover what the public educational system has lost. As one notable scholar has written:

> The strong religious and philosophical beliefs of those choosing unapproved options deserve both respect and protection under the Constitution. Thus, some educators wonder whether compulsory attendance is sufficiently important to justify criminal sanctions against parents who are doing what they believe to be in the best interests of their children. They note that the scant available evidence suggests that these children are able to perform adequately on standardized tests. They recognize the value of family choice to public educators, who cannot constitutionally provide a religious orientation to the program. Such options relieve the pressure on public schools to attempt such unconstitutional policies.[1]

Not Institutionalized Schooling

Institutionalized schooling, in public schools or formal private schools, is also clearly not the least burdensome means to achieve any perceived state interest in education. One legal commentator notes:

> [The state] should not be able to mandate a day-by-day, hour-by-hour directive of what a child's education should consist of and where his education should take place. Institutionalized schooling is not the least restrictive means, and it may not even bear a reasonable relation to the state's objective.[2]

Instead, several court decisions have noted that the real state interest, if any, is simply "that all children shall be educated, not that they shall be educated in any particular manner or place."[3]

Not Teacher Certification

A teacher certification requirement, which obviously disqualifies nearly all parents even if they are excellent teachers, is similarly not the least burdensome means. As an article in the *Willamette Law Review* states:

> It may be assumed that most parents are not state-certified teachers, that is, they are not graduates of programs designed for professional educators and approved by the state. Any requirement of state certification will therefore present a problem to the majority of parents wishing to educate their children themselves. . . .
>
> It does not appear unreasonable and would satisfy the concerns the state has in certification to allow a parent to produce proof of proficiency other than by a state certificate. Alternative proof of competency when administered reasonably would entail a cost. But the cost would be justifiable in view of the enhancement of the parent's interest and the always present possibility that a child's future may actually benefit from an alternative to the state-sanctioned teacher. Given the desirability of an alternative standard, adherence to certification as the exclusive method of teacher approval would appear untenable.[4]

Home Education as a Less Burdensome Means

Allowance for home education constitutes the least burdensome means for assuring any state interest in education. This is particularly so in view of the superiority of the tutorial method and the educational quality demonstrated by home education. As discussed in Chapter 11, numerous studies on a nationwide basis have demonstrated the educational quality of home education.

A requirement for annual standardized tests also has been found by several recent court decisions to provide a far less burdensome means than teacher certification and other intrusive regulations.[5] Standardized testing, because of grade inflation, is now considered by many as the most meaningful measure available of educational achievement. In fact, nonpublic school students (including home school students) generally score higher on the standardized tests than do public school students. As long as children's percentile scores on standardized tests are remaining substantially the same, or at least are not dropping precipitously, home instruction clearly is satisfying any state interest in education (and doing so at least as well as public school instruction would). Thus, home education with a testing requirement constitutes a less burdensome means, these courts have said.

We do not encourage the imposition of a testing requirement, because home education without such a requirement itself constitutes the least burdensome means. (Chapter 14 does encourage the use of standardized tests on a purely voluntary basis.) Although some home instructors differ, quite a few home educators support or do not oppose a testing requirement as long as it includes three important factors.

It is important to note that parents must *not* be required to meet the fiftieth percentile or average for public schools, because half of all children do not meet that level, and thus could not be educated by home instruction. It is also important to have a cushion of a probationary year if scores decline, because test scores are not perfect, and maturity changes can produce fluctuations in scores. Finally, it is critical to allow the parents to select the particular test out of the variety of available standardized tests, because tests are capable of being ideologically biased and thus objectionable on First Amendment grounds.

Permission for home education is the least burdensome means to achieve any state interests in nonpublic education, and therefore is constitutionally obligatory under the better line of cases. The following chapter on the educational effectiveness of home education shows that it indeed does fulfill these state interests.

Notes

1. Lines, *Private Education Alternatives and State Regulation*, 12 Journal of Law & Education 189, 190-91 (1983).
2. Beshoner, *Home Education in America: Parental Rights Reasserted*, 49 Univ. of Missouri (Kansas City) Law Review 191, 204 (1981).
3. *E.g., People v Levisen*, 404 Ill. 574, 575, 90 N.E.2d 213, 215 (1950); *Commonwealth v Roberts*, 159 Mass. 372, 374, 34 N.E. 402, 403 (1893).
4. Stocklin-Enright, *The Constitutionality of Home Education: The Role of the Parent, the State and the Child*, 18 Willamette Law Review 563, 606-07 (1982).
5. *Kentucky State Board for Elementary & Secondary Education v Rudasill*, 589 S.W.2d 877 (Ky. 1979), *cert. denied*, 446 U.S. 938 (1980); *State v Lundsten*, Nos. 7220 & 7221, slip op. at 14 (Minn. County Ct., Beltrami County, May 20, 1980).

11

The Educational Merit
of Home Education

In western New York State, five unrelated [home education] families submitted their children to testing. . . .
[T]he seven children averaged 90 to 99 percent on
Stanford Achievement Tests.

Dr. Raymond S. Moore

Educational Research on Quality

Numerous studies have demonstrated the educational
effectiveness of home education. For example, Dr. Raymond S. Moore, one of the leading academic authorities
on home education, a lecturer at Indiana University and
Western Michigan University, and president of Hewitt
Research Foundation, writes in a 1982 article in the
Teachers College Record of Columbia University: "A recent
national study of home schools confirmed among its other findings that youngsters educated at home achieved
higher than national averages in standardized measures."[1] The Hewitt Research team's clinical experience
with several thousand home schools verified this. As Dr.
Moore notes:

Rural and urban children from New York to California and Hawaii and from Alaska and North Dakota to Nebraska and Louisiana have often been performing in the seventy-fifth to ninety-ninth percentiles on Stanford and Iowa Achievement Tests. Frequently they are taught by high school-educated parents no more than an hour or two a day, usually utilizing readily available home-school or correspondence curriculum.[2]

Dr. Moore explains the academic success of home instruction in terms of several educational reasons:

This success should not be surprising in view of several factors that any objective observer can readily understand:

1. Home schools are characterized by parents who have enough concern for their children to take on the task of systematically teaching them.

2. Parents provide a partiality that young children need, but schools cannot allow.

3. Children thrive on routines that involve a few children who share the same family values.

4. A child in the home school daily experiences from ten to a hundred times as many personal adult-to-child responses as he would in a formal school; such responses—along with adult example—mean educational power far more than do books.

5. Without the all-day regimentation of the classroom, the child becomes more of a free explorer and thinker than a restricted regurgitator of books, which to him are often more barriers than facilitators to learning.

6. Parents who bring their children with them into the responsibilities of the home turn out independent, self-directed children.[3]

Dr. John Holt, author of several books on home education, concurs with Dr. Moore's assessment of the quality of home education. Holt writes:

> [T]he great majority of them learn to read much more quickly, enthusiastically, and efficiently than most children in conventional schools. . . .
>
> [E]ven the most attentive, perceptive, and thoughtful classroom teachers could never elicit from their students the amount and intensity of feedback that home-schooling parents typically get from their children, because parents know and understand their children so much better.[4]

Court Decision on Quality

The educational quality of home education has been noted in many decisions, such as *State v. Nobel.*[5] In that decision the court emphasized:

> Dr. George L. Hopkins of Florida, an educational psychologist, administered intelligence and psychological testing of the Nobel children. Dr. Hopkins' qualification as a psychologist and educational testing expert was stipulated to by the parties herein as were the findings of the results. . . .
>
> Dr. Hopkins' evaluations indicate that . . . the five Nobel children are above average intelligence, that each has obtained an educational level ahead of other children in their chronological age group. The results are given in detail in exhibit #6. In addition thereto, Mrs. Nobel was tested and found to possess the intelligence as well as the training and appropriate psychological makeup to perform well as a teacher.[6]

An important part of the educational effectiveness of home instruction is the proved tutorial method that it embodies, as well as the promised home computer revolution that is beginning, as discussed in Chapter 1. With home computers, the nation's best educators can be brought into the home by programmed instruction, just as they now can be brought in by good textbooks.

Notes

1. Moore, *Research and Common Sense: Therapies for Our Homes and Schools,* 84 Teachers College Record (Columbia University) 355, 372 (1982); Raymond Moore & Dorothy Moore, *School Can Wait* 27-48, 205-20 (Provo, Utah: Brigham Young University Press, 1979).
2. Raymond Moore & Dorothy Moore, *supra* note 1.
3. Moore, *supra* note 1, at 372.
4. Holt, *Schools and Home Schoolers: A Fruitful Partnership,* 64 Phi Delta Kappan 391, 393 (Feb. 1983).
5. No. S791-0114-A (Mich. Dist. Ct., Allegan County, Jan. 9, 1980).
6. *Id.,* slip op. at 3.

PART FIVE

Superseded and Erroneous Court Decisions

Part Five analyzes superseded court decisions, cases that are no longer valid precedent in light of recent cases. It also discusses erroneous court decisions, which have incorrectly construed or even ignored the constitutional guarantees that apply to home education. Numerous court decisions that are favorable to home instruction, and that are far better authority under current constitutional law, have been discussed in the preceding eleven chapters of this book.

12

Superseded Court Decisions

> In light of *Sherbert* the validity of such reasoning is to be doubted since the guarantee of free exercise of religion covers more than sacramental acts of worship.
>
> *State v. Yoder* (1971)

Some earlier decisions involving home education have been superseded by important United States Supreme Court decisions. For instance, some decisions were superseded by the Supreme Court's acknowledgment in 1925 of the constitutional right to nonpublic education. Later, some decisions were superseded by the Supreme Court's application of the First Amendment to the states in 1940. Other decisions were superseded by the Supreme Court's imposition of the compelling interest test in 1963. Finally, a few decisions were superseded by the Supreme Court's limitation on compulsory education in 1972.

Decisions Before 1940: *Pierce* and *Cantwell*
In 1925 in *Pierce v. Society of Sisters*,[1] the United States Supreme Court acknowledged the constitutional right

to nonpublic education, a matter which had been in considerable doubt in prior decisions.[2] Many decisions had been adverse to home education before 1925 and generally refused to consider constitutional rights, instead simply construing the language of compulsory education statutes.[3]

Next in 1940, in *Cantwell v. Connecticut*,[4] the Supreme Court first applied the First Amendment to the states, which had not theretofore been restricted by the Bill of Rights.[5] Originally, the Bill of Rights (the first ten amendments to the United States Constitution) were restrictions only on the actions of the federal government. With the Supreme Court's interpretation of the due process clause of the Fourteenth Amendment,[6] through such cases as *Cantwell v. Connecticut* and others, the original concept was altered to restrict actions of the states as well. Thus, with the coming of *Cantwell,* earlier decisions were superseded in which First Amendment rights were held inapplicable to the states.[7]

Decisions Before 1972: *Sherbert* and *Yoder*

In 1963 in *Sherbert v. Verner,*[8] the United States Supreme Court for the first time imposed a compelling interest test for the free exercise clause of the First Amendment. This now meant that a governmental requirement or law would override individual free exercise of religion *only* with a compelling state interest served by the least burdensome means.[9] Likewise, in the same year, the Supreme Court imposed the compelling interest test for freedom of speech, and subsequently for other First Amendment rights and fundamental freedoms.[10]

Sherbert and its judicial progeny superseded those

earlier decisions that had employed the much less strict, and much more easily met, "rational relation to a legitimate state interest" test.[11] Two of these earlier decisions were strongly and aptly criticized by the Wisconsin Supreme Court in the *Yoder* decision[12] (which was later affirmed by the United States Supreme Court). The Wisconsin court held:

> Two of these cases, *Hershberger* and *Beiler,* were decided before *Sherbert* and rely heavily on the dubious distinction between religious belief and religious conduct. See *Cantwell v. Connecticut* (1940), 310 U.S. 296. Thus the court in *Hershberger* reasoned that requiring the Amish to provide an education for their children would not abridge their right to worship, concluding therefrom that no question of infringement of religious freedom was involved. In light of *Sherbert* the validity of such reasoning is to be doubted since the guarantee of free exercise of religion covers more than sacramental acts of worship.
>
> In *Beiler* the court gave recognition to the conflict between compulsory education and religious liberty but having drawn the balance, proceeded to mechanically add to the state's side a series of cases upholding a restriction on religious conduct. Nor did the court consider the effectiveness of the regulatory purpose or the practicability of an exemption. The type of analysis used does not satisfy today's standards in dealing with constitutional questions. It is also significant that the *Beiler* decision has been modified by the Pennsylvania legislature.[13]

In 1972, the United States Supreme Court, in *Wisconsin v. Yoder,*[14] substantially limited the overpowering reach that many courts had given to compulsory education statutes.[15] The Court accomplished this important feat by sustaining a religious defense against the state's asserted interest in compulsory education.

One case, *State v. Garber*,[16] is generally viewed as having been overturned by the Supreme Court in *Yoder.* In fact, the *Garber* case was directly criticized by the Wisconsin Supreme Court decision[17] that was later affirmed by the United States Supreme Court in *Yoder.* The Wisconsin court, in particular, noted:

> In *State v. Garber,* the Kansas court considering the problem after *Sherbert,* held that the [compulsory education] law was to be enforced against the Amish. The appellants' contention that *Garber* reflects an insensitive consideration of the Amish religion is in part supported by a reading of the opinion. *Garber* followed the *Beiler* court's mechanical separation of religious conduct from religious belief, implying that the constitutional protection is afforded only to beliefs connected to the act of worship and held that since the compulsory attendance laws do not directly affect Amish worship, there was no abridgment of their religious freedom. But the Amish do not have a ritualistic form of worship. They have no churches as such. Their life style is dictated rather than motivated by their religion. The narrowness of the *Garber* concept of the scope of protection afforded by the Free Exercise Clause renders the case unpersuasive.
>
> *Garber* has also lost luster because an exemption was provided in 1968 by the Kansas Legislature. . . . This exemption enables the Amish to comply with the Kansas law with its unique educational program. These legislative exemptions evince the fact the important goals of education can be attained by alterna-

tive forms of regulation without infringing first amendment rights.[18]

Therefore, the plain meaning of the most recent and leading United States Supreme Court cases is that the earlier cases giving broad authority to the government through compulsory education laws have been superseded.[19] Although this is true, it is unfortunate that some modern courts yet cling to the older, outworn reasoning of the era that gave the government such an all-encompassing authority over education at the expense of individual freedom. As the next chapter discusses, these modern decisions are clearly erroneous.

Notes

1. 268 U.S. 510 (1925).
2. *Id.* at 534-35.
3. Beshoner, *Home Education in America: Parental Rights Reasserted,* 49 Univ. of Missouri (Kansas City) Law Review 191, 195 (1981). *E.g., Fogg v Board of Education,* 76 N.H. 296, 82 A. 173 (1912); *State v Jackson,* 71 N.H. 552, 53 A. 1021 (1902); *State v Counort,* 69 Wash. 361, 124 P. 910 (1912).
4. 310 U.S. 296 (1940).
5. *Id.* at 303.
6. The Fourteenth Amendment, in part, reads: "No state . . . shall . . . deprive any person of life, liberty, or property, without due process of law." The incorporation of the Bill of Rights by interpretation of the due process clause has received some critical comment. *E.g.,* Raoul Berger, *Government by Judiciary* (Cambridge: Harvard University Press, 1977); Hermine Herta Meyer, *The History and Meaning of the Fourteenth Amendment* (New York: Vantage Press, 1977).
7. *E.g., State v Hoyt,* 84 N.H. 38, 146 A. 170 (1929); *Stephens v Bongart,* 15 N.J. Misc. 80, 189 A. 131 (1937).
8. 374 U.S. 398 (1963).
9. *Id.* at 406.
10. *NAACP v Button,* 371 U.S. 415, 439 (1963).
11. *E.g., State v Lowry,* 191 Kan. 701, 383 P. 2d 962 (1963); *Commonwealth v Renfrew,* 332 Mass. 492, 126 N.E.2d 109 (1955); *Dobbins v Commonwealth,* 198 Va. 697, 96 S.E.2d 154 (1957); *Rice v Commonwealth,* 188 Va. 224,

49 S.E.2d 342 (1948); *State ex rel. Shoreline School District v Superior Court,* 55 Wash. 2d 177, 346 P. 2d 999 (1959), *cert. denied,* 363 U.S. 814 (1960); *People v Turner,* 121 Cal. App. 2d 61, 263 P.2d 685 (1953), *appeal dismissed,* 347 U.S. 972 (1954); *In re Shinn,* 195 Cal. App. 2d 683, 16 Cal. Rptr. 165 (1961); *State v Hershberger,* 103 Ohio App. 188, 144 N.E.2d 693 (1955); *People ex rel. Shapiro v Dorin,* 199 Misc. 643, 99 N.Y.S.2d 830 (Dom. Rel. Ct. 1950), *appeal dismissed,* 342 U.S. 884 (1953); *Knox v O'Brien,* 7 N.J. Super. 608, 72 A.2d 389 (1950); *Commonwealth v Smoker,* 177 Pa. Super. 435, 110 A. 2d 740 (1955); *Commonwealth v Beiler,* 168 Pa. Super. 462, 79 A. 2d 134 (1951); *Commonwealth v Bey,* 166 Pa. Super. 136, 70 A.2d 693 (1950). Note that quite a few of the above decisions are from within the same state. Note also that the *Shoreline* decision involved a narrow five to four margin, with a vigorous and solid dissent, and has been criticized as unconstitutional. Stocklin-Enright, *The Constitutionality of Home Education: The Role of the Parent, the State and the Child,* 18 Willamette Law Review 563, 601 (1982). The *Bongart* and *O'Brien* reasoning was rejected by New Jersey courts in *State v Massa,* 95 N.J. Super. 382, 231 A. 2d 252 (1967).

12. *State v Yoder,* 49 Wis. 2d 430, 182 N.W. 2d 539 (1971).
13. 49 Wis. 2d 430, 182 N.W. 2d at 546.
14. 406 U.S. 205 (1972).
15. *E.g., State v Garber,* 197 Kan. 567, 419 P. 2d 896 (1966), *cert. denied,* 389 U.S. 51 (1967).
16. *Id.*
17. *State v Yoder,* 49 Wis. 2d 430, 182 N.W. 2d 539 (1971).
18. 49 Wis. 2d 430, 182 N.W. 2d at 546-47.
19. This is true despite some arguments building on dictum (remarks in passing) in some of the United States Supreme Court cases. For example, the Supreme Court in *Pierce v Society of Sisters,* 268 U.S. 510 (1925), stated that "no question has been raised" about particular regulations of private education. 268 U.S. at 534. This clearly is not a holding, but a statement that the issue was not being reached. Moreover, the scope of permissible "reasonable regulation" has been considerably narrowed by the adoption of the compelling interest test in *Sherbert v Verner,* 374 U.S. 398 (1963).

In *Board of Education v Allen,* 392 U.S. 236 (1968), a reference was made to compulsory attendance and related regulations. This was dictum, because the issue in that case was a statute providing textbooks to students at religious schools, and it did not expressly consider the impact of the compelling interest test that had recently been adopted. Any similar references in other United States Supreme Court decisions constitute dictum, and in no way retreat from the holding in *Farrington v Tokushige,* 273 U.S. 284 (1927), that there are strict limits (even before application of the First Amendment to the states) on state regulation of teacher certification, textbooks, and curriculum. *Id.* at 298.

13

Erroneous Court Decisions

Despite unambiguous and concise constitutional rules enunciated by the United States Supreme Court, some courts have yet to afford home education full and complete legal protection. These cases are either distinguishable on their facts and issues or are so clearly in error that they deserve little precedential value.

Decisions Distinguishable on Their Facts or Issues
Several court decisions are plainly distinguishable on the basis of the legal issues argued (or *not* argued) or the factual situations involved.

In several cases involving home education, *no* constitutional arguments have been raised by the parties or discussed by the courts. In fact, in some of these cases such leading precedents as *Wisconsin v. Yoder*[1] and *Pierce v. Society of Sisters*[2] were not mentioned. Thus, such cases are not dispositive of the home education issue and properly have *no* value as precedents.

For example, in a 1982 Virginia decision, *Grigg v. Virginia*,[3] the only constitutional argument advanced in the case was an allegation that the compulsory education law was vague. Even on this issue, the Georgia Supreme Court and Wisconsin Supreme Court have reached the contrary result (as discussed in Chapter 7).

In another 1982 decision in Oregon, *State v. Bowman*,[4] the only constitutional issues raised were on an equal protection argument regarding statutory classification and a due process argument regarding proof beyond a reasonable doubt. Such key constitutional rights as parental liberty and free religious exercise (and others set forth in this book) were not even touched.[5]

Several cases have involved the absence of any home instruction at all, and so are distinguishable on their facts. For example, in one case, *State v. Kasuboski*,[6] although sometimes cited as a home education case, no actual instruction of the children took place at all. Also, this case involved a mail order church (for tax avoidance reasons), and thus no bona fide religious reasons were found to exist for the alleged home instruction. This case and a few others[7] are, in reality, not true home education cases. Because they are distinguishable, they are not legal precedent for discrediting valid home education programs.

Decisions Erroneous in Their Constitutional Law Approach

Several cases are incorrect as a matter of constitutional law, and should not be followed. The better line of authority and weight of authority is represented by the cases discussed earlier in this book.

One such case is *State v. Riddle*,[8] a 1981 West Virginia decision, wherein a court ruled against a home education program that was based on religious freedom. There are several reasons why *Riddle* was wrongly decided.

First, the court erroneously limited *Wisconsin v. Yoder* to ancient religions involving a community life. The court said:

> In the case before us we are not confronted by members of a recognized West Virginia community with a long history of successful preparation of its children outside of the public schools for a life in contemporary society.[9]

This reasoning is incorrect both in light of *Yoder* and of other free exercise of religion decisions, including recent United States Supreme Court decisions, involving individualistic religious beliefs and newly-formed religions.[10]

Second, the court in *Riddle* came to the erroneous conclusion that First Amendment defenses could not be validly raised to a criminal statute. The court said:

> Consequently, notwithstanding the strong language of *Yoder,* since that case arose out of an entirely different factual context, this Court holds that sincerely held religious convictions are never a defense to total non-compliance with the compulsory school attendance law.[11]

However, the United States Supreme Court in *Wisconsin v. Yoder*[12] implicitly rejected this approach, and explicitly has ruled in favor of a religious defense to other criminal prosecutions.[13] Moreover, it must be noted that the compulsory education law involved in the *Riddle* case explicitly permitted home education. The problem was that the Riddles had failed to file the required reports with the state.

In another disturbing decision, *Duro v. District Attorney*,[14] a United States Court of Appeals ruled on another home education program conducted because of religious belief. The court took a very similar tack to *State v. Riddle*, in holding that *Wisconsin v. Yoder* applies only to older and recognized religious beliefs and practices.[15] The court held:

> We find, therefore, that this case is factually distinguishable from *Yoder*. Despite Duro's sincere religious belief, we hold that the welfare of the children is paramount and that their future well-being mandates attendance at a public or nonpublic school.[16]

Moreover, in *Duro* the court made at least eight other critical errors of constitutional law. It erroneously gave significance to the lack of a formal stated command for home education in the Duros' religious faith (considered in Chapter 4). It erroneously placed the burden of proof on the parent (discussed in Chapter 8). It erroneously read *Yoder* to hold that a state generally has a compelling interest in compulsory education, and wrongly held that this state interest was sufficient to override the Duros' religious rights (assessed in Chapter 9). It totally ignored the least burdensome means requirement and the state's obligation to establish that (considered in Chapter 10). The court erroneously treated socialization as a legitimate and even important state interest (analyzed in Chapter 9). It erroneously concluded that home education necessarily would not prepare children to be self-sufficient participants in society or in the political system (discussed in Chapter 11). Finally, the court erroneously made the paternalistic argument that its chief consideration must be the welfare of the children, despite the absence of any disagreement between parents and children (who also wanted home education) and despite express rejection of that approach in *Yoder*.

In two other poorly reasoned cases, *Hanson v. Cushman*[17] and *Scoma v. Chicago Board of Education*,[18] the reason given by the parents for home education was parental liberty. The courts in these cases denied that such parental liberty is a fundamental constitutional right that requires use of the compelling interest test. These cases are clearly incorrect because parental liberty is indeed a fundamental right. As the United States Supreme Court in *Wisconsin v. Yoder* stated:

> Even more markedly than in *Prince*, therefore, this case involves the *fundamental interest* of parents, as contrasted with that of the State, to guide the religious future and *education* of their children.[19]

Moreover, in *State v. Whisner*,[20] the Ohio Supreme Court held:

> Thus, it has long been recognized that the right of a *parent* to guide the *education*, including the religious

education, of his or her child is indeed a *"fundamental right"* guaranteed by the due process clause of the Fourteenth Amendment.[21]

In a clearly erroneous decision, *State v. Moorhead*,[22] an Iowa court ruled against home instruction, and in doing so denied that the state has the ultimate burden of proof on the issue of equivalence under Iowa law. This ruling on the burden of proof was incorrect, because the United States Supreme Court has explicitly held that in a criminal prosecution the state must prove every element of a crime (even if statutorily worded as an exception) beyond a reasonable doubt.[23]

The above erroneous cases and others[24] present a dilemma to many parents conducting home education. Because of defects in reasoning and in application of the law, a portion of the American citizenry is being denied its rights. Clearly such errors in constitutional law, at the expense of fundamental constitutional rights, are inexcusable in our time.

Notes

1. 406 U.S. 205 (1972).
2. 268 U.S. 510 (1925).
3. 297 S.E. 2d 799 (Va. 1982).
4. 60 Ore. App. 184, 653 P. 2d 254 (1982).
5. *See also State v. M.M.*, 407 So. 2d 987 (Fla. Dist. Ct. 1981); *Akron v. Lane*, 65 Ohio App. 2d 90, 416 N.E. 2d 642 (1979); *In re Thomas H.*, 78 Misc. 2d 412, 357 N.Y.S. 2d 384 (Fam. Ct. 1974).
6. 87 Wis. 2d 407, 275 N.W. 2d 101 (1978).
7. *E.g., Hill v. State*, 381 So. 2d 91 (Ala. Ct. App. 1979), *rev'd on other grounds*, 381 So. 2d 94 (Ala. 1980), *on remand*, 410 So. 2d 431 (Ala. Ct. App. 1981); *T.A.F. v. Duval County,* 273 So. 2d 15 (Fla. Dist. Ct. 1973) (sham church with "principal tenet" of racial segregation). *State v. White*, 325 N.W. 2d 76 (Wis. Ct. App. 1982), was overruled in *State v. Popanz*, 112 Wis. 2d 166, 177, 332 N.W. 2d 750, 754-55 (1983).

8. 285 S.E. 2d 359 (W. Va. 1981).

9. *Id.* at 362.

10. *E.g., Widmar v Vincent,* 454 U.S. 263 (1981) (new religious group); *Heffron v International Society for Krishna Consciousness, Inc.,* 452 U.S. 640 (1981) (new religion); *Gillette v United States,* 401 U.S. 437 (1971) (individualistic religion); *Welsh v United States,* 398 U.S. 333 (1970) (individualistic religion); *United States v Seeger,* 380 U.S. 163 (1965) (individualistic religion).

11. 285 S.E. 2d at 365. *See also id.* at 362.

12. 406 U.S. 205 (1972).

13. *E.g., United States v Ballard,* 322 U.S. 78 (1944) (criminal fraud law); *West Virginia State Board of Education v Barnette,* 319 U.S. 624 (1943) (compulsory attendance law); *see also Wooley v Maynard,* 430 U.S. 705 (1977) (license tag law); *United States v Seeger,* 380 U.S. 163 (1965) (military draft evasion).

14. 712 F. 2d 96 (4th Cir. 1983).

15. *Id.* at 98.

16. *Id.* at 99.

17. 490 F. Supp. 109 (W.D. Mich. 1980).

18. 391 F. Supp. 452 (N.D. Ill. 1974).

19. 406 U.S. 205, 214 (1972).

20. 47 Ohio St. 2d 181, 351 N.E. 2d 750 (1976).

21. 47 Ohio St. 2d at 213-14, 351 N.E. 2d at 769. *Accord, In re Peirce,* 122 N.H. 762, 768, 451 A. 2d 363, 367 (1982) (concurring opinion).

22. 308 N.W. 2d 60 (Iowa 1981).

23. *E.g., Mullaney v Wilbur,* 421 U.S. 684, 704 (1975); *In re Winship,* 397 U.S. 358, 364 (1970).

24. The compelling state interest test was not used in two lower court decisions; *In re Franz,* 55 App. Div. 2d 424, 390 N.Y.S. 2d 940 (1977); *Jerningan v State,* 412 So. 2d 1242 (Ala. Ct. App.), *cert. denied,* No. 81-481 (Ala. S. Ct. 1982).

Conclusion

Home education has a venerable history of success, producing many world leaders and having been the basis of America's early schooling. It has been shown to be educationally successful in many studies, largely because it employs the tutorial method of individual instruction by genuinely caring parents.

The constitutional right to employ home education is protected by numerous provisions of the United States Constitution, including freedom of religious exercise, freedom of speech and philosophic belief, the right to privacy, and the right to parental liberty. The state lacks any compelling interest in prohibiting or intrusively regulating home education. Moreover, the state has not used the less burdensome means of permitting home education.

Numerous recent court decisions have upheld the right to home education under these constitutional provisions. The contrary cases, in the legal opinion of the authors, have been superseded or are erroneous.

Freedom to select home education is an important part of freedom in education and in family self-determination.

14

Practical Suggestions for Home Education

At this point in time, there are three primary avenues to pursue to ensure the protection of home instruction: education of the public at large, legislative efforts, and litigation. All of these, if necessary, should be pursued simultaneously.*

Educating the Public

Educating the general public on the many positive aspects of home education is important, not only in increasing general awareness but also in offering the alternative of home instruction to those who would otherwise be uninformed of its existence and viability. As empha-

---

* The constitutional position outlined in this book is believed by the authors to be accurate as a matter of correct constitutional interpretation, but it is not universally accepted by courts, as Chapters 12 and 13 indicate. Courts often are not solicitous of First Amendment rights, and this seems to be particularly true in regard to home education. Thus, home educators should not rely on the constitutional arguments given in this book as being accepted by all courts, and should not rely on the practical suggestions given in this chapter as assuring immunity from prosecution or conviction. Further, home educators who face potential or actual prosecution should retain a qualified attorney who understands their position and has First Amendment expertise. No reliance should be placed on this book as a substitute for individual legal counsel or for privately retained representation.

sized in preceding chapters, the validity of home education as an alternative to both public and private schools can be affirmed by historical precedents and court decisions, as well as by the empirical evidence provided by those parents and children actually involved in home instruction.

Moreover, home instruction adds to the richness of our culture by promoting a diversity in educational choice, thus adding to the pluralistic matrix of American society.

There are various methods of arousing public interest and awareness. One avenue is holding seminars and conferences that present competent and well-qualified speakers who can substantiate the value and legitimacy of home education. The distribution of books (such as this one), magazine and newspaper articles, and well-documented legal and educational articles published in professional journals can go a long way in raising the credibility of home education. Radio and television interviews with credible spokesmen can also accomplish much in building public awareness of home education.

We urge, however, that spokesmen for any media events be chosen with care. Such spokesmen should be articulate and careful in their public statements, relying on the wealth of factual data available and always avoiding gimmicks and overstatement. Much good can be said about home instruction, and that should be the focus.

Legislative Efforts

The educational process can, if effective, lead to legislative efforts in those states that do not affirmatively allow for home education in their state laws. Court litigation has also led those involved in home instruction to seek legislation to protect home education.

Obviously, there are state legislatures that are open to considering legislation to accommodate home schools. Such state legislatures would welcome factual information in support of home education. Those who teach their children at home should take advantage of legislative hearings to express their views and experience.

Testimony given before state legislatures and legislative committees, however, should be carefully planned by advocates of home instruction. The best expert witnesses possible should testify in support of home education before such committees. Parents involved in home instruction should testify, but the number testifying should be limited to avoid repetition. Moreover, the parents selected to testify should reflect, if possible, a wide range of religious faiths. Not only will these types of testimony supply the necessary information from which to draft the laws, but will also provide legislative, constitutional, and historical background that is so vital in the defense of laws when they are challenged in court.

Success in gaining favorable legislation requires that those in favor of home instruction be organized in their efforts. Effective home education lobbying groups are also important. Such organizations can monitor the legislatures and, upon competent legal advice, propose legislative measures to protect home instruction.

In fact, organizations already exist that can assist those wishing to organize. These organizations will also keep those interested in home education abreast of educational resources, court cases, and legislative activities concerning home instruction. See the organizations and programs listed at the end of this book.

Litigation

Finally, and with great caution, it may be necessary to pursue courtroom litigation in order to protect the right of home education. When possible, however, certain key cases must be selected that will set the needed precedent in protecting home instruction.

Because of this need for positive legal precedent, it is important that those involved in home education conduct their instruction efficiently, in the best possible educational environment, and in such a manner that they will be in the most advantageous position to contest state interference if they are brought to court. Therefore, for the best legal protection, a home instruction program should operate as closely as possible to a "traditional" school within the home.

This means that those involved in home instruction programs should, at least, do the following:

1. Annually have their children take standardized achievement tests. These tests should be administered by someone other than the parents, preferably some competent neutral person who is qualified to do so (such as a trained psychologist or testing expert).

2. Keep detailed records of actual days and hours of study.

3. Prepare a lesson plan that chronicles textbooks and the pages covered for each subject assignment given on each day of instruction. Some textbook publishers provide, along with purchase of the textbooks, professional lesson plans to assist the teacher.

4. Administer and maintain regular tests for each subject. These tests should be administered as frequently as those in the public schools and other private schools.

5. Provide a structured environment for instruction; that is, children should have desks, and a library should be established (a set of encyclopedias is almost essential for reference).

6. Read and be familiar with the state education laws.

Although some may question the necessity of such formal structures, parents must be practical in realizing what will have the greatest positive influence on a court or legislature. Moreover, state officials will often be more responsive to tangible evidence verifying that the child participating in home instruction is receiving an adequate education from competent teachers. Therefore, evidence showing that home education is as good as—if not superior to—public or traditional private education will carry more weight when based on accepted criteria.

Last, because a proper defense of home education in the courts is vital to a broad range of freedoms, it should be based upon competent legal advice. Effective legal action takes much time, effort, and money. Thus, careful consideration of legal counsel is essential. This means using, if at all possible, highly qualified attorneys with expertise in constitutional law and trial experience. Under no circumstances should parents attempt to represent themselves, and only in extraordinary circumstances should they accept free representation of volunteer attorneys unless the costs are underwritten by a foundation. An uncompensated attorney in a time-consuming matter virtually never does the quality work necessary for adequate constitutional litigation.

If freedom in education is to prevail, it will take a discerning vigilance on the part of those involved in home instruction. It will also require a sincere quest for the highest quality of children's education.

15

Freedom in Education

There is much wisdom in the Supreme Court's pronouncement that children are not the mere creatures of the state. This thought echoes the sentiments of an earlier time when freedom was at a pinnacle in our country.

Before the nineteenth century, education was considered primarily a family concern. Within the family, the child as student learned both religion and the necessary vocational and academic skills to become a self-sufficient individual.

Today, however, the family function of education and value orientation has been radically altered and largely replaced by the state-financed public education system. The child, as student, is no longer socially oriented solely by his family. Most children are now nurtured to a considerable degree by the state. Moreover, the compulsory nature of the public educational process has the effect of turning students into captive audiences for government-controlled curricula:

[E]ducation poses a constitutional problem because it has become (and was intended to become) a uniquely state activity: the state not only formally educates through the public school system but it also defines the end of education through its control over the curriculum and the certification of both public and private schools.[1]

Regardless of the legitimacy of a state's alleged interest in education, the state's authority over education must stop short of any measures or actions that conflict with fundamental rights guaranteed by the Constitution. The state should seek to avoid constitutional problems by allowing for freedom in education. In other words, within the context of the compulsory education laws, the state must permit those parents who so choose to develop intellectual and religious areas in the lives of their children beyond those developed in the public schools.

The state, then, should seek to protect the minority viewpoint that chooses the alternative of home education. It should seek to promote rather than to punish diversity and pluralism. This is the essence of our Constitution and particularly of the Bill of Rights. As James Madison told Congress, the Bill of Rights' limitations point "sometimes against the abuse of executive power, sometimes against the legislative, and in some cases, against the community itself; or, in other words, against the majority in favor of the minority."[2]

Notes

1. Note, *Freedom and Public Education: The Need for New Standards,* 50 Notre Dame Lawyer 530, 531 (1975).
2. 1 Annals of Congress 454 (Gales & Seaton eds. 1834).

Reading List

Legal Articles

Beshoner, *Home Education in America: Parental Rights Reasserted,* 49 University of Missouri (Kansas City) Law Review 191 (1981).

Stocklin-Enright, *The Constitutionality of Home Education: The Role of the Parent, the State and the Child,* 18 Willamette Law Review 563 (1982).

Tobak & Zirkel, *Home Instruction: An Analysis of the Statutes and Case Law,* 8 University of Dayton Law Review 1 (1982).

See generally Bird, *Freedom of Religion and Science Instruction in Public Schools,* 87 Yale Law Journal 515 (1978) (on free exercise and parental liberty).

See generally Toms & Whitehead, *The Religious Student in Public Education: Resolving a Constitutional Dilemma,* 27 Emory Law Journal 3 (1978) (on free exercise).

Education Books and Articles

Holt, *Schools and Home Schoolers: A Fruitful Partnership*, Phil Delta Kappan (Feb. 1983).

John Holt, *Teach Your Own* (New York: Delacorte Pubs., 1981).

_____. *The Underachieving School* (New York: Dell Pubs., 1970).

_____. *How Children Fail* (New York: Dell Pubs., 1967).

Moore, *Research and Common Sense: Therapies for Our Homes and Schools*, 84 Teachers College Record (Columbia University) 355 (1982).

Raymond Moore & Dorothy Moore, *School Can Wait* (Provo, Utah: Brigham Young University Press, 1979).

Organizations and Curricula

The following are *some* of the organizations and programs concerning home education. Most of these organizations have newsletters and should be contacted for those and other home education materials. No organization is intentionally omitted, and no endorsement is implied by listing herein. Always send a self-addressed and stamped envelope.

Largest Organizations

Hewitt Research Center
Dr. Raymond S. Moore, President
P.O. Box 9
Washougal, Washington 98671

Holt Associates, Inc.
Growing Without Schooling
729 Boylston St.
Boston, Massachusetts 02116

Other Organizations

Allegany Home Learning Out-Reach
350 Welsh Hill
Frostburg, Maryland 21532
301-689-8760

Alternatives in Education
Rt. 3 Box 305
Chloe, West Virginia 25235

Arizona Families for Home Education
639 E. Kino
Mesa, Arizona 85203
602-964-7435

Bay Area Unschoolers
San Jose, California
408-266-1494 or 408-243-7870

California Home Education Clearinghouse
8241 E. Hidden Lakes Dr.
Roseville, California 95678
916-791-4467

California Network News
Keys to Learning
2650 W. Trojan Pl.
Anaheim, California 92804
714-995-6059

Cape Cod Homeschooling Cooperative
36 Shorecrest Dr.
E. Falmouth, Massachusetts 02536

Christian Home Education Association
P.O. Box 226
Mabelvale, Arkansas 72103

Christian Home Schoolers of Ohio
P.O. Box 302
Cuyahoga Falls, Ohio 44221
419-289-8013

Christian Home Schools
8731 N.E. Everett
Portland, Oregon 97220

Citizens for Home Education
3404 Van Buren
Baker, Louisiana 70714
504-775-5472

Colorado Home Schooling Network
1902 S. Oneida
Denver, Colorado 80222

Colorado Springs Home Schoolers
2609 South Blvd.
Colorado Springs, Colorado 80904
303-473-3898

Florida Association for Schooling at Home
Rt. 3 Box 215
Marianna, Florida 32446
904-482-2568

Georgians for Freedom in Education
4818 Joy Lane
Lilburn, Georgia 30247

Home Centered Learning
34 Katrina Ln.
San Anselmo, California 94960

Home Education Resource Center
337 Downs St.
Ridgewood, New Jersey 07450
201-447-4044

HomeNet
25161 Jesmond Dene Rd.
Escondido, California 92026
714-741-5075

HOUSE
Box 2198
Chicago, Illinois 60657
312-929-6723 or 948-0665

Homeschoolers of Lane County
1315 Jay St.
Eugene, Oregon 97402
503-688-0794

Idaho Family Education Association
1821 Gallup St.
Idaho Falls, Idaho 83401

Independent Family Schools Resource Center
R.D. 1 Box 95
Smyrna, New York 13464
607-627-6670

Indiana Home Schoolers
707 E. Main
N. Judson, Indiana 46366

Life Education & Resource Network (LEARN)
601 Robin Dr.
Ellettsville, Indiana 47429

Maine Home Education
R.D. 1 Box 486
Bucksport, Maine 04416

Maryland Home Education Association
9085 Flamepool Way
Columbia, Maryland 21045

Michigan Association of Home Educators
P.O. Box 139
Oshtemo, Michigan 49077

Minnesota Home School Newsletter
9825 Aquila Rd.
Bloomington, Minnesota 55438
612-941-2494

Montana Homeschoolers Association
P.O. Box 1008
Belgrade, Montana 59714

National Association of Home Educators
P.O. Box 2487
Ft. Lauderdale, Florida 33303
305-525-6014

National Organization of Parent Educators
Mrs. Ruth Cannon, President
9403 Winding Ridge
Dallas, Texas 75238

National Parents League
P.O. Box 3987
Portland, Oregon 97208
503-628-1786

Nebraska Home School Association
4142 Adams St.
Lincoln, Nebraska 68504

Nebraska Home Schooling Exchange
Box 96
Rockville, Nebraska 68871

New Hampshire Home Schools Newsletter
R.F.D. 2 Box 255
Laconia, New Hampshire 03246

New Jersey Family School Association
R.D. 1 Box 7
Califon, New Jersey 07830
201-647-3506

New Jersey Unschoolers Network
2 Smith St.
Farmingdale, New Jersey 07727
201-938-2473

Northwest Unschoolers Newsletter
26611 S.R. 530 N.E.
Arlington, Washington 98223
206-435-5015

Ohio Coalition of Educational Alternatives Now
P.O. Box 094
Thompson, Ohio 44086

Oklahoma Home-Schoolers Association
Ada, Oklahoma 74820
405-332-9284

Organization to Keep Iowa Deschoolers Strong (OKIDS)
202 S.E. 8th St.
Ankeny, Iowa 50021

Parents Association of Christian Schools
6166 W. Highland
Phoenix, Arizona 85033

Pennsylvania Unschoolers Network
R.D. 2 Box 181
York Springs, Pennsylvania 17372
717-528-4049

Puerto Rico Home Schooling Association
503 Barbe St.
Santurce, Puerto Rico 00912

San Antonio Home Schoolers Association
512-533-9693

San Fernando Valley Homeschoolers
13610 Vanowen St.
Van Nuys, California 91405
213-786-8126

South Jersey Home Schooling Support Group
609-935-6253

Texas Family Schools Co-op
P.O. Box 466
Elgin, Texas 78621

Texas Home Education Coalition
1112 Millsprings
Richardson, Texas 75080
214-231-9838

Utah Home Education Association
P.O. Box 6338
Salt Lake City, Utah 84106
801-261-3521

Western Pennsylvania Homeschoolers
R.D. 2
Kittanning, Pennsylvania 16201
412-783-6512

Wisconsin Regional Coalition of Alternative Community Schools
Rts. 2 Box 230
New Auburn, Wisconsin 54757

Wyoming Home Schoolers
Box 1386
Lyman, Wyoming 82937
307-787-6728

Alberta Home Schooling Information Service
45 Haysboro Crescent S.W.
Calgary, Alberta T2V 3G1
Canada

Alternative Education Resource Group
101 Pleasant Rd., Hawthorn
Victoria 3121, Australia

Canadian Alliance of Home Schoolers
#1003-129 Wellington St.
Brantford, Ontario N3T 5Z9
Canada

Canadian Home Schooler Newsletter
R.R. 1
Dundas, Ontario L9H 5E1
Canada

Education Otherwise
25 Common Ln.
Hemingford Abbots
Cambs. PE T8 9AN, England

Newsletter About Alternatives
1/186 Stapleford Cres.
Browns Bay
Auckland 10, New Zealand

World-Wide Educational Service
Murray House, Vandon St.
London SW1H OAJ, England

Curriculum Material

Alpha Omega Publications
P.O. Box 3153
Tempe, Arizona 85281

American Home Academy Materials
R.F.D. 2. Box 106C
Brigham City, Utah 84302

Christian Home Education Association
P.O. Box 226
Mabelvale, Arkansas 72103

Christian Liberty Academy
203 East McDonald
Prospect Heights, Illinois 60070

Eagle Forum
P.O. Box 618
Alton, Illinois 62002

Hewitt Research Foundation
P.O. Box 9
Washougal, Washington 98671

Holt Associates, Inc.
729 Boylston Street
Boston, Massachusetts 02116

Pensacola Christian Correspondence School
P.O. Box 18000
Pensacola, Florida 32523

Rod & Staff Publishers
Crocket, Kentucky 41413

The Authors

John W. Whitehead, an attorney specializing in constitutional law, is president of the Rutherford Institute, headquartered near Manassas, Virginia. He has successfully litigated many constitutional law cases, including *People v. Nobel,* which involved the rights of a family to teach their children at home.

Mr. Whitehead has taught constitutional law and courses on the First Amendment. He has also lectured at various law schools throughout the United States.

He has served as counsel to numerous organizations. He has also served as counsel *amicus curiae* in the United States Supreme Court and various United States Circuit Courts.

Mr. Whitehead is a member of the bars of the Supreme Courts of Virginia and Arkansas; the United States Supreme Court; the United States Courts of Appeals for the Fourth, Seventh, and Ninth Circuits; and various United States District Courts. He has also been appointed Special Assistant Attorney General for the State of Louisiana.

Mr. Whitehead has authored eleven books and has

coauthored others. The film version of his book *The Second American Revolution* has been made by Franky Schaeffer V Productions of Los Gatos, California. The movie has been screened in the White House and before congressional staffs in Washington, D.C. It was nationally premiered in November 1982 at the National Archives in Washington, D.C.

Mr. Whitehead has also published articles in both *Emory Law Journal* and *Texas Tech Law Review.* Both concerned First Amendment issues.

He is married and the father of five children.

Wendell R. Bird, an Atlanta attorney with the firm of Parker, Johnson, Cook, & Dunlevie, specializes in constitutional law and nonprofit organization law and is president of the Rutherford Institute of Georgia. He teaches the "Constitutional Law: Church and State Law" course at a major law school as an Adjunct Professor of Law.

He is a member of the bars of the Supreme Courts of Georgia, California, Florida, and Alabama; the United States Supreme Court; the United States Courts of Appeals for the Fourth, Fifth, Eighth, Ninth, and Eleventh Circuits; and various United States District Courts.

Mr. Bird serves as general counsel to numerous religious and other exempt organizations and has participated in numerous First Amendment cases. He is recognized as the leading constitutional authority on creation science, having represented the state of Louisiana as Special Assistant Attorney General and lead counsel in the test case on that issue.

Mr. Bird's articles on First Amendment rights have been published in the *Yale Law Journal*, *Harvard Journal of Law & Public Policy*, and other publications.

He studied law at Yale Law School, where he was an Editor of the *Yale Law Journal* and received the Egger Prize of Yale for one of the two best student publications. His college study was at Vanderbilt University, from which he graduated *summa cum laude* and where he was the first student in Vanderbilt history to exempt the freshman year and enter as a sophomore.

He is married and the father of one child.

John W. Whitehead
Attorney at Law
President
The Rutherford Institute
P.O. Box 510
Manassas, Virginia 22110

Wendell R. Bird
Attorney at Law
Parker, Johnson, Cook &
Dunlevie
1275 Peachtree Street,
Suite 700
Atlanta, Georgia 30309

An Introductory Guide to
Post-structuralism and Postmodernism

An Introductory Guide to Post-structuralism and Postmodernism

Madan Sarup

Goldsmiths' College
University of London

The University of Georgia Press
Athens

Published in the United States of America in 1989 by the
University of Georgia Press, Athens, Georgia 30602

First published in Great Britain by Harvester-Wheatsheaf

Printed in Great Britain

Library of Congress Cataloging in Publication Data

Sarup, Madan.
  An introductory guide to post-structuralism and
postmodernism.

    Includes index.
    1. Structuralism. 2. Postmodernism. 3. Philosophy.
Modern—20th century. I. Title.
B841.4.S26   1989   149'.96   88–27962
ISBN 0–8203–1129–4
ISBN 0–8203–1130–8 (pbk.)

For Sita in reparation

Contents

Acknowledgements   viii

Introduction   1

Chapter 1   Lacan and psychoanalysis   6

Chapter 2   Derrida and deconstruction   34

Chapter 3   Foucault and the social sciences   63

Chapter 4   Some currents within post-structuralism   96

Chapter 5   Postmodernism   117

Conclusion   141

Notes   152

Notes on Further Reading   162

Index   169

Acknowledgements

My students at Goldsmiths' College wanted a short, accessible account that made links between the many discourses—philosophy, psychoanalysis, literature, the social sciences, politics, art—that are usually taught in isolation. I would like to thank them for encouraging me to write this textbook. I have drawn on the work of many people—all writing is intertextual—and they are acknowledged in the *Notes*. For intellectual stimulus and emotional support I would like to thank Elza Adamowicz, John Colbeck, Peter Dunwoodie, Eileen Jebb, Anne Kampendonk, Paul Maltby, Tasneem Raja and many others. I am particularly grateful to Bernard Burgoyne and Peter Dews, from whom I have learnt so much.

Introduction

During the last thirty years or so the structuralists and post-structuralists have made some very important contributions to human understanding. Lévi-Strauss, Lacan, Derrida, Foucault, Deleuze, Lyotard have produced an impressive body of work. Though structuralism and post-structuralism are very different—the latter theory, for example, does not use structural linguistics in its work—there are some similarities: both approaches make critiques.

Firstly, there is a *critique of the human subject*. The term 'subject' refers to something quite different from the more familiar term 'individual'. The latter term dates from the Renaissance and presupposes that man is a free, intellectual agent and that thinking processes are not coerced by historical or cultural circumstances. This view of Reason is expressed in Descartes's philosophical work. Consider this phrase: 'I think, therefore I am.' Descartes's 'I' assumes itself to be fully conscious, and hence self-knowable. It is not only autonomous but coherent; the notion of another psychic territory, in contradiction to consciousness, is unimaginable. In his work Descartes offers us a narrator who imagines that he speaks without simultaneously being spoken.

Lévi-Strauss, a leading structuralist, called the human subject—the centre of being—the 'spoilt brat of philosophy'. He stated that the ultimate goal of the human sciences is not to constitute man but to dissolve him. This became the slogan of structuralism. The leading philosopher of the Left, Louis Althusser, reacting against Sartrean voluntarism, dissolved the subject by reinterpreting Marxism as a theoretical anti-humanism.[1]

1

The advance of structuralism, far from being deflected or halted by the new reading of Marxism, was accelerated by it. After the events of 1968 Althusser tried to adjust his theory but, on the whole, he did not develop his work. The consequence was the gradual effacement and dissolution of Althusserian Marxism by the mid-seventies.

Post-structuralists, like Foucault, want to deconstruct the conceptions by means of which we have so far understood the human. The term 'subject' helps us to conceive of human reality as a construction, as a product of signifying activities which are both culturally specific and generally unconscious. The category of the subject calls into question the notion of the self synonymous with consciousness; it 'decentres' consciousness.

The post-structuralists, then, also want to dissolve the subject; in a sense it could be said that Derrida and Foucault do not have a 'theory' of the subject. The exception is Lacan, who is committed to the subject because of his Hegelian philosophical formation and his commitment to psychoanalysis. What most of these theorists do not understand is that structure and subject are interdependent categories. The notion of a stable structure really depends on a subject distinct from it. One can see that a wholesale attack on the subject was in due course bound to subvert the notion of structure as well.

Secondly, both structuralism and post-structuralism make a *critique of historicism*. They have an antipathy to the notion that there is an overall pattern in history. A famous example is Lévi-Strauss's criticism of Sartre in *The Savage Mind*, in which he attacks Sartre's view of historical materialism and his assumption that present-day society is superior to past cultures.[2] He then goes on to say that Sartre's historicist view of history is not a valid cognitive enterprise. We will see in later discussions that Foucault writes about history without having the notion of progress, and that Derrida says there is no end point in history.

Thirdly, there is a *critique of meaning*. While philosophy in Britain was heavily influenced by theories of language during the early years of this century (I am thinking of the work of Wittgenstein, Ayer and others), this was not the case in France. It could be said that, in a way, structuralism is the delayed entry of language in French philosophy. It may be remembered that Saussure emphasized the distinction between the signifier and the signified. The sound image made by the word 'apple' is the signifier, and the *concept* of an apple is the signified. The structural relationship between the signifier and the signified constitutes a linguistic sign, and language is made up of these. The linguistic sign is arbitrary; this means that it stands for something by convention and common usage, not by necessity. Saussure also stressed the point that each signifier acquired its semantic value only by virtue of its differential position within the structure of language.[3] In this conception of the sign there is a precarious balance between signifier and signified.

In post-structuralism, broadly speaking, the signified is demoted and the signifier made dominant. This means there is no one-to-one correspondence between propositions and reality. Lacan, for example, writes of 'the incessant sliding of the signified under the signifier'.[4] The post-structuralist philosopher Derrida goes further; he believes in a system of floating signifiers pure and simple, with no determinable relation to any extra-linguistic referents at all.[5]

Fourthly, there is a *critique of philosophy*. In his early work Althusser wrote of 'theoretical' practice and argued that Marxist philosophy was a science.[6] He made a clear distinction between the young Marx, who wrote within a Hegelian, ideological problematic, and the older Marx who, with his understanding of economic concepts and processes, was a great scientist. It should be noted that when the structuralists moved language into the centre of French thought this was done in an anti-philosophical way—an approach similar to that taken earlier by Comte and Durkheim.

Having outlined some of the similarities, the continuities, between structuralism and post-structuralism, I want to mention some of the characteristic features of post-structuralism. While structuralism sees truth as being 'behind' or 'within' a text, post-structuralism stresses the interaction of reader and text as a productivity. In other words, reading has lost its status as a passive consumption of a product to become performance. Post-structuralism is highly critical of the unity of the stable sign (the Saussurean view). The new movement implies a shift from the signified to the signifier: and so there is a perpetual detour on the way to a truth that has lost any status or finality. Post-structuralists have produced critiques of the classical Cartesian conception of the unitary subject—the subject/author as originating consciousness, authority for meaning and truth. It is argued that the human subject does not have a unified consciousness but is structured by language. Post-structuralism, in short, involves a critique of metaphysics, of the concepts of causality, of identity, of the subject, and of truth. All this may seem difficult and abstract at the moment, but these issues will be clarified in the chapters that follow.

There is more continuity between structuralism and post-structuralism than between structuralism and phenomenology. But there are many surprises and contradictions. Lacan, a Freudian psychoanalyst, has studied Hegel. Derrida, a post-structuralist, has studied Husserl and Heidegger deeply. Foucault's historical studies are based on philosophical assumptions drawn from Nietzsche.

The first half of this text is an introduction to the differing theories, the rival programmes, of the leading post-structuralists: Jacques Lacan, Jacques Derrida and Michel Foucault. These thinkers share a characteristic philosophical position which is incompatible with the concept of structure but is also quite radically anti-scientific. They question the status of science itself, and the possibility of the objectivity of any language of description or analysis. They reject the assumptions implicit in the Saussurian model of linguistics on which structuralism was based. The topics explored in Chapters 1, 2 and 3 include: psychoanalysis, the nature and role of language, the self and desire, deconstruction, the rise of instrumental reason, the expansion of apparatuses of social control, and the interconnections between knowledge and power.

In Chapter 4 I examine the work of the 'younger generation' of post-structuralists, such as Gilles Deleuze and Felix Guattari, Jean-François Lyotard, and others (the 'new philosophers'), and argue that many of the characteristic beliefs of post-structuralists have their roots in Nietzsche's thought. Chapter 5 explores Lyotard's thesis about the changing nature of knowledge in computerized societies, of what he calls the 'postmodern condition'. This is followed by a discussion on the current controversy about postmodernism and its critique of the Enlightenment project.

CHAPTER 1

Lacan and psychoanalysis

INTRODUCTION

It could be said that the Marxist dialogue with psychoanalysis began in 1963 when Louis Althusser, the leading communist philosopher in France, invited Jacques Lacan to hold his seminars at the École Normale.[1] During this period there must have been considerable interdisciplinary activity; at any rate, a year later Althusser published the famous article 'Freud and Lacan'.[2] He argued that both Marx and Freud invented new sciences. Each discovered a new object of knowledge. They both defined a new way of knowing about the social, but, not surprisingly, they were weighed down by the cultural baggage of their time. Freud 'thought' his discovery in concepts borrowed from biology, mechanics and the psychology of his day. Marx thought his discovery using Hegelian notions of the subject. It is fascinating to read how Althusser sees Lacan as being involved in a similar project to his own. Just as he, Althusser, is trying to rethink Marxism without any reference to Hegel's absolute subject, he sees Lacan as trying to think psychoanalysis without any reference to a unified conception of self or ego.

A few years later, during the May '68 uprising, it was felt by many students and workers that a liberated politics could only emerge from liberated interpersonal relationships, and there was an explosion of interest in Lacanian psychoanalysis—a movement which seemed to reconcile existentialism and Marxism. A part of existentialism's popular appeal may have been that it provided a way to think through the issues of choice and individual responsibility. But as a theory of the self existentialism remained within Cartesianism. Its psychology tended to portray the individual as a rational, conscious actor who could understand the basis for his action. It remained firmly rooted in a philosophy of individual autonomy and rational choice.

At the time of the May '68 events people were very concerned with questions of self-expression, desire and sexuality, and Lacan's theory offered a way of thinking about the social and the linguistic construction of the self, of thinking through the problem of *the individual and society*. For Lacan there is no separation between self and society. Human beings become social with the appropriation of language; and it is language that constitutes us as a subject. Thus, we should not dichotomize the individual and society. Society inhabits each individual.

It is often said that Lacan wants to be understood only by those who want to make an effort. I think we should make the effort. Lacan's writing, which exemplifies his views about language, is very allusive. His language fuses the theoretical and the poetic. His associative style is intended to slow the reader down. His text is not there to convince, but to do something to you. He relies heavily on punning and word games, and he uses symbols, signs etc. to express himself without referring to ordinary language. He wants to resist the over-simplification of much psychoanalytic writing. He also wants to subvert the normalization that everyday language imposes.

I believe that Lacan's unique achievement was that he fused phenomenology and structuralism. His early work coincided with the growth of French phenomenology and he was influenced by the thought of Hegel and Heidegger. Structuralism offered Lacan a way of talking about *systems* of interpretation. His work is fascinating in that it keeps sliding between phenomenology and structuralism. Phenomenology stresses the free self (the subject); structuralism emphasizes language determinism. Lacan uses structuralism but never rejects the subject.

Lacan also belongs, in part, to the hermeneutic tradition, which states that social phenomena always have meaning and that the task of the social sciences is not to explain (as traditional psychiatry seeks to do) but to understand. Psychoanalysis is a method of interpretation. However, Lacan is aware that in the act of interpretation we often impose our own assumptions.

His doctoral thesis 'On Paranoid Psychosis and its Relation to the Personality' is very interesting because he wrote it before Saussure's work on structuralist linguistics was available.[3] At that time he had not yet become a psychoanalyst; he was still a psychiatrist. What is revealing is the angle from which he approaches Freud and the way in which he repudiates physiological reductionism.

One of the main features of Lacan's work is that it is implacably anti-biological. The accepted view in the 1930s, for example, was that madness had organic causes. Lacan argues that organicist accounts cannot explain madness. Madness is a discourse, an attempt at communication, that must be interpreted. We have to understand rather than give causal explanations. He emphasizes that the personality is not 'the mind' but the whole being. We cannot separate a person's psychology from his or her personal history.

When Lacan became a psychoanalyst he made a few tentative criticisms of Freud. The main one was that Freud made a number of biologistic assumptions. Lacan's view is that biology is always interpreted by the human subject, refracted through language; that there is no such thing as 'the body' before language. It could be said that by shifting all descriptions from a biological-anatomic level to a symbolic one he shows how culture imposes meaning on anatomical parts.

Lacan denigrates not only behaviourist psychologists such as Pavlov and Skinner but also (American) ego psychologists such as Fromm and Horney. The latter stress the adaptation of the individual to the social environment. Lacan argues that they have watered down and sweetened Freud's ideas about the unconscious and infant sexuality.[4] Ego psychology asserts that 'self-improvement' is possible without calling society into question.

Lacan often asserts that he is returning to Freud, but this should not be taken too literally. He retains the main concepts but juggles with them to create a new system of thought. A subtle thinker, he offers us a rigorous reformulation of Freud. He is looking for objectivity, but not the objectivity of natural science. He is very interested in mathematical logic *and* poetry, and in his own writing tries to fuse them. His theory of language is such that he could not return to Freud: texts cannot have an unambiguous, pristine meaning. In his view, analysts must relate directly with the unconscious and this means that they must be practitioners of the language of the unconscious—that of poetry, puns, internal rhymes. In word play causal links dissolve and associations abound.

OVERVIEW

Lacan's psychoanalytic theory is partly based upon the discoveries of structural anthropology and linguistics. One of his main beliefs is that the unconscious is a hidden structure which resembles that of language. Knowledge of the world, of others and of self is determined by language. Language is the precondition for the act of becoming aware of oneself as a distinct entity. It is the I–Thou dialectic, defining the subjects by their mutual opposition, which founds subjectivity. But language is also the vehicle of a social given, a culture, prohibitions and laws. The young child is fashioned and will be indelibly marked by it without being aware of it. Let us look at some of the main stages in Lacan's theory.

In *Beyond the Pleasure Principle* Freud describes a child's game.[5] The child had a cotton reel with a piece of string tied to it. Holding the string he would throw the reel over the edge of his cot and utter sounds that Freud interpreted as being an attempt at the German '*fort*', meaning 'gone' or 'away'. He would then pull the reel back into his field of vision, greeting its reappearance with a joyful '*da*' ('there'). This game allowed the eighteen-month-old child to bear without protest the painful experience of his mother's absence, to cope with her disappearance and reappearance.

It illustrates the birth of language in its autonomy from reality and allows a better understanding of how language distances us from the lived experience of the Real. The distancing from the lived experience is effected in two stages: the child moves from the mother to the reel and finally to language.

The first articulation of the 'I' occurs in what Lacan calls the mirror stage. Lacan often refers to the mirror stage as it prefigures the whole dialectic between alienation and subjectivity.[6] Self-recognition in the mirror is effected (somewhere between the ages of six and eight months) in three successive stages. At first, the child who is together with an adult in front of a mirror confuses his own reflection with that of his adult companion. In the second phase the child acquires the notion of the image and understands that the reflection is not a real being. Finally, in the third stage, he realizes not only that the reflection is an image, but that the image is his own and is different from the image of the other.

Lacan sees, in a way similar to Lévi-Strauss, the Oedipus complex as the pivot of humanization, as a transition from the natural register of life to a cultural register of group exchange and therefore of laws, language and organization. Lacan contends that at first the child does not merely desire contact with the mother and her care; it wishes, perhaps unconsciously, to be the complement of what is lacking in her: the phallus. At this stage the child is not a subject but a 'lack', a nothing.

In the second stage the father intervenes; he deprives the child of the object of its desire and he deprives the mother of the phallic object. The child encounters the Law of the father. The third stage is that of identification with the father. The father reinstates the phallus as the object of the mother's desire and no longer as the child-complement to what is lacking in her. There is, then, a symbolic castration: the father castrates the child by separating it from its mother. This is the debt which must be paid if one is to become completely one's self.

It needs to be stressed that the Oedipus complex for Lacan is not a stage like any other in genetic psychology: it is the moment in which the child humanizes itself by becoming aware of the self, the world and others. The resolution of the Oedipus complex liberates the subject by giving him, with his Name, a place in the family constellation, an original signifier of self and subjectivity. It promotes him in his realization of self through participation in the world of culture, language and civilization.[7]

As I mentioned earlier, Lacan has rethought Freud in the wider framework provided by linguistics and structural anthropology. In his view the unconscious shows itself in dreams, jokes, slips of the tongue, symptoms. The unconscious is comparable in structure to a language. In fact, Lacan argues that language is the condition for the unconscious, that it creates and gives rise to the unconscious. Like conscious discourse, the formations of the unconscious (dreams etc.) are saying something quite different from what they appear to say. These formations are governed by the same mechanisms as language, namely metaphor and metonymy. At certain privileged points, such as in slips of the tongue and in some jokes, language seems to be torn apart. Conscious discourse is rather like those manuscripts where a first text has been rubbed out and covered by a second. In such manuscripts the first text can be glimpsed through the gaps in the second. The true speech—the unconscious—breaks through usually in a veiled and incomprehensible form.

Lacan suggests that, thanks to human beings' metaphoric ability, words convey multiple meanings and we use them to signify something quite different from their concrete meaning. This possibility of signifying something other than what is being said determines language's autonomy from meaning. Lacan insists on the autonomy of the signifier. He assimilates the metaphoric and metonymic processes of language to condensation and displacement respectively.[8] All the formations of the unconscious use these stylistic devices to outwit censorship.

Throughout his work Lacan strives to denounce the common illusion which identifies the ego with the self. In contrast to those who say 'I think, therefore I am' Lacan asserts: 'I think where I am not, therefore I am where I do not think.'[9] Or, 'I think where I cannot say that I am.'

Having provided a general introduction to Lacan's theory, I will now focus on some important aspects of his work: the relation between self and language; problems of self and identity; the main theoretical differences between Lacan and Freud; the influence on Lacan of Hegel; the meaning of need, demand and desire; the sense of loss.

SELF AND LANGUAGE

Lacan's theory cannot be presented coherently without a discussion of the function of language. He has a complete theory of language, which he links with subjectivity. He believes that there could not be a human subject without language but that the subject cannot be reduced to language. This is a circular (and not a reciprocal) relationship in which language has privilege. Lacan writes (in *The Mirror Stage*) that it is the ability to speak that distinguishes the subject. It is this feature that separates the social from the natural world. *There is no subject independent of language.* Lacan is highly critical of those encounter-therapy groups that tend to deny the role of verbal language and imply that the body and its gestures are more direct.

While Saussure implied that we can somehow stand outside language, Lacan insists that we are all immersed in everyday language and cannot get out of it. There is no such thing as metalanguage. We all have to represent ourselves in language. Indeed our only access to others is through language. (According to Lacan a psychotic person is someone who has not learnt what language is.)[10]

Saussure regarded the relationship between signifiers and signified as stable and predictable. He argued for the possibility of anchoring particular signifiers to particular signifieds in order to form linguistic signs. In Lacan's view, on the other hand, meaning emerges only through discourse, as a consequence of displacements along a signifying chain. Like Derrida, Lacan insists upon the commutability of the signified, upon the capacity of every signified to function in turn as a signifier. A consequences of the non-representational status of language is, of course, that the signified is always provisional.

In a Lacanian view of language a signifier always signifies another signifier; no word is free from metaphoricity (a metaphor is one signifier in the place of another). Lacan talks of *glissement* (slippage, slide) along the signifying chain, from signifier to signifier. Since any signifier can receive signification retrospectively, after the fact, no signification is ever closed, ever satisfied.[11] Each word is only definable in terms of other words. Moreover, each word uttered only makes complete sense when the sentence is finished; and it is perhaps only the very last word uttered which retrospectively establishes the full sense of each word that came before. From anything that is said it cannot be predicted what is going to be said. Any 'sentence' can always be added to. No sentence is ever completely saturated. There is no natural link between signifier and signified. In repression, for example, one signifier comes to substitute for another. The old signifier and what it signifies is 'pushed down' to the unconscious. In the course of a lifetime the individual builds up many chains of signification, always substituting new terms for old and always increasing the distance between the signifier that is accessible and visible and all those that are unconscious.

It is true that at the end of his life Lacan became interested in the possibility of expressing the laws of the unconscious in terms of mathematical statements called 'mathemes'; some people think that this was because he believed that through the process of formalization we might be able to find out what we *cannot* mathematize.

To illustrate that there is no unequivocal meaning, Lacan relates the following story:

A train arrives at a station. A little boy and a little girl, brother and sister, are seated in a compartment face to face next to the window through which the buildings along the station platform can be seen passing as the train pulls to a stop. 'Look', says the brother, 'we're at Ladies!'; 'Idiot!' replies his sister, 'Can't you see we're at Gentlemen'.[12]

In this story each child is able to see only one of the rooms;

each child sees a one-to-one correspondence between the word and the 'thing'—a way of understanding the relationship between signifier and signified that is totally inadequate. Note that it is the girl who sees 'Gentlemen' and the boy who sees 'Ladies', as if one could only see the sex one is not. Through the biological given of sitting on one side of the compartment or the other each sex is placed in a structure and as such is unable to see that structure. Lacan seems to be saying: we are all sitting on one side of the compartment or the other; we are all subject to the blindness imposed by our seats in the compartment; there is no other way of being on the train(chain).[13]

SELF AND IDENTITY

It should be stressed that Lacan uses the idea of a child before the mirror as a metaphor. The notion of reflection is a common one (especially in German Idealist philosophy), stemming from Hegel. In this philosophy there is a concern with questions such as: What is it to be conscious of oneself? How do we recognize the self? What is that 'something' that reflects consciousness back onto itself? In self-consciousness the subject and the object are identical; but can I reflect on the self and reflect on that reflection? Can the self that is self of consciousness grasp the self of consciousness? When we see ourselves we see only a look. We do not get nearer to what we are. This is called 'the infinity of reflection'.[14]

Another important Lacanian idea is 'the dialectic of recognition'. This refers to the idea that we get knowledge of what we are from how others respond to us. It is useful to compare D. W. Winnicott's discussion of the mirror role with Lacan's view. Winnicott suggests that the first mirror is the mother's face.[15] He argues that other people provide the stability of our self-identity. Some feminists have criticized him because he unquestioningly focuses only on the 'mother' role. (Moreover, what happens if the mother is ill or mentally disturbed and cannot send back an image?)

In contrast with Winnicott, Lacan says that we are never

going to get a stable image. We try to interpret our
relation to others but there is always the possibility of
misinterpretation. There is always a gap, a misrecognition.
We can never be certain of the meaning of the other's
response. We have an idea of our identity but it does not
correspond with reality: the mirror image is back to front.

Our notion of the self as an isolated self is in some
way connected with bourgeois individualism. (Lacan hints,
however, that it may always be like this.) Lacan continually
attacks the American psychologists (Erich Fromm and Karen
Horney again) who keep stressing the ego. In his view the
stable ego is illusory. We can shed the illusions of the ego
only asymptotically (in geometry an asymptote is a curve
approaching a straight line but never reaching it short of
infinity).[16]

Lacan insists that we do not have a fixed set of
characteristics. This is very much the view Sartre expressed
in *Being and Nothingness*.[17] In Sartre's theory consciousness
can never grasp itself. Reflection always turns the subject
into an object. Sartre rejects the idea that drives determine
consciousness. He suggests that as soon as we say, 'I'm like
that—that's me', we have made ourselves into an object.
We often build up a set of characteristics retrospectively.
Sartre insists that we are more than a fixed set of categories.
We should not think of ourselves as merely a set of
characterizations. Nor should we go to the other extreme
and conceive of ourselves as pure nothingness.

Lacan argues that we are never any one of our attributes.
There is no truth if by truth is meant that an individual
expresses an inherent characteristic. Sceptical of any 'underlying truth', he writes: 'If Freud had brought to man's
knowledge nothing more than the truth that there is such a
thing as the true, there would be no Freudian discovery.
Freud would belong to a line of moralists . . . .'[18]

Lacan stresses the point that there is no subject except in
representation, but that no representation captures us
completely. I can neither be totally defined nor can I escape
all definition. I am the quest for myself. Lacan believes that
how we present ourselves is always subject to interpretation
by others. On the other hand, any attempt to 'totalize'

someone else, to grasp the other completely, is bound to
fall short—no description does the other justice. Moreover,
one can only see onself as one *thinks* others see one.

There is an inherent tension, a feeling of threat, because
one's identity depends on recognition by the other. This is
the theme of Hegel's story of Master and Slave. I will give
a detailed exposition of it later in the chapter. For the
moment it is only necessary to say that Hegel argued that
consciousness cannot grasp itself without recognition by
others. The Master demands recognition from the Slave but
this is a self-defeating process. He feels threatened because
recognition of himself depends exclusively on the Slave. To
generalize from the story, we would like to reduce others
to an instrument—a mirror. There is a moment of aggression
when we want to overcome our dependency. (We often hear
people say: 'I've got to insist on my independence.')

But is there a possibility of mutual recognition? Lacan
suggests that intersubjectivity can never be fully attained
because we can never enter another person's consciousness
completely. Full mutual recognition is not possible partly
because of the ambiguity of signifiers. There is a gulf between
saying and meaning. All this is reminiscent of Sartre, who
says that when we love another we want that person's
love—and this attitude instrumentalizes love. As soon as
one person is the subject, the other is the object. Lacan
belongs to the tradition that believes that the subject and
the object are irreconcilably divided. Undoubtedly he has an
ontology: we all have a need for wholeness, a longing for
the state of unity, but the achievement of plenitude is a
logical impossibility.

FREUD AND LACAN

There are many differences between Freud and Lacan and
in this section I will discuss some of them. I will focus
particularly on their different conceptualizations of the ego,
the unconscious, the dream, and the Oedipus complex.

In Freud's early work the ego is connected with the reality

principle, and the unconscious is related to the pleasure principle. Later Freud reformulated his theory: the ego is formed through an identification with parental figures. The important point to note is that Freud never says the ego is illusory.

Lacan's argument is the opposite of this. He believes that identification stabilizes the individual but at the same time takes us away from ourselves. He says that Freud starts from individuals' drives and their satisfactions and that he neglects social dimensions. For Lacan, however, the subject-to-subject relation, what we call intersubjectivity, is there right from the beginning.

Freud believed that the aim of analysis was to integrate a drive into 'the harmony of the ego'. Lacan, of course, would never use such a phrase. While for Freud the unconscious has a threatening aspect, in Lacan it is the locus of 'truth', of authenticity. And yet Lacan believes that the unconscious cannot be an object of knowledge; the ego projects itself and then fails to recognize itself. Self-knowledge, the notion that the self can reflect on itself, is not possible.

While Freud seems to have believed in the unconscious as a substantive concept, for Lacan 'the unconscious is not the real place of another discourse'. Lacan proclaims that the unconscious is neither primordial nor instinctual. The unconscious is implicit in everything we say and do. However, in trying to grasp the unconscious we lose it—like 'twice-lost Eurydice'. The unconscious is that which we can never know, but this does not mean that the effort is not worth while.

Two processes are of central importance in Freudian theory: the primary process, which is associated with the unconscious (irrational thought), and the secondary process, which is associated with the conscious (logical thought).[19] When the object of satisfaction is denied and life is difficult we often retreat from reality and overcome frustration by hallucinating. But after a certain time, in order for us to survive, the reality principle comes into play. The ego intervenes, separates things out and puts a stop to the hallucination. This secondary process is continually being interrupted by the unconscious. Human rationality is a thin, fragile 'façade' which the unconscious keeps bursting asunder. Again, Lacan rejects Freud's view. For him the unconscious is neither primordial nor instinctual; the secondary process is more like the primary process than Freud thought.

It is in the dream that we can see the operation of the primary process. As Freud said, it is the dream that is 'the royal road to the unconscious'. For Lacan a dream is not a pictorial representation; though it happens to be an image *a dream is really a text*:

> The dream is like the parlour-game in which one is supposed to get the spectators to guess some well-known saying or variant of it solely by dumb show. That the dream uses speech makes no difference since for the unconscious it is only one among several elements of the representation. It is precisely the fact that both the game and the dream run up against a lack of taxematic material for the representation of such logical articulations as causality, contradiction, hypothesis, etc. that proves they are a form of writing rather than of mime.[20]

It is in dreams that the processes of condensation and displacement take place. According to Lacan, in condensation there is a superimposition of the signifiers which metaphor takes as its field. A simple image can thus have different meanings. Displacement, another means used by the unconscious to foil censorship, is associated with metonymy.

Though Lacan believes that the desire of the dream is to communicate, he does not ever say to an analysand 'this is what you really want', or 'this is what your dream really means'. If he did, this would be another alienation. In his view the subject is a process and cannot be defined.

Freud was very interested in the relationship between nature and culture and emphasized the dominance of culture over nature. Lacan rejects the notion of an innate human nature. Nature, for Lacan, is the Real which is out there but impossible to grasp in a pure state because it is always mediated through language. In Freud's work one is aware of a tragic element in the nature–culture dichotomy. In Lacan, tragedy lies in the fact that we have a perpetual lack of wholeness.

Freud and Lacan also have different views of the Oedipus

complex. In Freud's theory the Oedipus complex must be understood in the context of his theory of psychosexuality. In the first stage of infant sexuality, the oral stage, there are fantasies of incorporating and devouring. The second stage, the anal/sadistic, is associated with submission and domination. In the third, the phallic stage, the boy wants the mother exclusively. He is threatened with castration and develops an impotence fear. There is an introjection of the father's threat which leads, finally, to a resolution of the complex.

Lacan tries to rationalize Freud's thesis by not taking the Oedipus complex literally. Whereas Freud's Oedipal Father might be taken for a real, biological father, Lacan's Name-of-the-Father operates in the register of language. The Name-of-the-Father is the Law. The legal assignation of a father's name to a child is meant to call a halt to uncertainty about the identity of the father.

Lacan does not abandon the idea of the focus on the oral, the anal and the phallic, but he says that these stages are intersubjective. Freud's theory refers to the physical and not the symbolic. In Freud the penis is a guarantee of a possible union with the mother. Lacan transforms all this to the level of the symbolic. This is why he writes not of the penis but of the phallus.[21]

Lacanians, separating the two notions 'penis' and 'phallus', argue that there is no phallus inequity; that is, neither sex can be or have the phallus. The penis is what men have and women do not, the phallus is the attribute of power which neither men nor women have. Lacan suggests that all our fantasies are symbolic representations of the desire for wholeness. We tend to think that if we were the phallus or had the other's phallus we would then, somehow, be whole. In other words, the phallus is the signifier of an original desire for a perfect union with the Other. The phallus refers to plenitude; it is the signifier of the wholeness that we lack.

There is another difference between Freud and Lacan. The former held that rational discourse was possible, even though it was often distorted by unconscious forces. For Lacan discourse *constitutes* the unconscious. Language and desire are related. In Lacan desire is ontological, a struggle for wholeness rather than a sexual force. 'Desire is the metonymy of the desire to want to be.'

While Freud talks of instincts and drives Lacan talks of desire—a concept which comes from Kojève's lectures on Hegel. These lectures are important, as Lacan, Sartre and others were highly influenced by them. Kojève describes the development of self-consciousness. Hegel insists that self-consciousness develops out of the biological self. Self-consciousness would not be possible without an organic lack. A lack ('I feel hungry') makes us aware of ourselves as a being that needs something. Hegel continues that for a desire to develop in us we need to focus on a specific object. When we desire not a thing but another's desire we become human. Moreover, desire is mobile, not static; a desire can be continually negated, but it continues.

HEGEL AND LACAN

As what Lacan means by desire is drawn from Hegel, I want to retell in this section Hegel's metaphoric story of the Master and the Slave before I try to elucidate the Lacanian concepts of need, demand and desire.[22] What follows may seem a digression, but this 'detour' through Hegel is necessary because the Master/Slave theme, in both Marxist and Nietzschean versions, constantly reappears in contemporary social thought.

Hegel remarks that we all know that the person who attentively contemplates a thing is 'absorbed' by this thing and forgets himself. He may perhaps talk about the thing but he will never talk about himself; in his discourse the word 'I' will not occur.

For this word to appear, something other than purely passive contemplation must be present. And this other thing is, according to Hegel, Desire. Indeed, when man experiences a desire, when he is hungry, for example, and becomes aware of it he necessarily becomes aware of himself. Desire is always revealed to the individual as *his* desire, and to express desire he must use the word 'I'.[23]

Desire dis-quiets him and moves him to action. Action tends to satisfy desire but can do so only by the 'negation', the destruction or at least the transformation of the desired object: to satisfy hunger, for example, the food must be destroyed or in any case transformed. Thus, all action is 'negating'. The being that eats creates and preserves its own reality by overcoming a reality other than its own, by the 'transformation' of an alien reality into its own reality, by the 'assimilation', the 'internalization', of an 'external' reality. Generally speaking, the 'I' of Desire is an emptiness that receives a real positive content by a negating action that satisfies Desire in destroying, transforming and assimilating the desired non-I.

Desire, being the revelation of an emptiness, the presence of an absence, is something essentially different from the desired thing. Desire is directed towards another Desire, another greedy emptiness, another 'I'. Desire is human only if one desires not the body but the Desire of the other; that is to say, if one wants to be 'desired' or, rather, 'recognized' in one's human value. All Desire is desire for a value. To desire the Desire of another is really to desire 'recognition'.

MASTER AND SLAVE

If there is a multiplicity of desires seeking universal recognition, it is obvious that the action that is born of these desires can—at least in the beginning—be nothing but a life-and-death fight. It is assumed that the fight ends in such a way that both adversaries remain alive. Now, if this is to occur, one must suppose that one of the adversaries, preferring to live rather than die, gives in to the other and submits to him, recognizing him as the Master without being recognized by him. The Master, unable to recognize the other who recognizes him, finds himself in an impasse.

The Master makes the Slave work in order to satisfy his own desires. To satisfy the desires of the Master, the Slave has to repress his own instincts (for example, in the preparation of food that he will not eat), to negate or 'overcome' himself.[24] The Slave transcends himself by working, that is, he educates himself. In his work he transforms things and transforms himself at the same time. In becoming master of Nature by work, the Slave frees himself from Nature, from his own nature, and from the Master. It is because work is an auto-creative act that it can raise him from slavery to freedom. The future and history hence belong not to the warlike Master, who either dies or preserves himself indefinitely in 'identity to himself', but to the working Slave.

To summarize, according to Hegel it is a fight to the death for the sake of recognition that leads to a relation between a free man and a man who is enslaved to him. Hence man is necessarily either Master or Slave. But the difference between Master and Slave can be overcome in the course of time. Mastery and Slavery, then, are not given or innate characteristics. Man is not born slave or free but creates himself as one or the other through free or voluntary action. In short, the character of the Master/Slave opposition is the motive principle of the historical process. All of history is nothing but the progressive negation of Slavery by the Slave. Finally, the thesis of Mastery and the antithesis of Slavery are dialectically 'overcome'.

IDENTITY AND NEGATIVITY

Thanks to identity every being remains the same being, eternally identical to itself and different from the others. But thanks to negativity an identical being can negate or overcome its identity with itself and become other than it is, even its own opposite. Identity and negativity do not exist in an isolated state. Just like totality itself they are only complementary aspects of one and the same real being.[25]

The thesis describes the given material to which the action is going to be applied, the antithesis reveals this action itself as well as the thought which animates it ('the project'), while the synthesis shows the result of that action, that is, the completed and objectively real product. The new product is also given and can provoke other negating actions. Human beings are always negating the given. Negativity is the negation of identity. Human beings are truly free or really human only in and by effective negation of the given real. Negativity, then, is nothing other than human freedom. The freedom which is realized and manifested as dialectical or negating action is thereby essentially a creation. What is involved is not replacing one given by another given, but overcoming the given in favour of what does not (yet) exist. In short, man is neither identity nor negativity alone but totality or synthesis; that is, he 'overcomes' himself while preserving and sublimating himself.

In my view this discussion has a direct bearing on education. All education implies a long series of auto-negations effected by the child. As Kojève remarks, '. . . it is only because of these auto-negations ('repressions') that every "educated" child is not only a trained animal (which is 'identical' to itself and in itself) but a truly human or "complex" being; although in most cases, he is human only to a very small extent, since "education" (that is, auto-negations) generally stops too soon.'[26]

PARTICULARLITY AND UNIVERSALITY

Particularity refers to the individual agent. Every man, to the extent that he is human, would like—on the one hand—to be different from all others. But on the other hand he would like to be recognized, in his unique particularity itself, as a positive value; and he would like this recognition to be shown as many people as possible. Universality refers to the social aspect of man's existence. It is only in and by the universal recognition of human particularity that individuality realizes and manifests itself.

Individuality is a synthesis of the particular and the universal, the universal being the negation or the antithesis of the particular, which is the thetical given, identical to itself. In other words, individuality is a totality and the being which is individual is, by the very fact, dialectical. Man is and exists only to the extent that he overcomes himself dialectically (i.e. while preserving and sublimating himself). The opposition of particularity and universality is fundamental for Hegel. In his view history will develop by the formation of a society, of a state, in which the strictly particular, personal, individual value of each is recognized as such, in its very particularity, by all. The synthesis of particularity and universality is possible only after the 'overcoming' of the opposition between the Master and the Slave, since the synthesis of the particular and the universal is also the synthesis of Mastery and Slavery.[27]

THE DESIRE FOR DESIRE

What use does Lacan make of these Hegelian insights? We all have physical needs to satisfy. The child in the oral phase, for example, wants the mother's breast. It makes an appeal to its mother to have its needs met. This is the transformation from need to demand, but there is also the desire for love, for recognition. Needs, then, are biological. In demand the biological is mediated; a demand is always specific. Desire is what cannot be specified by demand.[28] A child cries. The mother gives a bar of chocolate; but the child can never know whether this action was performed for the satisfaction of its need or as an act of love. Lacan believes that such a response is inherently ambiguous. And because the response is ambiguous the demand is repeated, repeated . . . *ad infinitum.*

Need, demand, desire—how are these three categories interconnected? A child cries. It can use physical hunger as a vehicle for a communication. Sometimes the food satisfies a physical need but it can also become symbolically freighted. There can be a split between need and desire. In an account of anorexia Lacan states how a young woman is given food but wants love. The meaning of demand is not intrinsic but is partly determined by the response by the other to the demand. Though our demand is specific we can never be certain of other people's responses to ourselves. After all, how do you give love?

People can continually be making a demand but they need not be conscious of it. A demand is the means of revealing desire, but it is oblique. Desire is desire for the Other but it has to be interpreted. Lacan says that need is cancelled by demand which re-emerges on the other side of desire. We often want an object that could be given only to *us*, but there is no such object. A demand is for a response, but that response is never particular enough. We can never be certain that others love us for our unique particularity.

It could be said that some people are too confident that they are loved. Lacan suggests that their identities may become rather rigid. And there are other people who lack confidence. Desire emerges when satisfaction of need is not enough, when there is a doubt or gap which cannot be closed. Desire arises out of the lack of satisfaction and it pushes you to another demand. In other words, it is the disappointment of demand that is the basis of the growth of desire.

THE SENSE OF LOSS

In this section I will retell Lacan's story and will focus specifically on the sense of loss or lack that the subject undergoes. You will have noticed that Lacan's theory of the subject reads like a classic narrative; it begins with birth and then moves in turn through the territorialization of the body, the mirror stage, access to language and the Oedipus complex. Each of the stages of this narrative is conceived in terms of some kind of self-loss or lack.

Lacan situates the first loss in the history of the subject at the moment of birth. To be more precise, he dates it from the moment of sexual differentiation within the womb; but it is not realized until the separation of the child from the mother at birth. This lack is sexual in definition and has to do with the impossibility of being physiologically both male and female. The notion of an original androgynous whole is central to Lacan's argument. The subject is defined as lacking because it is believed to be a fragment of something larger and primordial.

Let me clarify this briefly. Lacan often makes references to a fable on the subject of love in Plato's *Symposium*.[29] Aristophanes speaks of beings that, 'once upon a time', were globular in shape, with rounded back and sides, four arms and legs and two faces. Strong, energetic and arrogant, they tried to scale the heights of heaven and set upon the gods. Zeus retaliated by cutting them all in half so that each one would be only half as strong.

Now, when the work of bisection was complete it left each half with a desperate yearning for the other and they ran together and flung their arms around each others' necks and asked for nothing better than to be rolled into one. So much so that they began to die. Zeus felt so sorry for them that he devised another scheme. He moved their genitals round to the front and made them propagate among themselves. So you see how far back we can trace our innate love for one another, and how this love is always trying to reintegrate our former nature, to make two into one and to bridge the gulf between one human being and another.

The second loss suffered by the subject occurs after birth but prior to the acquisition of language. The loss in question is inflicted by what might be called the 'pre-Oedipal territorialization' of the subject's body. For a time after its birth the child does not differentiate between itself and the mother upon whose nurture it relies. Then the child's body undergoes a process of differentiation; erotogenic zones are inscribed and the libido is encouraged to follow certain established routes. By indicating the channels through which that libido can move the mother or nurse assists in the conversion of incoherent energy into coherent drives which can later be culturally regulated. The drives possess a coherence which needs do not have, because they are attached to particular corporal zones. As a result of this attachment the drives provide only an indirect expression of the original libidinal flow. Thus very early in its history the subject loses unmediated contact with its own libidinal flows and succumbs to the domination of its culture's genital economy.

'Imaginary' is the term used by Lacan to designate that order of the subject's experience which is dominated by identification and duality. Within the Lacanian scheme it not only precedes the symbolic order, which introduces the subject to language and Oedipal triangulation, but continues to coexist with it afterwards. The imaginary order is best exemplified by the mirror stage.

Lacan tells us that somewhere between the ages of six and eighteen months the subject arrives at an apprehension of both its self and the Other—indeed of itself as Other. This discovery is assisted by the child seeing, for the first time, its own reflection in a mirror. That reflection has a coherence which the subject itself lacks. But this self-recognition is, Lacan insists, a mis-recognition. The mirror stage is a moment of alienation, since to know oneself through an external image is to be defined through self-alienation. The subject, then, has a profoundly ambivalent relationship to that reflection. It loves the coherent identity which the mirror provides. However, because the image remains external to it, it also hates that image. The subject experiences many radical oscillations between contrary emotions.

Lacan believes that once the subject has entered the symbolic order (language) its organic needs pass through the 'defiles' or narrow network of signification and are transformed in a way which makes them thereafter impossible to satisfy. The drives offer only a partial and indirect expression of those needs, but language severs the relationship altogether.

The *fort/da* game can be seen as the child's first signifying chain and hence its entry into language. It should be noted that whereas Freud describes the child's actions in the *fort/da* game as an attempt to diminish the unpleasure caused by his mother's absences, Lacan stresses instead the self-alienation which those actions dramatize. Lacan identifies the toy reel with which the child plays as an *objet petit autre*—that thing the loss of which has resulted in a sense of deficiency or lack. The breast, for example, certainly represents that part of himself that the individual loses at birth and which may serve to symbolize the most profound lost object. (Other objects which enjoy the same privileged status as the breast include the gaze and voice of the mother.) Lacan thus interprets the story as being more about the disappearance of the self than that of the mother. Like Freud Lacan reads the *fort/da* episode as an allegory about the linguistic mastery of the drives. Lacan describes this complete rupture with the drives as the 'fading' of the subject's being, as 'aphanisis'. Not only is the subject thereby split off or partitioned from its own drives, but it is subordinated to a symbolic order which will henceforth determine its identity and desires.

The formation of the unconscious, the emergence of the subject into the symbolic order and the inauguration of desire are all closely connected events. Desire is directed towards ideal representations which remain forever beyond the subject's reach. Since others will be loved only if they are believed to be capable of completing the subject, desire must be understood as fundamentally narcissistic. Object love is nothing more than the continued search for the lost complement.

Lacan conceptualizes the Oedipus complex as a linguistic transaction. He supports this claim by pointing out that the incest taboo can only be articulated through the differentiation of certain cultural members from others by means of linguistic categories like 'father' and 'mother'. Lacan defines the paternal signifier, what he calls the 'Name-of-the-Father', as the all-important one both in the history of the subject and the organization of the larger symbolic field.

This means that Lacan gives us a very different account of sexual difference from that provided by Freud, one in which the privileged term is no longer 'penis' but 'phallus'. The word 'phallus' is used by Lacan to refer to all of those values which are opposed to lack. He is at pains to emphasize its discursive (rather than its anatomical) status, but it seems to have two radically different meanings. On the one hand, the phallus is a signifier for those things which have been partitioned off from the subject during the various stages of its constitution and which will never be restored to it. The phallus is a signifier for the organic reality or needs which the subject relinquishes in order to achieve meaning, in order to gain access to the symbolic register. It signifies that thing whose loss inaugurates desire. On the other hand, the phallus is a signifier for the cultural privileges and positive values which define male subjectivity within patriarchal society but from which the female subject remains isolated. The phallus, in other words, is a signifier both for those things which are lost during the male subject's entry into culture and for those things which are gained.

Lacan believes that the discourse within which the subject finds its identity is always the discourse of the Other—of a symbolic order which transcends the subject and which orchestrates its entire history. An important part is played by sexual difference within that order, and this has made us aware of the phallocentricity of our current practices.

One Lacanian tenet is that subjectivity is entirely relational; it only comes into play through the principle of difference, by the opposition of the 'other' or the 'you' to the 'I'. In other words, subjectivity is not an essence but a set of relationships. It can only be induced by the activation of a signifying system which exists before the individual and which determines his or her cultural identity. Discourse, then, is the agency whereby the subject is produced and the existing order sustained.

CONCLUSION

I will now try to bring some of the threads together by briefly stating what Lacan means by the Imaginary, the Symbolic and the Real. This will also enable me to recapitulate some of the key points of this chapter. It is clear that the Imaginary—a kind of pre-verbal register whose logic is essentially visual—precedes the symbolic as a stage in the development of the psyche. Its moment of formation has been named the 'mirror stage'. At this stage there does not yet exist that ego formation which would permit a child to distinguish its own form from that of others. The child who hits says it has been hit, the child who sees another child fall begins to cry. (It is from Melanie Klein's pioneering psychoanalysis of children that the basic features of the Lecanian Imaginary are drawn.)

The Imaginary order is pre-Oedipal. The self yearns to fuse with what is perceived as Other. The child confuses others with its own mirror reflections; and since the self is formed from a composite of introjections based on such misrecognitions, it can hardly constitute a unified personality. In other words, we experience a profoundly divided self.

Lacan suggests that the infant's first desire for the mother signifies the wish to be what the mother desires. (*Désir de la mère* refers to the desire for the mother *and* to the mother's desire.) The infant wants to complete the mother, to be what she lacks – the phallus. The child's relationship with the mother is fusional, dual and immediate. Later, the child's desire to be its mother's desire gives way to an identification with the father.

The child's asocial, dual and fusional relationship with its mother is forsworn for the world of symbolic discourse. The father becomes the third term and we enter the symbolic order by accepting his name and interdictions. In the symbolic there is no longer a one-to-one correspondence between things and what they are called—a symbol evokes an open-ended system of meaning. Symbolic signification is social, not narcissistic. It is the Oedipal crisis which marks the child's entrance into the world of the symbolic. The laws of language and society come to dwell within the child as he accepts the father's name and the father's 'no'.

I said earlier that Lacan understands the Oedipus story in terms of language, not in terms of the body, and that there is no such thing as the body before language. Biology is always interpreted by the human subject. But not only biology, all experience is symbolically mediated and has to be interpreted (in the context of social convention).

The Lacanian notion of *the Symbolic order* is an attempt to create mediations between libidinal analysis and the linguistic categories, to provide, in other words, a transcoding scheme which allows us to speak of both within a common conceptual framework. The Oedipus complex is transliterated by Lacan into a linguistic phenomenon which he designates as the discovery by the subject of the Name-of-the-Father. Lacan feels that the apprenticeship of language is an alienation for the psyche but he realizes that it is impossible to return to an archaic, pre-verbal stage of the psyche itself.

I have underlined the point that Lacan places great emphasis on the linguistic development of the child. He argues that the acquisition of a name results in a thoroughgoing transformation of the position of the subject in his object world. There is a determination of the subject by language. The Freudian unconscious is seen in terms of language: 'The unconscious is the discourse of the Other'—a notion that tends to surprise those who associate language with thinking and consciousness.

Lacan's theory has attracted a good deal of interest among feminists because the emphasis on the production of gendered subjectivity via signification (the processes whereby meaning is produced at the same time as subjects are fabricated and positioned in social relations) implies that it is possible to escape the subordination of women inherent in Freud's recourse to biological difference. However, it could be argued that, in privileging the phallus as the sign of difference as opposed to the penis, Lacan's analysis is not any less deterministic than Freud's.[30] This is because Lacan relies heavily on Lévi-Strauss's structural analysis of the incest taboo which, it is said, underlies all human societies. The use of Lévi-Strauss's thesis means that the terms of the debate are fixed around the 'Law of the Father'. Because Lévi-Strauss's theory is a universalist one Lacan's account tends to collapse into an account of a universal subject who is not situated historically.

The third order is the Real. The reality which we can never know is the Real—it lies beyond language . . . the reality we must assume although we can never know it. This is the most problematic of the three orders or registers since it can never be experienced immediately, but only by way of the mediation of the other two: 'the Real, or what is

perceived as such, is what resists symbolization absolutely.'
Fredric Jameson, however, thinks that it is not terribly
difficult to say what is meant by the Real in Lacan: 'It is
simply History itself.'[31]

To conclude the chapter, let me now turn to some
criticisms of Lacan. It is often said that he intellectualizes
everything and does not consider the emotions. He is highly
critical, for example, of the Reichian approach which asserts
that we can get to the emotions directly.[32] For Lacan an
emotion is a signifier; it means something but what it means
is an open question. Secondly, as his writings lack clinical
material it is difficult to learn from his procedures or to test
their validity. He seems to be more interested in developing
theory in the university than in clinical practice. (On the
other hand, it could be argued that though Lacan fails to
provide case studies one way out of the problem is to
examine the work of his followers, for example child
psychologists such as Françoise Dolto and Maud Mannoni.)
As he believes that in analysis nothing should be routine or
predictable his sessions are sometimes only ten minutes long!
He argues that psychoanalysis is not a psychology. If it was
a psychology it would be like ethology (the study of animal
behaviour); but the salient difference is that we cannot
predict human behaviour. Moreover, Lacan holds that only
an analyst can authorize himself or herself as an analyst.
But, surely, self-authorization leads to problems about
standards? Is it enough to be told that becoming an analyst
is like becoming a poet, one who has a new, intimate
relationship with language?

There is also a feminist critique of Lacan. Some writers
have argued that his work reinforces Freud's phallocentrism,
albeit at the level of language and not that of anatomy.
Luce Irigaray, a fierce critic of Lacan, asks if the Freudian
reliance on the phallus as a symbolic law is not the result
of patriarchal culture rather than an inherent necessity of
language or biology.[33] She questions why the phallus alone
is guarantor of meaning, why there cannot be 'vagina envy'.
And is Lacan's phallocentric law (that the phallus alone can
represent the symbolic) really the universal law of mankind
or is this the law merely of men? It is clear that in Lacanian

theory certain symbols are privileged over others: the phallus, the Name-of-the-Father, the Law. There does not seem to be any convincing reason, however, why these signifiers in particular should play such a large role in defining and organizing the human psyche. The point of these feminist criticisms is not to deny the reality and current force of the law of the phallus; it is to question its universal and inevitable theoretical status and power.

And then there is also the question of Lacan's philosophical idealism. He proclaims, 'It is the world of words which creates the world of things.' This axiom is fundamental to his thought, since it gives primacy to language over social structure. While language certainly has a determining as well as mediating role in the formation of consciousness of the world, the social system, I would argue, also determines and limits linguistic possibility.

I often wonder whether the study of the Lacanian model of the subject can help us conceive of a different signification, a different subjectivity, and a different symbolic and social order. We certainly need a model that overcomes the opposition between individual and social phenomena.[34] It seems to me vital that some sort of integration be made between Lacanian psychoanalysis and Marxism. This is crucial because no political revolution can be completed until the very character structures inherited from the older, prerevolutionary society, reinforced by its instinctual taboos, have been utterly transformed.[35]

CHAPTER 2

Derrida and deconstruction

INTRODUCTION

Deconstruction, which has attained widespread recognition as one of the most important avant-garde intellectual movements in France and America, is essentially post-phenomenological and post-structuralist. In the history of contemporary deconstruction the leading figure is Jacques Derrida, who published three influential books in 1967: *Of Grammatology, Speech and Phenomena* and *Writing and Difference.*[1] Amongst other things these texts contain powerful critiques of phenomenology (Husserl), linguistics (Saussure), Lacanian psychoanalysis, and structuralism (Lévi-Strauss).

In this chapter I give an exposition of Derrida's thought. Beginning with an outline of his view of language I give an explanation of what he means by phonocentrism and logocentrism. I then present his arguments against the work of Jean-Jacques Rousseau, Claude Lévi-Strauss and Jacques Lacan. There are also sections on his 'predecessors' Freud and Nietzsche and an account of how they have influenced Derrida's thinking on reading texts and the nature of metaphor. After that I examine some metaphors in common use. Finally, after situating metaphor in the context of political and ideological struggle, I discuss the relationship between deconstruction and Marxism.

THE INSTABILITY OF LANGUAGE

In trying to understand Derrida's work one of the most important concepts to grasp is the idea of 'sous rature', a term usually translated as 'under erasure'. To put a term 'sous rature' is to write a word, cross it out, and then print both word and deletion. The idea is this: since the word is inaccurate, or rather, inadequate, it is crossed out. Since it is necessary it remains legible. This strategically important device which Derrida uses derives from Martin Heidegger, who often crossed out the word Being (like this: B̶e̶i̶n̶g̶) and let both deletion and word stand because the word was *inadequate yet necessary*. Heidegger felt that Being cannot be contained by, is always prior to, indeed transcends, signification. Being is the final signified to which all signifiers refer, the 'transcendental signified'.

In Derrida's view of language the signifier does not yield us up a signified directly, as a mirror yields up an image. There is no harmonious one-to-one set of correspondences between the level of the signifieds in language. Signifiers and signified are continually breaking apart and reattaching in new combinations, thus revealing the inadequacy of Saussure's model of the sign, according to which the signifier and signified relate as if they were two sides of the same sheet of paper. Indeed, there is no fixed distinction between signifiers and signified. Suppose you want to know the meaning of a signifier, you can look it up in the dictionary; but all you will find will be yet more signifiers, whose signifieds you can in turn look up, and so on. The process is not only infinite but somehow circular: signifiers keep transforming into signifieds, and vice versa, and you never arrive at a final signified which is not a signifier in itself.

In other words, Derrida argues that meaning is not immediately present in a sign. Since the meaning of a sign is a matter of what the sign is *not*, this meaning is always in some sense absent from it too. Meaning is scattered or dispersed along the whole chain of signifiers; it cannot be easily nailed down, it is never fully present in any one sign alone, but is rather a kind of constant flickering of presence and absence together. Reading a text is more like tracing this process of constant flickering than like counting the beads on a necklace.

Now, for Derrida the structure of the sign is determined by the trace (the French meaning carries strong implications of track, footprint, imprint) of that other which is forever absent. This other is, of course, never to be found in its full being. Rather like the answer to a child's question or a definition in a dictionary, one sign leads to another and so on indefinitely . . . .

What is the implication of this? That the projected 'end' of knowledge could ever coincide with its 'means' is an impossible dream of plenitude. No one can make the 'means' (the sign) and the 'end' (meaning) become identical. Sign will always lead to sign, one substituting the other as signifier and signified in turn. For Derrida the sign cannot be taken as a homogeneous unit bridging an origin (referent) and an end (meaning), as semiology, the study of signs, would have it. The sign must be studied 'under erasure', always already inhabited by the trace of another sign which never appears as such.

There is also the fact that language is a temporal process. When I read a sentence the meaning of it is always somehow suspended, something deferred. One signifier relays me to another; earlier meanings are modified by later ones. In each sign there are traces of other words which that sign has excluded in order to be itself. And words contain the trace of the ones which have gone before. Each sign in the chain of meaning is somehow scored over or traced through with all the others, to form a complex tissue which is never exhaustible.

Meaning is never identical with itself; because a sign appears in different contexts it is never absolutely the same. Meaning will never stay quite the same from context to context; the signified will be altered by the various chains of signifiers in which it is entangled.

The implication of this is that language is a much less stable affair than was thought by structuralists such as Lévi-Strauss. None of the elements is absolutely definable; everything is caught up and traced through by everything else. Nothing is ever fully present in signs. It is an illusion for me to believe that I can ever be fully present to you in what I say or write, because to use signs at all entails my meaning being always somehow dispersed, divided and never quite at one with itself. Not only my meaning, indeed, but I myself: since language is something I am made out of, rather than a convenient tool I use, the whole idea that I am a stable, unified entity must also be a fiction.[2]

PHONOCENTRISM–LOGOCENTRISM

Derrida is mainly concerned with the role and function of language and is famous for having developed a procedure called deconstruction. This is a method of reading a text so closely that the author's conceptual distinctions on which the text relies are shown to fail on account of the inconsistent and paradoxical use made of these very concepts within the text as a whole. In other words, the text is seen to fail by its own criteria; the standards or definitions which the text sets up are used reflexively to unsettle and shatter the original distinctions. Derrida has used this technique against Husserl, Rousseau, Saussure, Plato, Freud and others; but the method can be applied to any text.

The method of deconstruction is connected with what Derrida calls the 'metaphysics of presence'. It is Derrida's contention that Husserl, along with almost all other philosophers, relies on the assumption of an immediately available area of certainty. The origin and foundation of most philosophers' theories is presence. In Husserl's case the search for the form of pure expression is at the same time a search for that which is immediately present; thus implicitly, by being present in an unmediated way and present to itself, it is undeniably certain.

Derrida, however, denies the possibility of this presence and in so doing removes the ground from which philosophers have in general proceeded. By denying presence, Derrida is denying that there is a present in the sense of a single definable moment which is 'now'. For most people the present is the province of the known. We may be unsure of what took place in the past, of what may take place in the future, or of what is taking place elsewhere, but we rely on our knowledge of the present, the here and now—the present perceptual world as we are experiencing it. By challenging access to the present Derrida poses a threat to both positivism and phenomenology.

Husserl made an important distinction in *The Logical Investigations* between expression and indication. The expression, linked to the intention of the speaker, is what we might call the pure meaning of the sign, and as such is distinguished from indication, which has a pointing function and could occur without any intentional meaning. Now, Derrida has argued that pure expression will always involve an indicative element. Indication can never be successfully excluded from expression. Signs cannot refer to something totally other than themselves. There is no signified which is independent of the signifier. There is no realm of meaning which can be isolated from the marks which are used to point to it.

Having argued that a realm of the independent signified does not exist, Derrida concludes, first, that no particular sign can be regarded as referring to any particular signified and, second, that we are unable to escape the system of signifiers. In combination these conclusions imply that there can be no unqualified presence.

Now, it is because of the assumption of presence that a priority has been given to speech over writing. Derrida calls this phonocentrism. Speech has been regarded as prior because it is closer to the possibility of presence. It is closer because speech implies immediacy. In speech meaning is apparently immanent, above all when, using the inner voice of consciousness, we speak to ourselves. In the moment of speech we appear to grasp its meaning and are thereby able to capture presence, as if the meaning was decided once and for all. Thus, unlike writing, which is hopelessly mediated, speech is linked to the apparent moment and place of presence and for this reason has had priority over writing. For Derrida, therefore, phonocentrism is one of the effects of presence. Derrida's attempt to deconstruct the opposition between speech and writing is linked to the uncovering of the metaphysics of presence as a whole.

Derrida has also criticized Saussure for prescribing that linguistics should be a study of speech alone rather than of speech and writing. This is an emphasis shared by Jakobson, by Lévi-Strauss, indeed by all semiological structuralists. Derrida suggests in *Of Grammatology* that this rejection of writing as an appendage, a mere technique and yet a menace built into speech—in effect, a scapegoat—is a symptom of a much broader tendency. He relates this phonocentrism to logocentrism, the belief that the first and last thing is the Logos, the Word, the Divine Mind, the *self-presence of full self-consciousness*.

Derrida suggests that Husserl found evidence for self-presence in the voice (*phone*)—not the 'real' voice, but the principle of the voice in our interior soliloquy: 'When I speak I hear myself. I hear and understand at the same time that I speak.'

In the act of speaking I seem to coincide with myself in a way quite different from what happens when I write. My spoken words seem immediately present to my consciousness and my voice becomes their intimate spontaneous medium. In writing, by contrast, my meanings threaten to escape from my control. Writing seems to rob me of my being; it is a second-hand mode of communication, a pallid mechanical transcript of speech and so always at one remove from my consciousness. It is for this reason that the Western philosophical tradition, all the way from Plato to Lévi-Strauss, has consistently vilified writing as a mere lifeless, alienated form of expression and consistently celebrated the living voice. (This will be discussed in the next section when we consider Derrida's examination of specific texts by Rousseau and Lévi-Strauss.) Behind this prejudice lies a particular view of 'man': man is able spontaneously to create and express his own meanings, to be in full possession of himself, and to dominate language as a transparent medium of his inmost being. What this traditional theory fails to see is that speaking could be just as much said to be a second-hand form of writing as writing is said to be an inferior form of speaking.

Just as Western philosophy has been 'phonocentric', centred on the 'voice' and deeply suspicious of script, so also it has been in a broader sense 'logocentric', committed to a belief in some ultimate 'word', presence, essence, truth or reality which will act as the foundation of all our thought, language and experience. It has yearned for the sign which will give meaning to all others—the 'transcendental signifier'—and for the anchoring, unquestionable meaning to which all our signs can be seen to point (the 'transcendental signified'). Examples of such signs include: God, the Idea, the World Spirit, the Self, Matter, etc. Since each of these concepts hopes to found our whole system of thought and language, it must itself be beyond that system. It cannot be implicated in the very languages which it attempts to order and anchor; it must be somehow anterior to these discourses. It must act as a linchpin or fulcrum of a whole thought-system, the sign around which all others revolve. Derrida argues that any such transcendental meaning is a fiction.

Certain meanings are elevated by social ideologies to a privileged position, for example Freedom, Authority, Order. Sometimes such meanings are seen as the *origin* of all the others, the source from which they flow. But this is a curious way of thinking, because for the meaning to have been possible other signs must already have existed. It is difficult to think of an origin without wanting to go back beyond it. At other times such meanings may be seen not as the origin but as the goal towards which all other meanings are or should be steadily marching. Teleology (thinking of things in terms of their orientation to a *telos* or end) is a way of ordering and ranking meanings in a hierarchy of significance.

Derrida labels as 'metaphysical' any thought-system which depends on an unassailable foundation, a first principle or unimpeachable ground upon which a whole hierarchy of meanings may be constructed. If you examine such first principles closely, you can see that they may always be deconstructed. First principles of this kind are commonly defined by what they exclude, by a sort of 'binary opposition'. Deconstruction is the name given to a critical operation by which such oppositions can be partially undermined.

Derrida argues that all the conceptual oppositions of

metaphysics have for ultimate reference the presence of a present. (He often uses the word 'metaphysics' as shorthand for 'being as presence'.) For Derrida the binary oppositions of metaphysics include: signifier/signified, sensible/intelligible, speech/writing, speech (*parole*)/language (*langue*), diachrony/synchrony, space/time, passivity/activity. One of his criticisms of the structuralists, as we shall see, is that they have not put these concepts 'under erasure', that they have not put these binary oppositions into question.

Binary oppositions represent a way of seeing, typical of ideologies. Ideologies often draw rigid boundaries between what is acceptable and what is not, between self and non-self, truth and falsity, sense and non-sense, reason and madness, central and marginal, surface and depth. Derrida suggests that we should try to break down the oppositions by which we are accustomed to think and which ensure the survival of metaphysics in our thinking: matter/spirit, subject/object, veil/truth, body/soul, text/meaning, interior/exterior, representation/presence, appearance/essence, etc. Using deconstructive methods, we can begin to unravel these oppositions a little, demonstrate how one term of an antithesis inheres within the other.

Derrida argues that phonocentrism–logocentrism relates to centrism itself—the human desire to posit a 'central' presence at beginning and end. He states that it is this longing for a centre, an authorizing pressure, that spawns hierarchized oppositions. The superior term in these oppositions belongs to presence and the logos, the inferior serves to define its status and mark a fall. The oppositions between intelligible and sensible, soul and body seem to have lasted out 'the history of Western philosophy', bequeathing their burden to modern linguistics with its opposition between meaning and word. The opposition between speech and writing takes its place within this pattern.

ROUSSEAU AND LÉVI-STRAUSS

Derrida writes that many philosophers throughout history use the opposition nature/culture. It is often stated that archaic man, living in an innocent state of nature, comes upon a danger or insufficiency of one sort or another bringing about a need or desire for community. In the evolution of human beings from nature to society the latter stage of existence is pictured as an addition to the original happy stage of nature. In other words, culture supplements nature. Before long culture comes to take the place of nature. Culture, then, functions as a supplement in two ways: it adds and it substitutes. At the same time it is potentially both detrimental and beneficial. The structure of the nature/culture opposition repeats itself in other traditional polarities: for example, health/disease, purity/contamination, good/evil, speech/writing. The first term in each opposition traditionally constitutes the privileged entity, the better state.

Derrida argues that when Rousseau describes an event or phenomenon he invariably ends up relying on the supplement. Although nature is declared to be self-sufficient it needs culture. (In a similar way education for Rousseau aids the insufficiencies of the untrained intellect.) It is suggested by Derrida that there is no original, unsupplemented nature but that nature is always already a supplemented entity. This device, *sous rature*, indicates the equivocal status of the term erased, warning, as I suggested earlier, the reader not to accept the word at face value. The marks of erasure acknowledge both the inadequacy of the terms employed—their highly provisional status—and the fact that thought simply cannot manage without them. Similarly, Derrida has a mistrust of metaphysical language but accepts the necessity to work within that language.

Rousseau believed that speech was the originary, the healthiest and the most natural condition of language; writing was merely derivative and somehow debilitating. What Derrida does (by a close analysis of Rousseau's texts, particularly the *Essay on the Origin of Languages*) is to show that Rousseau contradicts himself, so that, far from proving speech to be the origin of language—and writing merely a parasitic growth—his essay confirms the priority of writing. In other words, Rousseau's text confesses what he is at such pains to deny; his text cannot mean what it says or literally say what it means.

The theme of lost innocence is also to be found in the work of Lévi-Strauss, to which I now turn. However before I outline Derrida's criticism of Lévi-Strauss, it may be useful to go over the main features of the latter's structuralist approach. Structuralism, an attempt to isolate the general structures of human activity, found its main analogies in linguistics. It is well known that structural linguistics performs four *basic* operations: it shifts from the study of conscious linguistic phenomena to the study of their unconscious infrastructure; second, it does not treat terms as independent entities, taking instead as its basis of analysis the relations between terms; third, it introduces the concept of system; finally, it aims at discovering general laws.

What are Derrida's criticisms of structuralism? Firstly, he doubts the possibility of general laws. Secondly, he questions the opposition of the subject and the object, upon which the possibility of objective descriptions rests. In his view the description of the object is contaminated by the patterns of the subject's desire. Thirdly, he questions the structure of binary oppositions. He invites us to undo the need for balanced equations, to see if each term in an opposition is not, after all, an accomplice of the other.

The structuralism of Lévi-Strauss can be characterized as a search for invariant structures or formal universals which reflect the nature of human intelligence. This approach lends support to the traditional idea of the text as a bearer of stable meanings and the critic as a faithful seeker after truth in the text. Derrida suggests that when Lévi-Strauss describes the life of the Nambikwara and their transition to civilization he takes upon himself the burden of guilt produced by this encounter between civilization and the 'innocent' culture it ceaselessly exploits.[3] Lévi-Strauss gives expression, like Rousseau, to an eloquent longing for the lost primordial unity of speech before writing. Writing for Lévi-Strauss is an instrument of oppression, means of colonizing the primitive mind. In Derrida's view there is no pure 'authenticity' as Lévi-Strauss imagines; the theme of lost innocence is a romantic illusion.

Derrida's critique of Lévi-Strauss follows much the same path as his deconstructive readings of Saussure and Rousseau.[4] Once again it is a matter of taking a repressed theme, pursuing its textual ramifications and showing how these subvert the very order that strives to hold them in check. The 'nature' which Rousseau identifies with a pure, unmediated speech, and Lévi-Strauss with the dawn of tribal awareness, expresses nostalgia for lost innocence, an illusory metaphysics of presence which ignores the self-alienating character of all social existence.

Derrida situates the project of Lévi-Strauss (like those of Saussure and Lacan) in logocentrism. One of the central problems of anthropology is the passage from nature to culture. Derrida argues that Lévi-Strauss regularly and symptomatically ends up privileging the state of nature over culture. He appears sentimental and nostalgic, trapped in a Rousseauistic dream of innocent and natural primitive societies. Beneath the guilt and nostalgia, endemic to the field of anthropology, lies a Western ethnocentrism masking itself as liberal and humane anti-ethnocentrism.

As for writing, Lévi-Strauss conceptualizes it as a late cultural arrival, a supplement to speech, an external instrument. Speech is endowed with all the metaphorical attributes of life and healthy vitality, writing with dark connotations of violence and death.[5]

Derrida has made similar comments on Saussure. He has criticized Saussure's *Course in General Linguistics* for the sharp distinction which it maintains between the signifier and the signified, a distinction which is congruent with the traditional opposition of matter and spirit, or substance and thought. (Traditionally, this opposition has always been elaborated in ways which privilege spirit and/or thought as something that precedes matter or substance.) Derrida suggests that the distinction between signifier and signified can only be maintained if one term is believed to be final, incapable of referring beyond itself to any other term. If there is no such term, then every signified functions in turn as a signifier, in an endless play of signification.

Derrida, in short, is critical of Saussure's notion of the sign and argues that the traditional concept of signifier and signified rests firmly within the phonocentric–logocentric *episteme*. One of the characteristics of the logocentric epoch is that there is a general debasement of writing and a preference for phonetic writing (writing as imitated speech). There is, then, a rooted Western prejudice which tries to reduce writing to a stable meaning equated with the character of speech. It is widely held that in spoken language meaning is 'present' to the speaker through an act of inward self-surveillance which assures a perfect, intuitive 'fit' between intention and utterance.

Derrida demonstrates that in Saussurean linguistics privilege is granted to speech as opposed to written language. Voice becomes a metaphor of truth and authenticity, a source of self-present 'living' speech as opposed to the secondary, lifeless emanations of writing. Writing is systematically degraded and is seen as a threat to the traditional view that associates truth with self-presence. This repression of writing lies deep in Saussure's proposed methodology and shows in his refusal to consider any form of linguistic notation outside the phonetic-alphabetical script of Western culture. Against this view Derrida argues that writing is, in fact, the precondition of language and must be conceived as prior to speech. Writing is the 'free play' or element of undecidability within every system of communication.

It should be pointed out that for Derrida 'writing' does not refer to the empirical concept of writing (which denotes an intelligible system of notations on a material substance); writing is the name of the structure always already inhabited by the trace. This broadening of the term, Derrida argues, was made possible by Sigmund Freud.

FREUD AND LACAN

Derrida argues that it is no accident that when Freud tried to describe the workings of the psyche he had recourse to metaphorical models which are borrowed not from spoken language but from *writing*.[6] (This, of course, raises the question of what a text is and what the psyche must be like if it can be represented by a text.)

At first, from about the time of *Project for a Scientific*

Psychology (1895), Freud used mechanical models, but these were soon discarded. As Freud moved from neurological to psychical modes of explanation he began increasingly to refer to metaphors of optical mechanisms. Then, in *The Interpretation of Dreams* (1900), Freud thought it more appropriate to compare dreams with a system of writing than with spoken language. In order to suggest the strangeness of the logico-temporal relations in dreams Freud constantly referred to alphabetic writing as well as non-phonetic writing (pictographs, rebuses, hieroglyphics) in general. Dream symbols, he wrote, frequently have more than one or even several meanings and, as with Chinese script, the correct interpretation can only be arrived at on each occasion from the context.

Later, in *Note on the Mystic Writing Pad* (1925) Freud used a writing apparatus as a metaphor for the working of the psyche. A child's toy had come on the market under the name of Mystic Writing Pad. You may have come across a modern version of it. Basically, it consisted of a celluloid covering-sheet which rested upon a wax slab. One could write on it with a pointed stylus and the writing could be erased by raising the double covering sheet by a little pull, starting from the free lower end. The pad, cleared of writing, is thus ready to receive fresh messages. Freud argued that its construction was very much like that of the perceptual apparatus. It had an ever-ready receptive surface and could retain permanent traces of the inscriptions made on it; the wax slab, in fact, represented the unconscious.

In short, Freud found in the Mystic Writing Pad a model that would contain the problematics of the psyche—a virgin surface that still retained permanent traces. The Freudian argument is that the establishment of permanent traces in the psychic apparatus precludes the possibility of immediate perception. In other words, we have 'memory-traces', marks which are not a part of conscious memory, which may be energized into consciousness long afterwards and so affect us.

Derrida's chief interest in Freudian psychoanalysis lies in the fact that it teaches and uses a certain method of deciphering texts. Freud lists the four techniques used by the 'dream-work' of the psychic apparatus to distort or refract the 'forbidden' dream-thoughts, to produce the pictographic script of the dream: condensation, displacement, considerations of representability and secondary revision. Condensation and displacement may be rhetorically translated as metaphor and metonymy. The third item on the list refers to the technique which distorts an idea so that it can be presented as an image. Secondary revision is a psychic force that smooths over contradictions and creates an apparent connectedness.

Freud suggested that the verbal text is constituted by concealment as much as by revelation. Freud suggests that where the subject is not in control of the text, where the text looks very smooth or very clumsy, is where readers should fix their gaze. Derrida develops this further; he suggests that we should fasten upon a small but tell-tale moment in the text which harbours the author's sleight of hand and which cannot be dismissed simply as contradiction. We should examine that passage where we can provisionally locate the moment when the text transgresses the laws it apparently sets up for itself, and thus unravel— deconstruct—the very text.

Freud's greatest contemporary interpreter is Jacques Lacan. Let me briefly remind you of the key features of Lacan's thought before outlining Derrida's critique of it. Like Freud, Lacan denies that there is a difference in kind between 'the normal' and 'the abnormal'. Moreover, he rejects the work of those American psychologists who stress that the ego is the primary determinant of the psyche. In his view 'the subject' can never be a total personality and is forever divided from the object of its desire. Lacan goes on to define the unconscious in terms of the structure of a language. This extends Freud in a direction that Derrida would endorse, but, nevertheless, the relationship between these thinkers is an uneasy one.

It would seem to an outside observer that Lacan and Derrida have a lot in common: they are both deeply concerned with anti-positivist theories of language and are highly aware of language's metaphoricity. Secondly, both thinkers have been influenced by Freud's theories of the unconscious and the dream as a text. This means that they are interested in (ways of) 'reading' and (styles of) 'writing'. Thirdly, they both draw attention, as did Freud, to the relationship between nature and culture.

And so, why is there an uneasy relationship between them? Derrida argues that the goal of Lacanian analysis is to draw out and establish 'the truth' of the subject, and it appears to him that in spite of giving to the unconscious the structure of a language Lacan has entrenched some of Freud's (metaphysical) suggestions by making the unconscious the source of 'truth'. Derrida believes that Lacan sees himself as unveiling 'the true' Freud and is sceptical of Lacan's notions of 'truth' and 'authenticity', seeing them as remnants of a post-war existentialist ethic, the unacknowledged debts to Hegelian phenomenology.

Derrida believes that Lacan simplifies Freud's text. In Lacanian analysis the truth (logos) systematically shines forth as spoken or voiced. Psychoanalysis remains 'the talking cure' founded on spoken truth.[7] Derrida cautions us that when we learn to reject the notion of the primacy of the signified (of meaning over word) we should not satisfy our longing for transcendence by giving primacy to the signifier (word over meaning). He feels that Lacan has done precisely this.

I stated earlier that Derrida is attempting to subvert the logocentric theory of the sign. Traditionally, the signifier refers to the signified, that is, an acoustic image signifies an ideal concept, both of which are present to consciousness. The signifier 'dog' indicates the idea 'dog'; the real dog, the referent, is not present. In Derrida's view *the sign marks an absent presence*. Rather than present the object we employ the sign; however, the meaning of the sign is always postponed or deferred.

Derrida has developed a concept which he calls 'différance' and which refers to 'to differ'—to be unlike or dissimilar in nature, quality or form—and to 'to defer'—to delay, to postpone (the French verb *différer* has both these meanings). Spoken French makes no phonetic distinction between the endings '-ance' and '-ence'; the word registers as *différence*. This undetected difference shows up only in writing.

The advent of the concept of writing, then, is a challenge to the very idea of structure; for a structure always presumes a centre, a fixed principle, a hierarchy of meaning and a solid foundation; and it is just these notions which the endless differing and deferring of writing throws into question.

As we have seen, Derrida's analysis of Husserl led him to portray language as an endless play of signifiers. Once an independent signified was abandoned signifiers referred to other signifiers which yet again referred to signifiers. Language is thus the play of differences which are generated by signifiers which are themselves the product of those differences. Derrida incorporates into the meaning of *différance* the sense of deferring. *Différance* is itself endlessly deferred.

NIETZSCHE AND METAPHOR

Derrida's acknowledged 'precursors' were Nietzsche, Freud and Heidegger. They all felt a need for the strategy of '*sous rature*'. Heidegger put 'Being' under erasure, Freud 'the psyche', and Nietzsche 'knowing'.[8] It seems that post-structuralists such as Derrida have not so much followed in Nietzsche's footsteps as rediscovered his philosophical stance, a stance that owes its character to an all-pervasive reflexivity.

The current emphasis on reflexivity (a form of self-awareness, a turning back on oneself) is in part due to a critical shift of focus from the individual subject to the text. Thus from Nietzsche to Derrida we see the human subject—traditionally the focus of philosophical thought as the place of experience, morality, choice and will—gradually abandoned.

Derrida suggests that the main characteristics of Nietzsche's work are a systematic mistrust of metaphysics and a suspicion of the values of 'truth' and 'meaning'. Many cultural relativists believe that, although we may interpret the world differently according to our social context, there is a single world which we are all interpreting. For Nietzsche, however, there is no single, physical reality beyond our interpretations. There are only perspectives.

Rooted in Nietzsche's philosophy is the implicit stance that there are no final conclusions; the text can never be fixed and as a result it can never be deciphered either. Nietzsche believes that we are unable to escape the constraints of language and thus have no alternative but to operate within language. He is aware of the reflexive problem: if we say 'we are trapped within language and its concepts', that claim is in itself, of course, part of language. We wish to express our 'trappedness' but we are unable to do so other than in the very concepts which trap us. The original thought therefore eludes us, for if we could express it, we would not, after all, be trapped.[9]

Nietzsche, then, was deeply aware of the problem that one is bound by one's perspective. One of his ways of coping with this was by the strategy of intersubstituting opposites. If one is always bound by one's perspective, one can at least deliberately reverse perspectives as often as possible, in the process undoing opposed perspectives, showing that the two terms of an opposition are merely accomplices of each other. In this way Nietzsche problematized, for example, the opposition between 'metaphor' and 'concept', 'body' and 'mind'. I mention this because Nietzsche's undoing of opposites is rather like Derrida's undoing of them as a part of deconstructive practice.

For Nietzsche there is no possibility of a literal, true, self-identical meaning. (Derrida, too, is deeply committed to the view that philosophical discourse is something to be deciphered.) Nietzsche described the figurative drive as the impulse towards the formation of metaphors. Every idea, he said, originates through an equating of the unequal. Metaphor is the establishing of an identity between dissimilar things:

> What, therefore, is truth? A mobile army of metaphors, metonymies, anthropomorphisms; truths are illusions of which one has forgotten that they are illusions . . . coins which have their obverse effaced and now are no longer of account as coins but merely as metal.[10]

In his later work Nietzsche gave this figurative drive the

name 'will to power'. Our so-called will to truth is the will
to power because the so-called drive for knowledge can be
traced back to a drive to appropriate and conquer. Sometimes
Nietzsche places this abstract will to power, an incessant
figuration, not under the control of any knowing subject
but rather in the unconscious. Indeed, for Nietzsche the
important main activity is unconscious, that is, it takes place
in that vast arena of the mind of which the so-called 'subject'
knows nothing. Derrida has remarked that both Nietzsche
and Freud questioned, often in a very similar way, the self-
assured certitude of consciousness.

In many ways, then, Nietzsche anticipates both the style
and the strategy of Derrida's writing. Nietzsche held that
philosophy from Plato to the present had suppressed the
fact that language is radically metaphorical in character.
Philosophy utilized metaphors but disguised this fact. All
philosophies, whatever their claim to logic or reason, rested
on a shifting texture of figurative language, the signs of
which were systematically repressed. In Nietzsche's view the
Sophists, a school of rhetorician-philosophers in ancient
Greece, came closer to wisdom by implicitly acknowledging
what Socrates has to deny: that thinking is always and
inseparably bound to the rhetorical devices that support it.

Following Nietzsche, Derrida makes the point that all
language is ineradicably metaphorical, working by tropes
and figures. It is a mistake to believe that any language is
literally literal. Literary works are in a sense less deluded
than other forms of discourse, because they implicitly
acknowledge their own rhetorical status. Other forms of
writing are just as figurative and ambiguous but pass
themselves off as unquestionable truth.

One of the implications of this view is that literature can
no longer be seen as a kind of poor relation to philosophy.
There is no clear division between literature and philosophy,
nor between 'criticism' and 'creation'. Since metaphors are
essentially 'groundless', mere substitutions of one set of signs
for another, language tends to betray its own fictive and
arbitrary nature at just those points where it is offering to
be most intensively persuasive. In short, philosophy, law,
and political theory work by metaphor just as poems do,
and so are just as fictional.

UNDERSTANDING METAPHOR

The study of metaphor is becoming important as it is being realized that language does not simply reflect reality but helps to constitute it. Attention is now being increasingly given to how rhetorical devices shape our experience and our judgements, how language serves to promote the possibilities of certain kinds of action and exclude the practicability of others.

In the past, metaphor was often studied as an aspect of the expressive function of language, but it is actually one of the essential conditions of speech. Language works by means of transference from one kind of reality to another and is thus essentially metaphorical. Some people have urged that technical and scientific language should be purged of metaphor but, as we have seen, metaphorical expressions are rooted in language itself. For example, we habitually think of organizations spatially, in terms of up and down. We tend to think of theories as though they were buildings, and so we talk of foundations, frameworks etc. 'Base' and 'superstructure' are fundamental concepts in Marxism. As Derrida has shown, even philosophy is permeated with metaphor without knowing it.

Meaning shifts around, and metaphor is the name of the process by which it does so. It is a threat to orderly language and allows for the proliferation of meaning. First, there is no limit to the number of metaphors for any given idea. Second, metaphor is a sort of rhetorical double-bind, which states one thing but requires you to understand something different. (I found it interesting to learn that many schizophrenics cling to the literal and avoid metaphors because these are ultimately undecidable.) Metaphors evoke relationships and the making of the relationships is very much the task of the hearer or reader. Indeed, understanding a metaphor is as much a creative endeavour as making a metaphor, and as little guided by rules. Metaphor is ubiquitous and ineradicable.

I want to stress the point that metaphors are not just the

concern of the poet or the literary critic, not just figures of
speech; they represent one of the ways in which many kinds
of discourse are structured and powerfully influence how
we conceive things. I would like you to consider for a
moment the metaphor 'time is money'. In our culture time
is money in many ways; we calculate telephone calls, hourly
wages, interests on loans. But not only do we *act* as if time
is a valuable commodity, we also *conceive* of time that way.
'I don't have the time to give you.' 'How do you spend
your time these days?' Thus we understand and experience
time as the kind of thing that can be spent, wasted, budgeted,
invested wisely or foolishly, saved or squandered. 'Time is
money', 'time is a limited resource' and 'time is a valuable
commodity' are all metaphorical concepts. They are metaphorical since we are using our everyday experiences with
money, limited resources and valuable commodities to
conceptualize time. But this is not the only way in which
human beings may conceptualize time; it is tied to our
culture. There are cultures where time is none of these
things.

Let us consider another example: the organizing metaphors
surrounding work and leisure. One does a full day's work;
one is in or out of work. Leisure time, on the other hand,
is to be filled; holiday weekends are breaks between work.
We associate the metaphor of work with plenitude, with
something of importance, and that of leisure with emptiness,
with a vacuum. The metaphors reinforce the idea of life as
first and foremost the life of work, while activities outside
of it belong to the frivolous and not to the main business
of life. Metaphors like these are particularly insidious since
they are so interwoven into our speech that their flavour
of metaphor is lost upon speakers and hearers.

THE POLITICS OF METAPHOR

Our ordinary language is saturated with metaphor. For
example, in our society argument is in part structured,
understood, performed and talked about in terms of war.

There is a position to be established and defended, you can win or lose, you have an opponent whose position you attack and try to destroy and whose argument you try to shoot down. The language of argument is basically, the language of physical combat. That 'argument is war' is built into the conceptual system of the culture in which we live. Lakoff and Johnson have pointed out that it need not be so; that one can easily imagine societies in which argument is conceived differently—for example as theatrical perform-ance.[11] In such a society both argument itself and the criteria for success or failure in argument would be quite unlike our own.

Some metaphors, in certain historical periods, have been liberating. The historian Christopher Hill has described how in the seventeenth century nature came to be thought of as a machine to be understood, controlled and improved upon by knowledge.[12] Nature as a machine was (at that time) a tremendously exciting, liberating idea. Human beings were freed from Providence or divine will and could not only understand the world better but could begin to change it.

I think that the creative or imaginative aspect of sociologi-cal theories often lies in their use of metaphor. Parsons likens society to a biological organism; Marx uses the metaphor of a building, the base and superstructure; Goffman uses the metaphor of a stage 'performance'. Metaphors serve to draw attention not only to similarities but to differences. As the theory develops and becomes more precise, concepts emerge that sometimes have little to do with the original metaphor.

An influential post-structuralist thinker, Michel Foucault (whose work on the social sciences and the relations between power and knowledge will be discussed in the next chapter), is particularly fond of using 'geographical' metaphors such as territory, domain, soil, horizon, archipelago, geopolitics, region, landscape. He also makes profuse use of spatial metaphors—position, displacement, site, field. Althusser, too, in *Reading Capital* uses many spatial metaphors (terrain, space, site, etc.). Foucault suggests that, since Bergson perhaps, there has been a devaluation of space. Space has been treated as the dead, the fixed, the undialectical, the immobile; time, on the contrary, was richness, fecundity, life, dialectic. But to talk in terms of space does not mean that one is hostile to time. Althusser believed that the use of spatial metaphors in his work was necessary but at the same time regressive, non-rigorous. Foucault, on the other hand, is more positive. He has said that *it is through these spatial obsessions that he came to what he was looking for*: the relations that are possible between power and knowledge. 'Once knowledge can be analysed in terms of region, domain, implantation, displacement, transposition, one is able to capture the process by which knowledge functions as a form of power and disseminates the effects of power.'[13]

I believe the metaphors determine to a large extent what we can think in any field. Metaphors are not idle flourishes—they shape what we do. They can help to make, and defend, a world view. It is important that the implications of the metaphors we employ or accept are made explicit and that the ways in which they structure our thought and even our action are better understood. I also want to stress that metaphors can be productive of new insights and fresh illuminations. They can promote unexpected or subtle parallels or analogies. Metaphors can encapsulate and put forward proposals for another way of looking at things. Through metaphor we can have an increased awareness of alternative possible worlds.

DECONSTRUCTION AND MARXISM

The metaphor most often used by deconstructionists is that of the palimpsest; reading texts resembles the X-raying of pictures which discovers, under the epidermis of the last painting, another hidden picture. Deconstructive criticism takes the 'metaphoric' structure of a text seriously. Since metaphors are not reducible to truth, their own structures 'as such' are part of the text. The deconstructive procedure is to spot the point where a text covers up its grammatical structure. Gayatri Spivak puts it like this:

> If in the process of deciphering a text in the traditional way we come across a word that seems to harbour an unresolvable contradiction, and by virtue of being one word is made sometimes to work in one

way and sometimes in another and thus is made to point away from
the absence of a unified meaning, we shall catch at that word. If a
metaphor seems to suppress its implications, we shall catch at that
metaphor. We shall follow its adventures through the text coming
undone as a structure of concealment, revealing its self-transgression,
its undecidability.[14]

Derrida has provided a method of 'close-reading' a 'text'
very similar to psychoanalytic approaches to neurotic
symptoms. Deconstructive 'close-reading', having 'interrogat-
ed' the text, breaks through its defences and shows that a
set of binary oppositions can be found 'inscribed' within it.
In each of the pairs, private/public, masculine/feminine,
same/other, rational/irrational, true/false, central/peripheral,
etc., the first term is privileged. Deconstructors show that
the 'privileged' term depends for its identity on its excluding
the other and demonstrate that primacy really belongs to
the subordinate term instead.

Derrida's procedure is to examine the minute particulars of
an undecidable moment, nearly imperceptible displacements,
that might otherwise escape the reader's eye. He tries to
locate not a moment of ambiguity or irony ultimately
incorporated into the text's system of unified meaning but
rather a moment that genuinely threatens to collapse that
system. Derrida's method is not that of Hegel. Hegel's
idealist method consists in resolving by sublation the
contradictions between the binary oppositions.

Derrida stresses the point that it is not enough simply to
neutralize the binary oppositions of metaphysics. Deconstruction involves reversal and displacement. Within the familiar
philosophical oppositions there is always a violent hierarchy.
One of the two terms controls the other, holds the superior
position. The first move in deconstructing the opposition is
to overthrow the hierarchy. In the next phase this reversal
must be displaced, the winning term put 'under erasure'.
Deconstruction, then, is the attempt

> to locate the promising marginal text, to disclose the undecidable
> moment, to pry it loose with the positive lever of the signifier, to
> reverse the resident hierarchy, only to displace it; to dismantle in order
> to reconstitute what is always already inscribed.[15]

Before making some critical remarks, let me try to sum up.

Derrida has made a close study of many philosophers: Nietzsche, Rousseau, Husserl, Heidegger and others. He argues that they have been able to impose their various systems of thought only by ignoring or suppressing the disruptive effects of language. One of the ruling illusions of Western metaphysics is that reason can somehow grasp the world without a close attention to language and arrive at a pure, self-authenticating truth or method. Derrida's work draws attention to the ways in which language deflects the philosopher's project. He does this by focusing on metaphors and other figurative devices at work in the texts of philosophy. In this way Derrida underlines the rhetorical nature of philosophical arguments.

Deconstruction stresses the irreducibility of metaphor, the difference at play within the very constitution of literal meaning. It should be remembered that deconstruction is not simply a strategic reversal of categories which otherwise remain distinct and unaffected. It is an activity of reading in which texts must be read in a radically new way. There must be an awareness of ambivalence, of the discrepancy between meaning and the author's assertion. Derrida discovers a set of paradoxical themes at odds with their manifest argument. His method consists of showing how the privileged term is held in place by the force of a dominant metaphor and not, as it might seem, by any conclusive logic.[16] Metaphors often disrupt the logic of an argument.

Derrida writes that we have a metaphysical desire to make the end coincide with the means, create an enclosure, make the definition coincide with the defined, the 'father' with the 'son'; within the logic of identity to balance the equation, close the circle. In short, he is asking us to change certain habits of mind; he is telling us that the authority of the text is provisional, the origin is a trace. Contradicting logic, we must learn to use and erase our language at the same time. Derrida wants us to 'erase' all oppositions, undoing yet preserving them.

Deconstructionists tend to say that if a text seems to refer beyond itself, that reference can finally be only to another text. Just as signs refer only to other signs, texts can refer only to other texts, generating an intersecting and indefinitely expandable web called *intertextuality*. There is a proliferation of interpretations, and no interpretation can claim to be the final one. Now, Derrida is sometimes taken to be denying the possibility of truth. This is not so. It is more plausible to think of him as trying to avoid assertions about the nature of truth.

The usual superficial criticism of Derrida is that he questions the value of 'truth' and 'logic' and yet uses logic to demonstrate the truth of his own arguments. The point is that the overt concern of Derrida's writing is the predicament of having to use the resources of the heritage that he questions.

Derrida's work confronts us with many problems. Having argued that there cannot be a realm of the signified independent of the signifier, he opens up the vista of an endless play of signifiers that refer not to signifieds but to other signifiers, so that meaning is always ultimately undecidable. Derrida gives as an example of undecidability Plato's frequent presentation of writing as a drug, *pharmakon*. This Greek word can mean either 'poison' or 'cure' and, as with a drug, which way it is taken (translated) makes a lot of difference. Consider another important case of undecidability: an isolated note found amongst Nietzsche's unpublished manuscripts, a single sentence in quotation marks: 'I have forgotten my umbrella.' In a sense, we all know what this phrase means, and yet we have no idea of what its meaning is in this instance. Is it a jotting to himself, a citation, or a phrase overheard and noted for further use? Perhaps the umbrella is seen as some sort of defence, a protection from the weather? Nietzsche, on the verge of breakdown, has left his defences behind; caught in a rainstorm, he has forgotten his umbrella. Of course, it could also be analysed in Freudian terms, as psychoanalysis often focuses on the significance of forgetting and phallic objects. 'I have forgotten my umbrella': the phrase is undecidable. This illustration could be a metaphor for the whole of Derrida's text.

As we saw with Derrida's work on Saussure and Lévi-Strauss, deconstruction questions the self-identity of signifier and signified and the self-presence of the speaking subject and the voiced sign. There is an abandonment of all reference to a centre, to a fixed subject, to a privileged reference, to an origin, to an absolute founding and controlling first principle.

Deconstruction disarticulates traditional conceptions of the author and the work and undermines conventional notions of reading and history. Instead of mimetic, expressive and didactic theories of 'literature' it offers textuality (*écriture*). It kills the author, turns history and tradition into intertextuality and celebrates the reader.[17]

One of the main features of post-structuralist theory is the deconstruction of the self. In place of a unified and stable being or consciousness we get a multifaceted and disintegrating play of selves. The reader, like the text, is unstable. With deconstruction the categories 'criticism' 'philosophy' and 'literature' collapse, borders are overrun. The work, now called 'text', explodes beyond stable meaning and truth towards the radical and ceaseless play of infinite meanings. Critical writing, formerly analytical and coherent, becomes playfully fragmented.

Is this a result of Derrida's view of language? It has been suggested by Terry Eagleton that

> meaning may well be ultimately undecidable if we view language contemplatively, as a chain of signifiers on a page; it becomes 'decidable' and words like 'truth', 'reality', 'knowlege', and 'certainty' have something of their force restored to them when we think of language rather as something we *do*, as indissociably interwoven with our practical forms of life.[18]

The deconstructor's method often consists of deliberately inverting traditional oppositions and marking the play of hitherto invisible concepts that reside unnamed in the gap between opposing terms. In the move from hermeneutics and semiotics to deconstruction there is a shift of focus from identities to differences, unities to fragmentations, ontology to philosophy of language, epistemology to rhetoric, presence to absence. According to one recent commentator 'deconstruction celebrates dissemination over truth, explosion and fragmentation over unity and coherence, undecidable spaces over prudent closures, playfulness and hysteria over care and rationality.[19]

It is said that every boundary, limit, division, frame, or margin installs a line separating one entity or concept from another. That is to say, every border marks a difference. The question of the border is a question of difference. Derrida writes, 'No border is guaranteed, inside or out.' Applied to texts, this finding becomes 'no meaning can be fixed or decided upon.' According to deconstructionists there is nothing other than interpretation.[20] As there is neither an undifferentiated nor a literal bottom or ground, the activity of interpretation is endless. It is also a fact that every text tends itself to deconstruction and to further deconstruction, with nowhere any end in sight. Finally, no escape outside the logocentric enclosure is possible since the interpreter must use the concepts and figures of the Western metaphysical tradition. The term used to describe the impasse of interpretation ('there is no way out') is *aporia*. 'The supreme irony of what Derrida has called logocentrism is that its critique, deconstruction, is as insistent, as monotonous and as inadvertently systematizing as logocentrism itself.'[21]

Having given a few criticisms of Derrida and deconstruction, I now want to ask, 'Are his methods allied or opposed to Marxism?' When faced with new approaches such as deconstruction it is very hard to try to work out whether they are useful aids in building a new socialist order or are just other forms of bourgeois recuperation and domination. I think I am right in saying that deconstruction is, for Derrida, ultimately a political practice, an attempt to dismantle the logic by which a particular system of thought and, behind that, a whole system of political structures and social institutions maintains its force. But in practice it cannot be denied that his work has been grossly unhistorical and politically evasive.[22] One post-structuralist, Michel Foucault, has argued that Derrida's own decision to avoid questions about the extent to which the text arises out of and reflects underlying social practices itself reflects a social practice. He has said that by deliberately restricting himself to textual analysis the question of evaluating textual analysis as a social and political practice cannot be raised. In so far as textual undecidability precludes raising questions about truth it perpetuates the status quo.

On the other hand, some commentators have suggested that deconstruction, by unsettling the theories with which we have surrounded ourselves, serves to indicate that our account of the world *could* be different but that it cannot tell us how it would be different. Derrida seems to believe that deconstruction is able gradually to shift the structures within which we operate 'little by little to modify the terrain of our work, and thereby produce new figurations'. Is this enough? Is Derrida playing among the webs of language, 'parodying himself, and then parodying the parody'?[23]

Derrida has himself observed that certain American uses of deconstruction work to ensure 'an institutional closure' which serves the dominant political and economic interests of American society. He has also said that Marxist texts are shot through with metaphors disguised as concepts, themes that carry along with them a whole unrecognized baggage of presuppositions. But on the whole Derrida has been silent about Marx—a silence that can be construed as a prolonged postponement, a refusal as yet to engage with Marxist thought.

There are some critics, like Fredric Jameson, who feel that the claims of synchronic thought must somehow be reconciled with those of historical understanding, that there must be a *rapprochement* between rhetoric and Marxist dialectic.[24] But other critics have suggested that the Marxist model of representation, however refined in theory, is caught up in a rhetoric of tropes and images that entirely controls its logic. Christopher Norris, for example, has argued that deconstruction is inimical to Marxist thought. In his view the insights of deconstruction are inevitably couched in a rhetoric which itself lies open to further deconstructive reading: 'Once criticism enters the labyrinth of deconstruction it is committed to a sceptical epistemology that leads back to Nietzsche, rather than Marx.'[25]

Some of the most trenchant criticisms of deconstruction have been made by the English Marxist critic Terry Eagleton. According to Eagleton the main characteristics of deconstruction are that it rejects any notion of totality and that it is against the privileging of the unitary subject. Deconstructionism asserts that literary texts do not have relations to something other than themselves. It follows that deconstruction is not concerned with blaming anybody for the exploitation that exists, since this would entail some kind of vantage point from which definite judgements could be delivered. Eagleton, in 1981, wrote that

> many of the vauntedly novel themes of deconstruction do little more than reproduce some of the most commonplace topics of bourgeois liberalism. The modest disownment of theory, method and system; the revulsion from the dominative, totalising and unequivocally denotative; the privileging of plurality and heterogeneity; the recurrent gestures of hesitation and indeterminacy; the devotion to gliding and process, slippage and movement; the distaste for the definitive—it is not difficult to see why such an idiom should become so quickly absorbed within the Anglo-Saxon academies.[26]

It is suggested by Eagleton that deconstruction is not only reformist but ultra-leftist too. On the one hand, deconstruction is a sort of patient, probing reformism of the text. Because it can only imagine contradiction as the external warring of two monistic essences, it fails to comprehend class dialectics. On the other hand, deconstruction is ultra-left in that it is 'a problematic that sees meaning itself as terroristic'. Both left reformism (social democracy) and ultra-leftism are among other things antithetical responses to the failure or absence of a mass revolutionary movement.

CHAPTER 3

Foucault and the social sciences

INTRODUCTION: FOUCAULT'S VIEW OF HISTORY

Foucault is against any form of global theorizing. He wants to avoid totalizing forms of analysis and is critical of systemacity. Though his works do not constitute a system, nevertheless there is an underlying coherence which stems from the fact that Foucault's works are based on a vision of history derived from Nietzsche. Indeed, he has expressed his indebtedness to Nietzsche for having outlined a conception of history called genealogy.[1]

Nietzsche's book *On the Genealogy of Morals* was an effort to delegitimize the present by separating it from the past. This is what Foucault tries to do. Unlike the historian who traces a line of inevitability, Foucault breaks off the past from the present and, by demonstrating the foreignness of the past, relativizes and undercuts the legitimacy of the present.

Foucault rejects the Hegelian teleological model, in which one mode of production flows dialectically out of another, in favour of a Nietzschean tactic of critique through the presentation of *difference*. The Nietzschean historian begins with the present and goes backward in time until a difference is located. Then s/he proceeds forward again, tracing the transformation and taking care to preserve the discontinuities as well as the connections. This is the method used by Foucault. The alien discourses/practices are explored in such a way that their negativity in relation to the present explodes the 'rationality' of phenomena that are taken for granted.

When the technology of power of the past is elaborated in detail, present-day assumptions which posit the past as 'irrational' are undermined.

The gap between the past and the present underlines the principle of difference at the heart of Foucault's historiography. He allows the discontinuity to remain unexplained. The role of cause or explanation is severely reduced in most post-structuralist texts, since it leads to evolutionist conclusions and works against the purposes of the genealogy of difference.

Genealogical analysis, then, differs from traditional forms of historical analysis in several ways. Whereas traditional or 'total' history inserts events into grand explanatory systems and linear processes, celebrates great moments and individuals and seeks to document a point of origin, genealogical analysis attempts to establish and preserve the singularity of events, turns away from the spectacular in favour of the discredited, the neglected and a whole range of phenomena which have been denied a history. According to Foucault there has been an insurrection of subjugated knowledges, of a whole set of knowledges that have been disqualified as inadequate—naïve knowledges located low down on the hierarchy, beneath the required level of scientificity. Foucault often uses the term genealogy to refer to the union of erudite knowledge and local memories which allows us to establish a historical knowledge of struggles and to make use of this knowledge tactically today. Genealogies focus on local, discontinuous, disqualified, illegitimate knowledges against the claims of a unitary body of theory which would filter, hierarchize and order them in the name of some true knowledge.

Genealogy, I repeat, is a form of critique. It rejects the pursuit of the origin in favour of a conception of historical beginnings as lowly, complex and contingent. It attempts to reveal the multiplicity of factors behind an event and the fragility of historical forms. In this view of history, which Foucault's writings exemplify, there can be no constants, no essences, no immobile forms of uninterrupted continuities structuring the past.

REASON AND UNREASON

Foucault's early work is mainly concerned with the growth of those disciplines which are collectively known as the social or human sciences. His books are an answer to the question of how the human sciences are historically possible and what the consequences of their existence are. His studies repeatedly centre on the eighteenth century—the period in which the human sciences in their modern forms were constituted and certain new 'technologies' elaborated. Both of these developments were linked to a new philosophical conception of Man as a simultaneous subject and object of knowledge.

Throughout his life Foucault has been interested in that which reason excludes: madness, chance, discontinuity. He believes that the literary text allows 'otherness' to speak. In philosophy and law this otherness is silent, whereas in madness it is not listened to. Foucault values the literature of transgression—it attempts to subvert the constraints of all other forms of discourse by its difference. And so he admires the literary tradition that includes writers such as de Sade, Nerval, Artaud, and Nietzsche.

In his first well-known book 'Madness and Civilization' Foucault describes how madness, along with poverty, unemployment and the inability to work, comes in the seventeenth century to be perceived as a 'social problem' which falls within the ambit of responsibility of the state.[2] There is a new conception of the state as preserver and augmenter of the general welfare. In the book there is an important discussion of the emergence of 'humanitarian' attitudes towards the insane at the end of the eighteenth century. The opening of Tuke's Retreat at York and Pinel's liberation of the insane at Bicêtre are protrayed as leading to a 'gigantic moral imprisonment', more oppressive than the former practices of brutal incarceration since they operate on the mind rather than merely on the body.

THE GREAT CONFINEMENT

At the end of the Middle Ages leprosy disappeared from the western world. Foucault suggests a connection between this and some of the attitudes then taken towards madness. As leprosy vanished a void was created and the moral values had to find another scapegoat. He shows how in the 'classical period' (1500–1800) madness attracted that stigma.

During the Renaissance madmen led an easy, wandering existence. The towns drove them outside their limits and they were allowed to wander in the open countryside. One common way of dealing with the mad was to put them on a ship and entrust them to mariners, because folly, water and sea, as everyone then 'knew', had an affinity with each other. These 'Ships of Fools' were to be found criss-crossing the seas and canals of Europe. Many texts and paintings, for example the works of Brueghel, Bosch and Dürer, refer to the theme of madness. These works of art express an enormous anxiety about the relationships between the real and the imaginary. Then, within the space of a hundred years, the 'madship' was replaced by the 'madhouse'; instead of embarkation there was *confinement*. Men did not wait until the seventeenth century to 'shut up' the mad, but it was in this period that they began to 'confine' them.

Why was this? Foucault argues that during the second half of the seventeenth century social sensibility, common to European culture, began to manifest itself; a 'sensibility to poverty and to the duties of assistance, new forms of reaction to the problems of unemployment and idleness, a new ethic of work'.[3] And so, enormous houses of confinement (sometimes called 'houses of correction') were created throughout Europe. To these places a (strangely) mixed group of people, poor vagabonds, the unemployed, the sick, the criminals, and the insane were sent. No differentiation was made between them.

Confinement was a massive phenomenon, a 'police' matter whose task was to suppress beggary and idleness as a source of disorder.

> The unemployed person was no longer driven away or punished; he was taken in charge, at the expense of the nation but at the cost of his individual liberty. Between him and society an implicit system of obligation was established: he had the right to be fed, but he must accept the physical and moral constraint of confinement.[4]

The repressive function of the houses of confinement was combined with a new use: the internees were made to work. In the Middle Ages the great sin had been pride, in the seventeenth century it was sloth. Since sloth had become the absolute form of rebellion, the idle were forced to work. Labour was instituted as an exercise in moral reform. Confinement played a double role: it absorbed the unemployed in order to mask their poverty and it also avoided the social or political disadvantages of agitation.

In the Renaissance madness had been present everywhere, but the houses of confinement hid it away. Confinement marked a decisive event: 'The new meanings assigned to poverty, the importance given to the obligation to work, and all the ethical values that are linked to labour, ultimately determined the experience of madness and inflected its course.'[5] Most of Foucault's book is a detailed description of how madness was thought about in the seventeenth and eighteenth centuries: he writes about mania and melancholia, hysteria and hypochondria; how it was thought that the savage danger of madness was related to the danger of the passions, and how madness was conceived as a form of animality to be mastered only by discipline.

Gradually in the eighteenth century confinement came to be seen as a gross error; it began to be said that charity was a cause of impoverishment and that vagabonds should seek employment. Moreover, legislators were beginning to be embarrassed because they no longer knew where to place mad people—in prison, hospital or the family. Measured by their functional value alone, the houses of confinement were a failure: when the unemployed were herded into forced-labour shops, there was less work available in neighbouring regions and so unemployment increased. Thus the houses of confinement, a social precaution clumsily formulated by a nascent industrialization, disappeared throughout Europe at the beginning of the nineteenth century.

THE BIRTH OF THE ASYLUM

The legislation passed to segregate criminals and poor people from fools was prompted, as often as not, by a desire to protect the poor and the criminal from the frightening bestiality of the madman. A hallowed tradition has associated Tuke in England and Pinel in France with the liberation of the insane and the abolition of constraint. But, Foucault argues, we must be sceptical of this claim. In fact, Tuke created an asylum where the partial abolition of physical constraint was part of a system whose essential element was the constitution of a self-restraint. 'He substituted for the free terror of madness the stifling anguish of responsibility .... The asylum no longer punished the madman's guilt, it is true, it did more, it organized that guilt.'[6]

The Quaker Samuel Tuke organized his Retreat so that it had a religious ethos. In it work was imposed as a moral rule, a submission to order. Instead of repression there was surveillance and judgement by 'authority'. Everything at the asylum was arranged so that the insane were transformed into minors and given rewards and punishments like children. A new system of education was applied; first the inmates were to be subjugated, then encouraged, then applied to work: 'The asylum would keep the insane in the imperative fiction of the family; the madman remains a minor, and for a long time reason will retain for him the aspect of the Father.'[7]

During the 'classical period' poverty, laziness, vice, and madness mingled in an equal guilt within unreason. Madness during the nineteenth century began to be categorized as social failure. The doctor gained a new social status and increasingly the patient surrendered to the medical profession. In short, the asylum of the age of positivism was not a free realm of observation, diagnosis and therapeutics. In the hands of Tuke and Pinel it became a juridical space where one was accused, judged and condemned—an instrument of moral uniformity. Invoking the names of those who have gone mad, such as Artaud, Hölderlin, Nerval, Nietzsche, and van Gogh, Foucault reminds us that we are in the habit of calling this gigantic moral imprisonment the 'liberation' of the insane.

Foucault's book has a sense of great loss. It states that during the Middle Ages mad people were not locked up; indeed they possessed a certain freedom. There was a notion of the 'wise fool'—like the character in *King Lear*. Even in the eighteenth century madness had still not lost its power; but in the nineteenth century the dialogue between reason and unreason was broken. There is now only the monologue of reason *on* madness. Foucault suggests that there are dimensions that are missing in reason or, to put it in another way, there may be a wisdom in madness.

Human beings have been released from the physical chains, but these have been replaced by mental ones. One of the main themes of the book is how external violence has been replaced by internalization. The birth of the asylum can be seen as an allegory on the constitution of subjectivity. It is an indictment of modern consciousness. *Madness and Civilization* is as much concerned with the plight of everyday consciousness in the modern world as with the specific fate of those labelled insane. Foucault implies that modern forms of public provision and welfare are inseparable from ever tighter forms of social and psychological control. From the beginning, intervention and administrative control have defined the modern state.

According to Foucault madness can never be captured; madness is not exhausted by the concepts we use to describe it. His work contains the Nietzschean idea that there is more to madness than scientific categorization; but in associating freedom with madness he seems to me to romanticize madness. For Foucault to be free would be *not* to be a rational, conscious being. Though Foucault's position is a relativist one, he actually has deep-seated preferences. Critics of Foucault have asked, 'How can Foucault capture the spirit of madness when he is so obviously writing from the viewpoint of reason?'[8] Shouldn't he, logically, give up writing altogether?

Most of Foucault's books are really analyses of *the process of modernization*. One of the characteristics of his work is the tendency to condense a general historical argument into a tracing of the emergence of specific institutions. His second main work, *The Birth of the Clinic*, is subtitled 'An Archaeology of Medical Perception'.[9] This perception or 'gaze' is formed by the new, untrammelled type of observation made possible for the doctor at the bedside of the hospitalized patient intersecting with a system of monitoring the state of health of the nation through the new teaching hospital.

Foucault's subsequent books, *The Order of Things* and *The Archaeology of Knowledge*, deal largely with the structure of scientific discourses.[10] (Discourses are perhaps best understood as practices that systematically form the objects of which they speak.) Foucault is concerned with the question, what set of rules permit certain statements to be made?

In *The Order of Things* Foucault argues that in certain empirical forms of knowledge such as biology, psychiatry, medicine, etc. the rhythms of transformation do not follow the continuist schemas of development which are normally accepted. In medicine, for example, within a period of about twenty-five years there arose a completely new way of speaking and seeing. How is it that at certain moments and in certain knowledges there are these sudden transformations? There seem to be changes in the rules of formation of statements which are accepted as scientifically true. There is a whole new 'regime' of discourse which makes possible the separation not of the true from the false but of what may be characterized as scientific from what may not be characterized as scientific.

Unlike most of Foucault's other work, *The Order of Things* and *The Archaeology of Knowledge* are not concerned with the emergence of modern forms of administration. One reason for this may be that the structuralists during the 1960s veered away from any form of political analysis and that he was influenced by them.

Looking back on his early work, Foucault concedes that

what was missing was a consideration of the effects of power:

> When I think back now, I ask myself what else it was that I was talking about, in *Madness and Civilization* or *The Birth of the Clinic*, but power? Yet I'm perfectly aware that I scarcely ever used the word and never had such a field of analysis at my disposal.[11]

In his later work, where Foucault is concerned with power and knowledge, he is much more inclined to talk about 'apparatuses'. An apparatus is a structure of heterogeneous elements such as discourses, laws, institutions, in short, the said as much as the unsaid. The apparatus contains strategies of relations of forces supporting, and supported by, types of knowledge.

A STRUGGLE OVER MEANING

Foucault returned to some of the topics discussed in *Madness and Civilization* in a book which he edited twelve years later called *I, Pierre Rivière . . . A Case of Parricide in the 19th Century*.[12] One of the main themes of this 'dossier' is the problematic division between the innocence of unreason and the guilt of crime. This work is truly interdisciplinary in that one can approach it from the point of view of history, politics, literature, psychiatry, or the law.

It raises many important questions about these forms of knowledge and their interrelationship. The case of Pierre Rivière marked the border where many types of discourse, institutions and powers confronted one another. To anyone wishing to read a case study of a struggle over meaning or wanting to understand what Foucault means by a 'battle among discourses through discourses' I would recommend this book.

Pierre Rivière was, in two different ways but in virtually a single deed, an 'author'. In 1835 the twenty-year-old peasant killed his mother, his sister and his brother. While he was detained he wrote a memoir giving particulars and an explanation of the crime. Though he had received only a village education he produced a text that has beauty and eloquence. The memoir is of interest to historians and others because it raises so many questions. Frightful crimes were being committed in the countryside at that time, but what were those acts saying and why did they speak such a terrifying language? Why was parricide equated with regicide?

The life story of this obscure peasant (who resembles Julien Sorel) has considerable literary value; and as there are so many interpretations it raises the question, 'How do we read a text?' What is fascinating is that the book shows how two conflicting arguments (that advanced by the doctors and that put forward by the lawyers) could be constructed from two different accounts of Rivière's life, both of them based on the *same* sources of information. Of course, the frontier between rationality and madness is hard to establish, but can they coexist in the form of a partial delusion and the lucid interval? While some people saw in Rivière's memoir a proof of rationality and therefore wanted to condemn him to the guillotine, other people saw in the memoir a sign of madness and hence wanted to isolate him in an asylum.

Some said that the same signs of madness could be found alike in the fact of premeditated murder and in the particulars of what was narrated; others said that the same signs of lucidity could be found both in the *preparation and circumstances* of the murder and in the fact that Rivière had written it down. In other words, the fact of killing and the fact of writing, the deeds done and the things narrated, coincided since they were elements of a like nature.

While the doctors presented Rivière as always having been mad, the lawyers claimed that he was always sane. The doctors stressed his 'bizarre behaviour' as a sign of his madness; lawyers, by stressing Rivière's intelligence, ascribed to him full responsibility for his crime. What was really happening in this competition between the medical and the penal authorities was an attempt to pathologize a sector of criminality. Emergent psychiatry was attempting to gain a space for its intervention and create a new apparatus. There is an interesting section in the book on how the development of the theory of limited responsibility, the existence of extenuating circumstances, opened the way in introducing not merely psychiatry but all the social and human sciences, psychology, sociology, genetics and so on, into judicial procedure.

This book, then, gives us an idea of how a particular kind of knowledge such as medicine or psychiatry is formed. Foucault tells us that the documents in the book give us a key to the relations of power, domination and conflict within which discourses emerge and function, and hence provide material for a potential analysis of discourse which may be both tactical and political and therefore strategic. In short, the book exemplifies one of Foucault's main preoccupations: the attempt to rediscover the interaction of discourses as weapons of attack and defence in the relations of power and knowledge.

DISCIPLINARY POWER

I have mentioned several times that Foucault's work owes much to Nietzsche. Many of the themes that have reappeared in post-structuralism, such as relativism and the relationship between knowledge and power, can be found in Nietzsche's work. Foucault inverts, following Nietzsche, the common-sense view of the relation between power and knowledge. Whereas we might normally regard knowledge as providing us with power to do things that without it we could not do, Foucault argues that knowledge is a power over others, the power to define others. In his view knowledge ceases to be a liberation and becomes a mode of surveillance, regulation, discipline.

Foucault's masterpiece *Discipline and Punish* focuses on the moment when it became understood that it was more efficient and profitable to place people under surveillance than to subject them to some exemplary penalty. This transition in the eighteenth century corresponds to the formation of a new mode of exercise of power.[13] The book begins with a horrifying description of a regicide's torture and public execution. The author then describes how within eighty years vast changes occurred: torture disappeared, there was regulation of prisoners, and the new mechanisms of surveillance began to be applied in barracks, hospitals, prisons and schools.

Foucault suggests that under a feudal and monarchical system individualization is greatest at the summit of society. Power is visibly embodied in the person of the king, who has unlimited power over an anonymous body of subjects. Under this type of regime the notion of crime is still not fully distinguished from that of sacrilege, so that punishment takes the form of a ritual intended not to 'reform' the offender but to express and restore the sanctity of the law which has been broken. In general, power in feudal societies tends to be haphazard and imprecise, whereas in modern societies the agencies of punishment become part of a pervasive, impersonal system of surveillance and correction which pays an ever-increasing attention to the psychology of the individual. Intention rather than transgression now becomes the central criterion of culpability.

Let me restate Foucault's argument. In feudal societies, under *monarchical power*, the judiciary only arrested a very small proportion of criminals and it was argued that punishment must be spectacular so as to frighten the others. The new theorists of the eighteenth century objected to this: such a form of power was too costly in proportion to its results. In contrast to monarchical power, there is *disciplinary power*, a system of surveillance which is interiorized to the point that each person is his or her own overseer. Power is thus exercised continuously at a minimal cost.

Once you suppress the idea of vengeance, which previously was the act of a sovereign threatened in his very sovereignty by the crime, punishment can only have a meaning within a technology of reform. Foucault's hypothesis is that the prison was linked from its beginning to a project for the transformation of individuals. The failure of the project was immediate and this was realized virtually from the start. People knew that prisons did not reform but on the contrary manufactured criminals and criminality. It was soon

discovered that criminals could be put to good use as
informers, pimps, policemen. Foucault writes that at the end
of the eighteenth century people dreamed of a society
without crime. And then the dream evaporated. Crime was
too useful to dream of anything as dangerous as a society
without crime. 'No crime means no police. What makes the
presence and control of the police tolerable for the population, if not fear of the criminal?'[14] In short, supervised
illegality was directly useful. It provided a justification and
a means for the general surveillance, the policing of the
entire population.

The transformation of Western societies from monarchical
(or sovereign) power to disciplinary power is epitomized in
Foucault's description of the Panopticon, an architectural
device advocated by Jeremy Bentham towards the end of
the eighteenth century. In this circular building of cells no
prisoner can be certain of not being observed from the
central watch-tower, and so the prisoners gradually begin
to police their own behaviour.

This new mode of power, which we can call panopticism,
was used first of all in schools, barracks and hospitals.
People learned how to establish dossiers, systems of marking
and classifying. Then there was the permanent surveillance
of a group of pupils or patients; and at a certain moment
in time these methods began to be generalized.

If you have already read *Discipline and Punish* you will
have noticed the likeness between the Panopticon (the 'all-
seeing') and the Christian God's infinite knowledge. It is
also similar to Freud's concept of the super-ego as the
internal monitor of unconscious wishes. Another parallel is
between the Panopticon and the computer monitoring of
individuals in advanced capitalism. Foucault hints that the
new techniques of power were needed to grapple with the
increase in population: to undertake its administration and
control because of newly-arising problems of public health,
hygiene, housing conditions, longevity, fertility, sex. As we
shall see in a moment, sex is politically significant because
it is located at the point of intersection of the discipline of
the body and the control of the population.

At times *Discipline and Punish* regresses to a totalizing

logic in which the Panopticon becomes the model for all forms of domination. Moreover, though Foucault makes a powerful case against the modern prison system, he offers nothing as a constructive alternative to it. One point that puzzles me is that, according to Foucault, the Panopticon is a machine in which everyone is caught and which no one knows. What, then, is the origin of this strategy, how do these tactics arise? Foucault does not give a clear answer; he merely states that all these tactics were invented and organized from the starting points of local conditions and particular needs, that they took shape in piecemeal fashion, prior to any class strategy.

TECHNICAL RATIONALITY

What is the problem that really worries Foucault? Bourgeois thought stresses the idea of the conscious subject who calculates means and ends. The subject is rational, autonomous and capable of initiating action. But the more autonomous one becomes the more important the criterion of means and ends becomes. Now, the work of Foucault has often been compared with that of Max Weber, one of whose central themes was rationalization. Weber held that action could be rational in its ends or its means. Bureaucracies stressed efficiency of means. In impersonal, bureaucratic organizations reason was shaped into scientific rationality. The objective of scientific rationality is to gain mastery over the physical and the social environment. Weber, following Nietzsche, argued that scientific rationality focused on means but not on ends. Instrumental reason cannot tell us anything about how to live our lives. In a sense Foucault reiterates the fears of (Nietzsche and) Weber: science uncovers the mythology in the world; but science itself is a myth which has to be superseded. Scientific knowledge has brought about a disenchantment with the world. Means can be calculated with efficiency—this is what is called technical rationality—but ends, values, become increasingly problematic to determine. One effect of the rise of technical or instrumental rationality is the process of reification which has produced disenchantment.

This analysis is in some ways close to the one made by the 'critical theorists' of the Frankfurt School. Theodor Adorno and Max Horkheimer, much influenced by Weber, analysed the capitalist economy as merely one form of the autonomous dynamic of a means–end rationality. This makes possible not only an unprecedented increase in the forces of production, and therefore in the domination of external nature, but also in the domination of human beings who are adapted to the system of production through social engineering and psychological manipulation. According to Adorno and Horkheimer the calculating instrumental rationality required of the subject in its struggle to gain independence from the overwhelming powers of external nature requires a corresponding repression of the spontaneity of inner nature.[15] For Weber and the Frankfurt School the social forms engendered by (technical or) instrumental rationality represent a profounder threat to human freedom than class oppression. Adorno and Horkheimer believed that even the space for individual responsibility and initiative, which was opened during the early phases of capitalism, is now closed by the administered society.

Foucault, too, is worried about the productivity and efficiency of those instrumental–rational forms of organization which Weber detected in modern bureaucracies and in the capitalist organization of the labour process. Foucault's view that power cannot be considered a possession of groups or individuals should be understood in the light of Weber's account of the transition from 'traditional' to 'legal–rational' forms of domination. That is to say, power in modern societies does not depend upon the prowess and prestige of individuals but is exercised through an impersonal administrative machinery operating in accordance with abstract rules.

SEXUALITY AND POWER

Foucault is generally known as the historian who stresses discontinuities. But in fact, when he writes about other thinkers he often emphasizes the continuities in their work. For example, at the time Althusser was emphasizing the epistemological break in Marx's work (separating the early 'ideological' texts from the later anti-humanist, economic work) Foucault argued that Marx's concepts were only a development of those of David Ricardo and, what is more, that Marxism fitted into nineteenth-century thought like a fish in water; that is, it was unable to breathe anywhere else. Similarly, Freud's work does not represent a radical break; psychoanalysis is, in fact, an episode in the machinery of the confession. (By confession Foucault means all those procedures by which subjects are incited to produce a discourse of truth about their sexuality which is capable of having effects on the subjects themselves.) In the usual histories one reads that sexuality was ignored by medicine and psychiatry and that at last Freud discovered the sexual origin of neuroses. Now everyone knows, says Foucault, that that is not true; the problem of sexuality was massively inscribed in the medicine and psychiatry of the nineteenth century.

Psychoanalysis was established in opposition to a certain kind of psychiatry, the psychiatry of degeneracy, eugenics and heredity. In relation to that psychiatry psychoanalysis played a liberating role; some of its activities, however, have the function of control and normalization. In Foucault's view psychoanalysis grew out of the institutionalization of confessional procedures which has been so characteristic of our civilization. Viewed over a shorter span of time, it forms part of that medicalization of sexuality which is another phenomenon of the West.

These are some of the views expressed in *The History of Sexuality; Volume One: An Introduction.*[16] One of the main points of the book is that sexuality is far more a positive product of power than power was ever repression of sexuality. Foucault states that we have only had sexuality since the eighteenth century, and sex since the nineteenth. What we had before that was, no doubt, the flesh.

Foucault argues that at one time the Christian confession was the locus of sexuality. In the Middle Ages the priest was concerned with what people did; the faithful were asked in detail about their sexual activities. In that period sexuality, in the understanding of society, concerned only the body. With the Reformation and the Counter-Reformation the discourse on sexuality takes another form. In the confession the priest begins to inquire not only about actions but also about intentions. Sexuality begins to be defined in terms of the mind as well as the body. This is similar to the pattern of change discovered by Foucault in his history of crime and punishment; there also, discourse intensifies from a concern with action and the body to a concern with the mind and its intentions.

Foucault's work shows how in the eighteenth century processes of training and regulation of human bodies emerged in a wide range of specific institutional locations: in factories, prisons and schools. The overall outcome of these disciplinary practices were bodies that were useful and docile, productive and subjected. And then, at the beginning of the twentieth century, the discourse on sex became a matter of science. Foucault's main example of a modern discourse on sexuality, a new scientific confessional, is psychoanalysis. He says that by positing a sexual instinct Freud opened up a new realm for the domination of science over sexuality.

Foucault draws attention to the dissolution of the forms of group identity characteristic of traditional societies, and their replacement by a form of identity which depends increasingly upon the capacity of the individual to reflect upon and articulate the domain of private experience. It is an attack on what he calls 'the repressive hypothesis', the assumption that the asceticism and work discipline of bouregois society demanded a repression of sexuality. The sexual-repression hypothesis is associated with Wilhelm Reich and the Frankfurt School. Reich's story, to put it simply, is that with the onset of capitalism there was an increasing repression and confinement of (natural) human

sexuality. The authoritarian bourgeois father, devoted obsess-
ively to accumulating capital, hoarded his energies for the
market place and the factory. Foucault's *The History of
Sexuality* opens with an attack on this Freudo-Marxist
position. He claims that it was precisely during this period
that there was 'a veritable explosion' of discourses about
sexuality in, for example, medical, psychiatric and educational theories and the practices that were both informed
and presupposed by these discourses.

Foucault's main objection to the repressive hypothesis is
its reliance upon a negative conception of power as
prohibition or limitation. Against this he maintains that
since the eighteenth century power has become increasingly
positive or productive, involving the careful construction of
new capacities rather than the repression or removal of pre-
existing ones. The fundamental thesis of the book is that
sexuality is not a natural reality but the product of a system
of discourses and practices which form part of the intensifying
surveillance and control of the individual. Foucault suggests
that liberation is a form of servitude, since our apparently
'natural' sexuality is in fact a product of power.

Foucault's primary objective is to provide a critique of
the way modern societies control and discipline their
populations by sanctioning the knowledge claims and
practices of the human sciences: medicine, psychiatry,
psychology, criminology, and sociology. The human sciences
have established certain norms and these are reproduced
and legitimized through the practices of teachers, social
workers, doctors, judges, policemen and administrators. The
human sciences have made man a subject of study and a
subject of the state. There has been an unrelenting expansion
of rationalized systems of administration and social control.
It is time to examine Foucault's theory of power.

POWER AND KNOWLEDGE

In structuralism all relations were seen as linguistic, symbolic,
discursive. After a while such a linguistic model was seen

to be limited and some theorists became increasingly interested in power. Foucault's writings are an example of this trend. His work in the 1960s focused on language and the constitution of the subject in discourse. The individual subject was an empty entity, an intersection of discourses. In his later work Foucault has shifted from linguistic determination to the view that individuals are constituted by power relations, power being the ultimate principle of social reality.

Foucault has remarked that Nietzsche's contemporary presence is increasingly important. It was Nietzsche who specified the power relation as the general focus, whereas for Marx it was the production relation. Nietzsche is the philosopher of power, a philosopher who managed to think of power without having to confine himself within a political theory in order to do so. Historians have studied those who held power and there have been many anecdotal histories of kings and generals; contrasted with this there has been the history of economic processes. Again distinct from this we have histories of institutions. But power in its strategies and its mechanisms has never been studied. What has been studied even less is the relation between power and knowledge. It is, of course, the interdependence of power and knowledge (*pouvoir–savoir*) that constitutes the strategic fulcrum of Foucault's later work.

Traditionally, power has often been thought of in negative terms and been seen as an essentially judicial mechanism: as that which lays down the law, which limits, obstructs, refuses, prohibits and censors. It presupposes a sovereign whose role is to forbid: to have power is to say no. And the challenging of power thus conceived can appear only as transgression.

This is the view that Foucault accepted in his early work; but by around 1971–2 he realized that the question of power needed to be reformulated. He replaced a judicial, negative conception of power with a technical and strategic one. This positive view can be seen in *Discipline and Punish* and *The History of Sexuality*. Modern power operates through the construction of 'new' capacities and modes of activity rather than through the limitation of pre-existing ones.

Foucault argues that power is not a possession or a capacity.[17] It is not something subordinate to or in the service of the economy. He insists that relations of power do not emanate from a sovereign or a state; nor should power be conceptualized as the property of an individual or class. Power is not simply a commodity which may be acquired or seized. Rather it has the character of a network; its threads extend everywhere. Foucault suggests that an analysis of power should concentrate not on the level of conscious intention but on the point of application of power. In other words, he wants to shift attention from questions such as 'Who has power?' or 'What intentions or aims do power holders have?' to the processes by which subjects are constituted as effects of power.

He rejects analyses which locate the source of origin of power within a structure or an institution at a centre or summit. Foucault's view calls into question the Marxist notion of conflict between a ruling class and a subordinate class. Foucault states that the mechanisms, techniques and procedures of power were not invented by the bourgeoisie, were not the creation of a class seeking to exercise effective forms of domination; rather they were deployed from the moment that they revealed their political and economic utility for the bourgeoisie.

For Foucault, then, conceiving of power as repression, constraint or prohibition is inadequate: power 'produces reality'; it 'produces domains of objects and rituals of truth'. Foucault remarks that we often hear the cliché 'power makes mad', but we should consider the fact that the exercise of power itself creates and causes to emerge new objects of knowledge. Conversely, knowledge induces effects of power. It is not possible for power to be exercised without knowledge, it is impossible for knowledge not to engender power.

FOUCAULT AND ALTHUSSER

Foucault's thesis that subjects are constituted by power derives from Nietzsche (who remarked that an internalized moral control of behaviour can only be inculcated through threats and violence).[18] Like Nietzsche Foucault analyses the transition from a state of overt violence and brutality to a condition of internalized restraint. As I said earlier, Foucault argues that the physical confinement and repression that occurred in the sixteenth, seventeenth and eighteenth centuries left a greater power and freedom to madness than modern methods of treatment, which aim at transforming the consciousness of the insane. Where formerly there had been the 'free terror of madness' there now reigns the 'stifling anguish of responsibility'. This regime of incessant observation and judgement forms the conditions for the internalization of morality. As Peter Dews has observed, what Foucault is really talking about here is not the specific regime of the modern asylum but the makings of modern subjectivity.[19]

Foucault is against the philosophical tradition which takes for granted that human subjects are responsible and autonomous. He is critical of the notion of the subject throughout his work. You will remember that in *Discipline and Punish* Foucault wrote that the Panopticon creates subjects responsible for their own subjection. Self-enslavement is the moment of horror. The book can be read as a parable about human subjectivity. At one time the ruler was individualized and the mass was anonymous. Now the bureaucracy is anonymous and the subject is individualized. Foucault is ambiguous about whether the Panopticon is power or an apparatus of power. He believes, like Althusser, that ideology will not end in the future, that there will never be a transparent society.

It could be argued that Foucault's notion of the Panopticon is in some ways rather like Althusser's account of ideology. In Althusser there are many small subjects in subordinate positions in relation to the absolute subject.[20] Similarly, in Foucault there are many separate, individual prisoners who are subject to 'the look', the gaze. The inmates in the circular building do not know when they are being observed from the central tower, and so they tend to behave as if they were always under surveillance.

I think this may be a good place to consider some of the similarities—and the differences—between Foucault and Althusser that are often overlooked but which are really quite important. One of the most obvious similarities is their *anti-humanist* approach. You may remember that Althusser attempted to make a distinction between ideology and science and argued that humanism has an ideological character. Let me quickly distinguish some of the characteristic features of humanism. There is, firstly, the Cartesian notion of the subject: 'I think, therefore I am. I have intentions, purposes, goals, therefore I am the sole source and free agent of my actions.' Humanism is also associated with 'methodological individualism' (the idea that societies consist only of individuals). Humanism is sometimes accompanied by the belief that social relations in a socialist society will be transparent. Anti-humanists argue that unconditional emancipation is a fantasy—and that fantasies are dangerous. Althusser and Foucault regard humanism as an error; and yet there is the irony that, in a sense, we are all humanists. We experience the world as humanists, but this is not necessarily the way we theorize.

Another similarity between Althusser and Foucault is that they both emphasize the necessity of applying certain anti-humanist theories to the reading of texts. It must be said, however, that just as there is no clear way of deciding what is idealist and what is materialist, there is no simple way of deciding what is humanist and what is anti-humanist.[21] Thirdly, both Althusser and Foucault have produced work that raises problems rather than provides solutions. Althusser's books *For Marx* and *Reading Capital* are good examples of this.[22] Many of Foucault's writings are polemical and his concepts are unstable because of their provisional character.

Indeed, Foucault is often depicted as some sort of freewheeling relativist in contrast to Althusser, the guardian of Marxist truth; but it has been argued by Mark Cousins and Athar Hussain that both Foucault and Althusser are against a rigid notion of truth and falsity.[23] One of

Althusser's main points is that science produces its own objects and that it is itself the product of social practices. Foucault argues that the character of the knowledge of the human sciences is different from that of the natural sciences. In the human sciences (what Foucault calls) Man is both subject and object.

There are also many *differences* between Foucault and Althusser which must be remembered. Althusser is committed by his espousal of Marxist materialism both to a strong view of the mind-independent reality of the objects of scientific knowledge *and* to a positive valuation of the cognitive authority of science. Ted Benton has perceptively suggested that many of the inner tensions and oscillations in Althusser's work stem from his difficulties in synthesizing the French epistemological tradition, which stresses that knowledge is culturally produced, with Marxist materialism with its stress on the existence of a mind-independent reality.[24]

Althusser makes a sharp distinction between ideology and science. He believes that, historically, ideology precedes the science, that is produced when there is an 'epistemological break', but that it survives alongside science as an essential element of every social formation. Foucault, however, rejects the concept of ideology. What he tries to do is to talk about the social function of ideology but without an epistemological dimension; it is as if he did not want to get trapped in the interminable debates about reality and illusion.

What are Foucault's objections to the concept of ideology? In Marxist thought ideology is usually conceived as a form of mystification; it does not have the status of scientific knowledge. From Foucault's Nietzschean viewpoint, however, all discourses are merely perspectives. I think Foucault's objection to the concept of ideology derives from his anti-humanism. The humanist notion of ideology places the sources of ideas in subjects, but Foucault's project is not to study Man but the mechanisms of the human sciences. He believes that by taking a point of view other than that of the subject one can decipher the mechanisms through which the human sciences come to dominate, not liberate, the subject. Furthermore, Foucault is opposed to the central feature of historical materialism upon which the concept of ideology rests: the distinction between base and superstructure. He believes that ideas are not reducible to the mode of production. In his view discourses are already powers and do not need to find their material force somewhere else, as in the mode of production. Let us look in more detail at Foucault's criticisms of Marxism.

FOUCAULT'S CRITIQUE OF MARXISM

Foucault is very concerned about the inhibiting effect of global, totalitarian theories (Marxism and psychoanalysis) and argues that the attempt to think in terms of a totality has in fact proved a hindrance to research. As I mentioned earlier, Foucault believes that Marx's analysis of the formation of capital is for a large part governed by the concepts he derives from the framework of Ricardian economics. In short, Marx did not escape from the epistemological space established by Ricardo.[25]

What are Foucault's criticisms of the Marxist conception of the state and of the revolutionary movement? Firstly, in order to be able to fight a state which is more than just a government, the revolutionary movement must possess equivalent politico-military forces and hence must constitute itself as a party, organized internally in the same way as a state apparatus with the same mechanisms of hierarchies and structures of power. This consequence is heavy with significance. Secondly, during the period of the dictatorship of the proletariat the state apparatuses must be kept sufficiently intact for them to be employed against the class enemy. In order to operate these state apparatuses which have been taken over but not destroyed it is necessary to use specialists from the bourgeoisie. (This is what happened in the USSR.) But, Foucault argues, power is not localized in the state apparatuses and nothing in society will be changed if the mechanisms of power that function outside, below and alongside the state apparatuses on a much more minute and everyday level are not also changed.

Power is not located in the state apparatus; it passes through much finer channels and is much more ambiguous, since each individual has at his or her disposal at least some power. Moreover, it should be remembered that the reproduction of the relations of production is not the only function served by power. The systems of domination and the circuits of exploitation certainly interact, intersect and support each other, but they do not coincide. Excessive insistence on the state playing an exclusive role leads to the risk of overlooking all the mechanisms and effects of power which do not pass directly via the state apparatus, yet often sustain the state more effectively than its own institutions. In fact, the state can only function on the basis of other already existing power networks such as the family, kinship, knowledge, and so forth. Of course, the critics of Foucault argue against this position because in their opinion he neglects the state and focuses only on the micro-powers that are exercised at the level of daily life.

Foucault is deeply antagonistic to the Marxist concept of ideology; he says that it is difficult to make use of it for three reasons. Firstly, it always stands in virtual opposition to something else which is supposed to count as truth. What interests him, of course, is how effects of truth are produced within discourses which in themselves are neither true nor false. Secondly, analyses which prioritize ideology trouble him because they always presuppose a human subject on the lines of the model provided by classical philosophy. Foucault wants to dispense with the constituent subject. Thirdly, ideology stands in a secondary position relative to something which functions as its base, as its material economic determinant. Perhaps I should add here that Foucault is also highly critical of the concept 'repression', which he regards as negative, psychological and insufficiently analytical. What makes power accepted is that it not only weighs on us as a force that says no, but it produces things: it induces pleasure, forms of knowledge, produces discourse.

Foucault has little to say about class consciousness, class ideology, class interest or class struggle for the simple reason that he does not believe in class. He writes '. . . one should not assume a massive and primal condition of domination, a binary structure with "dominators" on one side and "dominated" on the other, but rather a multiform production of relations of domination . . . .'[26]

Foucault therefore stresses the importance of *local, specific struggles* and believes that they can have effects and implications which are not simply professional or sectoral. In his view the universal intellectual (usually a writer), the bearer of values in which all can recognize themselves, has become outmoded. Intellectuals now tend to work within specific sectors such as housing, the hospital, the asylum, the laboratory, the university, family and sexual relations. He refers to these people as 'specific' intellectuals. They do not formulate the global systematic theory which holds everything in place, but analyse the specificity of mechanisms of power. He writes: 'The project, tactics, and goals to be adopted are a matter for those who do the fighting. What the intellectual can do is to provide instruments of analysis, and at present this is the historian's essential role.'[27]

Foucault thinks that many people are obsessed with a determination to make a science out of Marxism. He is particularly critical of those Marxists who say, 'Marxism, as the science of sciences, can provide the theory of science and draw the boundary between science and ideology.'[28] To those who are trying to establish the scientificity of Marxism he asks, 'What types of knowledge do you want to disqualify in the very instant of your demand: "Is it a science?"'[29] In his view the method of genealogy involves a painstaking rediscovery of struggles, an attack on the tyranny of what he calls 'totalizing discourses' and a rediscovery of fragmented, subjugated, local and specific knowledge. It is directed against great truths and grand theories. But he provides no grounds for distinguishing between different struggles and does not seem to be able to commit himself to a conception of the human good.[30]

SOME CRITICISMS OF FOUCAULT'S WORK

Having outlined some of Foucault's arguments against Marxism, I now want to make some criticisms of his work.

The first criticism is this: Foucault refuses to be committed to a general ontology of history, society or the human subject, or to advance any general theory of power. Many commentators, however, believe that this is precisely his strength; his value lies in *particular* analyses (of the clinic, the asylum, the prison). While there is much that is valuable and insightful in these studies, it must be admitted that Foucault's refusal to deal with epistemological questions means that it is difficult to evaluate them. As he does not present his own methodological protocols we do not know what standards should be used to assess his work.[31] What are the procedures by which one archaeologist of knowledge can confirm or question the analyses of another? If we are to engage seriously with Foucault's writings, considerable theoretical work on his epistemological and ontological protocols will have to be done.

In his writings Foucault often describes a coherent rational strategy, but it is not possible to identify a person who conceived it. It seems to be *a strategy without a subject*. In an interview Foucault was asked who or what it is that co-ordinates the activities of agents. His reply, in my opinion, does not answer the question:

> Take the example of philanthropy in the early nineteenth century: people appear who make it their business to involve themselves in other people's lives, health, nutrition, housing; then, out of this confused set of functions there emerge certain personages, institutions, forms of knowledge: public hygiene, inspectors, social workers, psychologists. And we are now seeing a whole proliferation of different categories of social work.[32]

Consider another example: the strategy for the moralization of the working class. Foucault insists that one cannot say that the bourgeois class (on the level of its ideology or its economic project) invented and forcibly imposed this strategy on the working class.[33] The objective existed and the strategy was developed with ever-growing coherence but without it being necessary to attribute to it a subject.

The Panopticon is Foucault's apt metaphor for the anonymous centralization of power. But what is the principle, force or entity which power crushes or subdues? In other words, what does this modern power operate against? How would a situation change if an operation of power was cancelled? Foucault is vague in his replies to these questions. He has difficulty in defining what this power operates against. It seems that power is almost a metaphysical principle. Power is everywhere: it filters up from below, it is produced at every moment. Now, though he remarks that wherever there is power there is resistance, he offers no grounds for encouraging resistance or struggle. This is partly because he believes that there is no constant human subject in history. History does not reveal the gradual triumph of human rationality, nor does it fulfil an ultimate goal. History is uncontrolled and directionless.

In an interview Foucault was asked: 'Given that there are relations of forces and struggles, the question inevitably arises of who is doing the struggling and against whom?' He replied: 'This is preoccupying me. I'm not sure what the answer is.' The interviewer persisted: 'So who ultimately are the subjects who oppose each other?' Foucault answered:

> This is just a hypothesis, but I would say it's all against all. There aren't immediately given subjects of the struggle, one the proletariat, the other the bourgeoisie. Who fights against whom? We all fight each other. And there is always within each of us something that fights something else.[34]

Underlying Foucault's work there seem to be the following presuppositions: One, social power is omnipotent with respect to the psychic formation of the individual. Two, human individuals exist merely as an embodied nexus to be transformed by the deployment of external causal powers. This ontology is immediately qualified by Foucault. Power, he says, always produces resistance. But the question is, why should it? If power cannot be identified with repression (Foucault insists that it is both productive and regulative), what is the mechanism that generates resistance? Why do people resist? Why do they obey? People obey laws because of external reasons (physical force) or because of internal reasons (ideology). Foucault says that people obey or resist for *many* reasons. This may not seem very helpful, but perhaps his work reminds us that we should avoid easy answers.

When Foucault has been pressed to explain resistance he has been forced back to saying that there is 'something in the social body, in classes, groups, and individuals themselves which in some sense escapes relations of power ... an inverse energy, a discharge ... a plebeian quality or aspect'.[35] It is not surprising that Nicos Poulantzas scorned this attempt to ground resistance in an essentialized, absolutized, externalized spirit of refusal. In short, though the phrase 'wherever there is power there is resistance' is an appealing one, there is no doubt that 'resistance' is really a residual category in Foucault's work. It remains unanalysed.

One useful way of thinking about Foucault has been provided by Poulantzas, who found Foucault helpful *as a theorist of specific techniques of power* and of aspects of the state, but who carefully rejected his more general theoretical project. Poulantzas conceded that Foucault's analysis of normalization and the state's role in shaping corporality was superior to his own. Indeed, there are several interesting parallels between the work of Poulantzas and Foucault.[36] The latter considered that power is immanent in all social relations; Poulantzas also argued that all social relations are relations of power. Both theorists adopt a relational approach to power and explore the links between power and strategies. They also agree that power is productive rather than simply repressive and negative. Another similarity is their interest in 'micro-revolts'. Foucault emphasized that there is a multiplicity of dispersed micro-power relations. Poulantzas, too, was interested in the autonomous role of new social movements but he focused more on the question of how such micro-diversity culminates into the macro-necessity of bourgeois domination.

In spite of these similar interests Poulantzas goes on to make some trenchant criticisms. In his view Foucault neglects to study the modern form of the state and how it is derived from capitalist relations of production. He does not see that all social phenomena always occur in relation to the state and class division. To put this in another way, Foucault disregards the fact that domination has its basis in the relations of production and exploitation and in the organization of the state.

Foucault exaggerates the importance of disciplinary techniques in the modern state and thus neglects the continued importance of violence, legal coercion and law in general. Poulantzas argues that law and the state are each characterized equally by negative and positive features. The law is not only involved in organizing repression but is also essential for reproducing consent. Likewise the state is not only involved in repression and police measures, it is also active in constituting social relations and winning mass support.

According to Poulantzas Foucault emphasizes only the repressive, prohibitive side of law and the positive productive side of (state) power. In emphasizing the internalized repression achieved through disciplinary normalization, Foucault ignores the direct role coercion plays in sustaining the web of disciplinary and ideological mechanisms as well as the continued importance of overt violence in the state's activities. On the other hand, some commentators have remarked that the tacit social theory of *Discipline and Punish* describes all social relations in terms of power, domination and subordination and that Foucault neglects aspects of human sociability, in the family and in civil society generally, which are based on co-operation and reciprocity.[37]

Let me now try to summarize the main points. Foucault's historical analyses of specific institutions focus on the themes of centralization, increasing efficiency (technical rationality), and the replacement of overt violence by moralization. Power in modern societies is essentially orientated towards the production of regimented, isolated and self-policing subjects. According to Foucault power is everywhere. The idea that 'power' is located at, or emanates from, a given point seems to him to be based on a misguided analysis. In his view power is not always exercised from above in a negative or repressive way but is an open cluster of relations. Power is not an institution, a structure, or a certain force with which certain people are endowed; it is a name given to a complex strategic relation in a given society. All social relations are power relations. But if all social relations are power relations, how do we choose between one society and another?

When Foucault has to answer a question such as this he becomes evasive. Theoretically he has put himself in a situation where he cannot use terms like equality, freedom, justice. These concepts are merely tokens in a game, in an interplay of forces. This is a viewpoint very much like that of Nietzsche (who wrote 'when the oppressed want justice it is just a pretext for the fact that they want power for themselves'). History, according to this view, is an endless play of domination.

I said earlier that Foucault does not conceptualize power in terms of the state or the intentionality of an agent, as a property or a possession, or as purely repressive. His analyses of power employ a conception of power as positive, productive and relational. It has been said that Foucault is trapped within a logical 'impasse'. Given his conception of power, there can be no escape, no locus of opposition or resistance, because *power itself has no specific basis or ground.*[38]

According to Foucault the existence of power relations presupposes forms of resistance. Just as power is present everywhere in the social network, so is resistance; there are a multiplicity of resistances which are constantly shifting and regrouping. Foucault does not say more than this. *The concept of resistance remains undeveloped.*

Additionally, *an analysis of the state is absent from his work.* Foucaldians like Donzelot have deliberately decentred the question of the state. They do not believe that the state is the locus or prime operator of power. To put it in another way, they have suspended assumptions concerning the unity, functionality and importance of the state.

Moreover, Foucault believes that it is no longer feasible to conceptualize relations of power simply in terms of the state, class struggle, relations of production and capitalist exploitation. And so it is not surprising that Foucault *underestimates the significance of social class and class struggle* and *neglects the role of law and physical repression.* He is so concerned with the anonymity of modern forms of administration that he neglects class domination.

Foucault's philosophy is embedded in the historical analyses that have been described. It is rooted in story-telling. Foucault neither claims nor seeks scientific status for his analyses. I refer to the fact that he has said that his histories—which seek to forge connections, establish relationships and transgress the established—are fictions:

> I am well aware that I have never written anything but fictions. I do not mean to say, however, that truth is therefore absent. It seems to me that the possibility exists for fiction to function in truth, for a fictional discourse to induce effects of truth ....[39]

There are different systems or 'regimes' of truth; truth is conventional. Foucault wants to avoid questions of epistemology and so in his work truth plays no part in the transformation of knowledges. Instead he celebrates, like Nietzsche, the perspectivity of knowledge.

Foucault is acutely aware that there are different sorts of knowledge; there is disqualified knowledge, knowledge not only from above but from below. His claim that truth is always relative is not easy to accept. It is because of this position that he cannot say that one historical period or society or theory is better than another. This, of course, raises the question: from what position is Foucault able to write his own descriptions? What is the status of his own theory?

In this chapter I have tried to show that Foucault is especially concerned with how knowledge is enmeshed in disciplinary power. He rejects the traditional liberal view that power interferes with the free formation of truth. For Foucault power is necessary for the production of knowledge and is an inherent feature of all social relationships. I want particularly to stress the fact that Foucault and his many followers, both in France and in this country, have been propagating the view that Marxism is authoritarian and outmoded: '... one must try to think of struggle and its forms, objectives, means and processes in terms of a logic free of the sterilising constraints of the dialectic.'[40] Nietzsche's thought has influenced Foucault so deeply that it is not surprising that he rejects Marx's view of economics, history, politics and method. In the next chapter I will consider the influence of Nietzsche's thought on some of the 'younger generation' of post-structuralist thinkers.

CHAPTER 4

Some currents within post-structuralism

NIETZSCHE CONTRA HEGEL

Many post-structuralist thinkers have been greatly influenced by the philosophy of Nietzsche, with its denunciation of the 'illusion' of truth and static notions of meaning, its belief in the will to power, its affirmation of the Dionysian way of life, and its hostility to egalitarianism. To give only a few examples, Michel Foucault was influenced by Nietzsche's thought in the late 1950s, and he began to be critical of historicism and humanism. Another writer, Jean-François Lyotard, who had been a left-wing militant for a long time, denounced the Soviet Union and turned to Nietzsche's ideas. Jacques Derrida constantly invokes Nietzsche in his writing. Gilles Deleuze, too, has been deeply swayed by Nietzsche. Many writers suggest that Marx sublates Hegel by appropriating the radical form (the dialectical method) and dispensing with the conservative content. Deleuze rejects completely both the form and content of Hegel's philosophy and claims that Nietzsche was the first real critic of Hegel and dialectical thought.

Let us try to see how certain features of Nietzsche's philosophy are being used in the polemic against Hegel and Marx. Nietzsche is often misunderstood; he often speaks of 'war' even when he is evidently thinking of 'strife', of 'power' rather than 'self-perfection', and of the 'Dionysian' rather than the 'classical'. I can see that there is much that is appealing in his thought. In Nietzsche's philosophy, for example, there is a sustained celebration of creativity—all genuine creation is a creation of new values and norms. I think that perhaps we should make a distinction between Nietzsche and Nietzscheanism. To be a Nietzschean is in a sense a contradiction in terms; to be a Nietzschean one must not be Nietzschean.

Nietzsche opposed both the idolatry of the state and political liberalism because he was basically anti-political. He loathed the idea of belonging to any 'party' whatever. Nietzsche objects to the state because it appears to him as the power that intimidates men and women into conformity. However, Nietzsche opposes not only the state but any overestimation of the political. In short, the leitmotiv of his life and thought is *the anti-political individual who seeks self-perfection* far from the modern world. He thus thinks that the Goethean man embodies the great contemplative type who is essentially unrevolutionary, even anti-revolutionary.

Nietzsche had strong philosophical reasons for not having a system. He held that a system is reducible to a set of premises which cannot be questioned within the framework of the system: 'The will to a system is a lack of integrity.' All assumptions have to be questioned. No one system reveals the entire truth; at best each adopts one point of view or perspective. We must consider many perspectives and not imprison our thought in one system. Nietzsche held that the coherence of a finite system could never be a guarantee of its truth. His entire attack on systems is based on his objection to the irrationality which he finds in the failure to question premises. For him science is not a finished and impersonal system but a passionate quest for knowledge, an unceasing series of small, courageous experiments. He has in mind the 'gay science' of fearless experiment and the goodwill to accept new evidence and to abandon previous positions if necessary.

There are many important differences between the philosophies of Hegel and Nietzsche. In Hegel's dialectic, concepts are inadequate and contradictions lead to a more adequate concept at a higher level. This process continually repeats itself as the dialectic moves towards the Absolute. In Nietzsche, however, the dialectic undercuts, undermines itself. Hegel always stressed the result of the process, the synthesis, and the larger unit, while Nietzsche concerned himself with the negative and the individual. A consequence of Nietzsche's emphasis on the negative may be seen in the tremendous importance he attached to suffering and cruelty—the negative aspect of self-overcoming. Nietzsche was much concerned with the individual and his/her attempts at self-realization. He was, unlike Hegel, more of a psychologist than a historian. In the end, Nietzsche's emphasis on individuality led him to the conception of a vast plurality of individual wills to power. He asserted that not all people are equally capable of being good and creating the beautiful. It seems that some people are more favoured by nature than others. This is the basis of his opposition to socialism and democracy.

I turn now to a crucial point in Nietzsche's philosophy of history and theory of values. One of his hypotheses was the doctrine of the eternal recurrence. It refers to the unconditional and infinitely repeated circular course of all things. This conception depends on Nietzsche's denial of definite progress, of a plan or goal to give meaning to history or life. He deprecated any faith that pins its hopes on the future. Empirical facts do not seem to him to warrant the belief that history is a story of progress: 'The goal of humanity cannot lie at the end of time but only in its highest specimens' (*Thoughts out of Season*).

In contrast to this view Hegel believed that there was an Absolute Spirit that was working itself through all the concrete manifestations of the world. He held that reality unfolded itself through its contradictions and rose to ever higher levels until Spirit at last became conscious of itself. For all its philosophical idealism this view compels one to see human culture and history as a part of a total process. This is why political institutions, works of art and social customs so often appear as the varied expression of a single inner essence.

Marx abolished the idealism of Hegel's system and stressed the material laws of historical development. He replaced Spirit with Economy; in his view economic forces determined the particular system of social relations that characterizes each stage of historical development. Class struggle became the central principle of historical development.

One of the reasons why I have given the above outline is that many thinkers are opposed to this sort of 'teleological' Marxism. The French right-wing 'new philosophers' assert that Marxism of this sort transforms Marx into the teller of a salvational story rather than a scientific theorist of historical laws. But they say more than this—they contend that there is a direct line from Hegel to the Gulag. The stages are these: first of all there is Hegel's invention of the notion of Absolute Spirit with its teleology of history. Then Marx relocates this teleology within history conceived in materialist terms. Finally, the annulment of contradiction at the end of the teleological process becomes (with Stalinism) an abolition of differences through sheer force. The Absolute Spirit becomes the knock at the door, in the name of history, of the secret police.

DELEUZE AND GUATTARI: THE RETURN TO THE IMAGINARY

One source of the ideas mentioned above is the book *Anti-Oedipus: Capitalism and Schizophrenia.*[1] Its authors, Gilles Deleuze and Félix Guattari, have combined the three concepts 'desire', 'production' and 'machine' from Freud and Marx into a new idea: we are desiring machines. They call the outward, linguistic manifestation of desire *délire*. *Délire* is an effect produced by the machinery of desire. *Anti-Oedipus* stresses the collective nature of *délire* (even if it is produced by an individual) and its social character. At the present time the dominant tendency is to privatize *délire*. Against this trend Deleuze and Guattari have implicitly adopted one of the slogans of the French Left of the 1970s: the personal is the political. There is no separation between the personal and the social, the individual and the collective. Both the political and the psychological field are permeated by the same form of energy, libido, which has effects both political (the class struggle) and individual (*délire*). Libido and politics interpenetrate.

Deleuze and Guattari distinguish two types of desire, the paranoid and the schizophrenic, corresponding to two main forms of society: the fascist and the revolutionary. In social terms, the contrast is between authoritarian and libertarian organizations: on the one hand there are states with their insistence on centralized power; on the other hand looser organizations of smaller groups—imagine a society of nomads—without territorial limits or a system of hierarchy. The authors assert that there are two poles to *délire*: the real *délire* of schizophrenia, centred on flight, and the reactionary *délire* of paranoia based on the authoritarian structure of the hierarchical state.

Politically Deleuze and Guattari are against the process of generalization by which a class is elevated into an abstraction above its members and the party becomes representative of a class. In contrast they believe that revolutionary desire flows through small groups and produces collective action. In other words, it is not enough to fight fascism in the street; we must also fight it in our own heads, setting our revolutionary schizophrenia against our own fascist paranoia. Influenced by the ideas of Wilhelm Reich's *Mass Psychology of Fascism*, they believe that the unconscious is a political force and that fascism dwells in it as much as on the historical stage or in political parties.

The authors of *Anti-Oedipus* argue that Freudian psychoanalysis is an example of 'interpretation as impoverishment'. It is what happens when the lived complexity of a patient's life is 'rewritten' within the confined limits of the Freudian 'family romance'. They go on to attack the reductiveness of all schemes that seek to limit and thus impoverish a complex reality in the name of interpretation. Complex reality is always rewritten in terms of a 'mastercode' or 'master narrative' which is then given as the 'meaning' of what is interpreted. Marxism is one such 'mastercode'. In teleological Marxism there is a providential or salvational account of history as a 'master narrative'.

In a sense, Deleuze and Guattari perceive all explanation or interpretation as an expression of the Nietzschean will to power. But they insist that their attack is not directed against interpretation as such but against Marxism as a 'transcendent' interpretation. *Transcendent interpretation* is transcendent in the sense that its significance is based on going outside the text, on some extratextual set of norms. Against this notion of transcendent interpretation they counterpose their demand for *immanent interpretation*, a mode of analysis that respects the internal norms and values and the complexity as it is given of the reality to be interpreted.

Not only Deleuze and Guattari but also Foucault and the 'new philosophers' have argued that traditional Marxism has been 'transcendent' in the sense that it has produced 'meaning' by allegorizing in terms of the 'mastercode' provided by Marx. They all see in Marxism a prime example of an interpretative system that inevitably transforms itself into an instrument of political and physical domination.

I mentioned just now that Deleuze and Guattari are anti-Freudian. Their arguments against the Oedipus complex are these: since the Oedipus complex is supposed to be universal, the results of any interpretation are known in advance. Freud was just a clairvoyant; he recognized the predictable character of his interpretations. Secondly, the richness of the patient's productions is reduced to ready-made explanations. Hence, Freudian interpretation is a form of repression. Thirdly, there is a patriarchal bias in the Oedipus complex (the reduction of desire to the male sexual organs). These arguments are part of a more general criticism of psychoanalysis. Psychoanalysis imposes Lack, Culture and Law on the unconscious, thus structuring, reducing and repressing desire. The unconscious, on the other hand, is productive; it produces desire and threatens to smother the body politic with it; hence its revolutionary character and the necessity for its repression by psychoanalysis, the watch-dog of the modern state.

Psychoanalysis, it is argued, is basically an interpretation-machine. It translates all the patient says into another language and thus turns the patient into a subject in both senses of the term. Moreover, psychoanalysis depends upon a form of power: the patient submits to the analyst and his flow of libido is reduced to words and interpretations.

An important current within post-structuralism explores the possibilities and potentialities of *desire*. For Deleuze and Guattari desire emerges as a mysterious and disruptive, all-pervading, productive force of libido. The authors idealize Lacan's concept of the imaginary (the stage before the acquisition of language) and emphasize his theory of desire. They see the transition into the symbolic (language, structure and society) as a loss. Entrance into structure and society is seen as a tragedy. Only a return to the imaginary can spell the end of socio-political repression, of the dictatorship of the symbolic. For Deleuze and Guattari the really important condition is schizophrenia. Indeed, attacking classical psycho-analysis and Marxism, they develop a new theory, provoca-tively named schizoanalysis.

Deleuze and Guattari envisage a politics of the Lacanian imaginary. The goal of politics is to return to humankind's freedom, to a sense of being a passionate animal. They glorify the pre-symbolic stage of direct, fusional relationships, of spontaneity, of primitive, unmediated desire. They reject phallocentrism and denounce the family as the bearer of hierarchy and taboo. They look to children, primitive peoples and, most of all, to the mad as examples of people in touch with the power of the pre-symbolic. What these marginal groups are assumed to have in common is that they have not yet been fully 'oedipalized', that is, that the symbolic has not yet entered them. The book is a diatribe against oedipalization. Although the authors' attack on oedip-alization is also an attack on psychoanalysis, the book relies on Lacan's particular way of theorizing the Oedipus complex as the process by which society enters the indivi-dual.

Psychiatric theory is usually based on a negative concept of madness, in which madness is perceived as a deficit, a lack of rationality, a state of being less than one could be. Lacan has never supported this pejorative view. He has spoken of the analyst as someone deeply in touch with the knowledge 'that it is possible for each of us to go mad'. Man's being, he says, cannot be understood without reference to madness, nor would man be man without his carrying madness within as the limit of his freedom. Lacan, then, is sympathetic to the anti-psychiatrists who identify themselves with the mad in so far as they claim to have a message that cannot be communicated in ordinary ways. Like the schizophrenic they have to destroy ordinary language in order to communicate. In the case of anti-psychiatry Lacan's support comes from the way he demolishes the notion that there is a 'normal' self that is autonomous, coherent, its own 'centre'. The notion of the decentred subject is a crucial link between Lacan and the anti-psychiatric movement, which refuses to view madness as something alien to 'normals'.

Deleuze and Guattari are sympathetic to madness. They argue in *Anti-Oedipus* that in modern life there is an incompatibility between reason and impulse—spontaneity is being squeezed out. The authors take Lacan's ideas about the decentred subject and carry them several steps further than he does. They believe that the schizophrenic makes no separation between personal and social experience; his or her personal expressions are themselves political expressions. For the schizophrenic, word and thing are one, saying is doing. The relationship between word and action, wish and action, is direct and immediate. In a way, Deleuze and Guattari advance 'a politics of schizophrenia'. They regard schizophrenia as a privileging experience and believe that the schizophrenic is not trapped within the oedipal prison, in which the complexity and fluidity of the unconscious are distorted, frozen and flattened, but that he is in touch with fundamental truths about society. In short, they exalt the schizophrenic's proximity to the imaginary, to fusional relationships and to flux. The self is all flux and fragmentation, collection of machine parts. In human relationships one whole person never relates to another whole person because there is no such thing as the 'whole person'. There are only connections between 'desiring machines'. Fragmentation is a universal of the human condition, not something specifc to the schizophrenic.

It will not have escaped notice that the work of Deleuze and Guattari proceeds through conceptual dichotomies: the hierarchical state and the nomadic tribe, paranoia and schizophrenia. It is often said that desire differs from need in that it cannot attain fulfilment; it is an ever-renewed failure, a constant yearning. But there are several ways of conceiving desire. In the Lacanian psychoanalytic tradition, for example, it is a striving after a lost primary object. Deleuze and Guattari, however, reject the Lacanian definition of the real as the impossible. They invert it: 'in reality everything becomes possible.' Reality is what my desire fabricates.

Deleuze and Guattari are Nietzschean in the sense that their book is a celebration of 'the numinous energies of existence in a joyous activity of free play'. The schizo

> produces himself as a free man, irresponsible, solitary, and joyous, finally able to say and do something simple in his own name, without asking permission; a desire lacking nothing, a flux that overcomes barriers and codes, a name that no longer designates any ego whatever. He has simply ceased being afraid of becoming mad.[2]

In criticism of Deleuze and Guattari I would argue that their conception of desire culminates in sheer idealism. As a sympathetic commentator on *Anti-Oedipus* has remarked:

> The advice is let yourself go. Do your own thing, scream your own screams. In other words, take risks and go against the grain of common sense. This thesis offers no objective assessment of a state of affairs; it is rather a call for action.[3]

Their notion of productive desire is none other than the Nietzschean will to power. In their view there is only one class, that of the slaves, in which some dominate the others. One consequence of all this is that the class struggle is politely consigned to the museum. Though the vocabulary of *Anti-Oedipus* is sometimes Marxist, sometimes Freudian, the main critical strand is Nietzschean from start to finish.[4]

PRISONERS OF DISCOURSE

In one of its developments post-structuralism became a convenient way of evading political questions altogether. The work of Derrida and others had cast great doubt upon the classical notions of truth, reality, meaning and knowledge. If meaning, the signified, was a passing product of words or signifiers, always shifting and unstable, part-present and part-absent, how could there be any determinant truth or meaning at all? If reality was constructed by our discourse rather than reflected by it, how could we ever know reality itself, rather than merely knowing our own discourse? According to this dogma we can never know anything at all; we are the prisoners of our discourse.

One of Foucault's main concerns is the transition from the classical age to nineteenth-century culture. In all of his works there is a similar narrative framework: the relatively open and freewheeling world of the sixteenth century gives way to the classical age, which is superseded by the densely regulated, 'disciplined' society of today. Serious thinking about modern life has polarized into two sterile antitheses which Marshall Berman has called 'modernolatry' and 'cultural despair'.[5] For the practitioners of the former, from Marinetti and Mayakovsky to Le Corbusier, all the personal and social dissonances of modern life can be resolved by technological and administrative means. The means are all at hand, and the only thing needful is leaders with the will to use them. For the intellectuals of cultural despair, from Eliot and Ezra Pound to Marcuse and Foucault, all of modern life seems uniformly hollow, sterile, flat, 'one-dimensional', empty of human possibilities. Anything that looks or feels like freedom or beauty is really only a screen for more profound enslavement and horror.

There is no freedom in Foucault's world, nor does he have a theory of emancipation. The more powerful the vision of some increasingly total system or logic, the more powerless the reader comes to feel. The critical capacity of Foucault's work is paralysed because the reader is made to think that the project of social transformation is vain, trivial, hopeless. I think Habermas is correct when he argues that Foucault's later work 'replaced' the model of repression and emancipation developed by Marx and Freud with a pluralism of power/discourse formations. 'These formations intersect and succeed one another and can be differentiated according to their style and intensity. They cannot, however, be judged in terms of validity.'[6]

It is largely because of the impact of Foucaldian discourse that many intellectuals feel that they cannot use general concepts any more; they are taboo. The system as a whole cannot be combated because there is in fact no 'system as a whole'. Nor is there any central power; power is everywhere.[7] The only forms of political action now felt to be acceptable are of a local, diffused, strategic kind. The worst error is to believe that such local projects should be brought together.

I want to argue that some of the Nietzschean themes in Foucault's thought are the basis of his anti-Marxist position. He insists that any general theory should be renounced and that life cannot be grasped from a single perspective. Believing that truth and power are linked, he adopts a relativist position; modern society is not necessarily better than past ones. We are not progressing from the dark to the light. Foucault attacks Marxists because they believe that they have deciphered the secret of history. For him history is discontinuous and Marxism is a global totalitarian theory which is out of date.

THE CELEBRATION OF INTENSITY

One can also see the shift away from Marxism if one looks at the political trajectory of Jean-François Lyotard. He was a militant for fifteen years in a small left-wing group called *Socialisme ou Barbarie*. This group, which contained well-known theorists such as Cornelius Castoriadis and Claude Lefort, came out of Trotskyism and developed a critique of Soviet bureaucracy.[8] It argued that both the US and the Soviet Union were state capitalist countries.

Lyotard's first book was a monograph on phenomenology, and traces of this commitment are still very apparent in his work. He has never accepted all the injunctions of structuralism and has criticized aspects of the work of Lévi-Strauss. During the events of 1968 Lyotard was a professor of philosophy at Vincennes. He has written that the

preoccupations of *Socialisme ou Barbarie* were expressed in
'68; in many ways the student revolt was libertarian and
anarchist rather than Marxist. One has only to look at the
posters and the graffiti ('it is forbidden to forbid') to
realize that the movement was largely a protest against
bureaucratization, depersonalization, routinization, repression, and not wholly an expression of class antagonism.
In Lyotard's view people began to feel that there was a
discrepancy between the rhetoric of Marxism and the actual
content of the students' movement. 1968 was the year many
people turned away from Marxism.

Lyotard next wrote about the tension between the
discursive and the figural (the verbal and the visual) in his
book *Discours/figure*.[9] He has always been fascinated by
the non-linguistic, is critical of Lacan's view that the
unconscious is structured like a language and suggests that
it is the Other of language. He associates the unconscious
with figural representation and the preconscious with
language. Language is on the side of censorship and
repression; figural representation is on the side of desire and
transgression. Lyotard thinks of modern art as being
fragmented and believes that it is liberatory. Fragmentation
and disruption are attempts to make the unconscious process
visible. Art, then, involves the disruption of convention; but
this raises the question, 'Can art exist for ever as a
transgression of previous assumptions?'

During the time of *Discours/figure* Lyotard was still
writing from within the Marxist tradition, but he was
beginning to be critical of some aspects of it. He argued
against the Hegelian notion that there is a coincidence
between the movement of thought and the movement of
reality. He also rejected the Lukácsian view that Marxism
is the expression of the revolutionary consciousness of the
proletariat, the 'voice of history'.[10] Lyotard argued against
this view because he believed that the bureaucratic communist
parties often claimed to speak in just such an authoritative
(and authoritarian) way. Nevertheless, during this period he
wanted to retain the concept of alienation because he was
concerned with the individual, unlike Althusser, who rejected
it as being an ideological remnant from the work of the
young Marx.[11]

In recent years Lyotard has supported symbolic protest actions because he believes that through such actions societal veils are dropped. But it has often been noticed that this sort of activity, an interruption of routine, gradually comes to replace revolutionary political activity itself. Once a political act is severed from revolution and becomes symbolic, then all it does is produce a shock effect, which is also a stylistic device of many artists. In detaching action from political goals this sort of activity becomes a self-defeating convention.

The younger generation of post-structuralist thinkers are very concerned not only with the spontaneous but also with the subjective. Lyotard, for example, values the intensity of experience and suggests that if we are always thinking of what we are, we cannot 'let go'. If we are always theorizing about things, we cannot enjoy them for their own sake. In Lyotard's view there should be a shift from the dominance of dry, abstract thinking to a greater appreciation of the emotional. The main message seems to be that we should move from criticism of the present to hedonistic affirmation. It could be argued against Lyotard that he has forgotten that Nietzsche's affirmative view implies that we have to affirm suffering as well. The importance of Nietzsche is that he tells us to put reason *and* impulse together.

Basically, what the post-structuralists like Lyotard are saying is that there is more to life than politics. If we are totally immersed in the political, we miss what is going on here and now. Marxists are always criticizing the status quo in the name of an ideal. Militants are so inflexible that they have no time to enjoy life as it is now. Ideals cut us off from the present.

Instead of having a nostalgia for an unalienated community that may have existed in the past we should celebrate aspects of contemporary life—its anonymity, its fragmentation, its consumptionism. The post-structuralists also want to extol everything that has been left out in the totalizing theories. And so they focus on the marginal, the excluded. But for how long can a group or movement stress the marginal without becoming marginal itself? Furthermore, it could be argued that if all that matters is intensity (the quest for 'kicks'), then one can get as much intensity acting within the system as outside it.

THE 'NEW PHILOSOPHERS'

Some intellectuals, though not strictly post-structuralists themselves, have been deeply influenced by the post-structuralists and have used their ideas in their attack on Marxism. Ten years after the events of 1968 a group of French intellectuals achieved notoriety by making criticisms of Marxism and the socialist societies. This group, which includes Bernard-Henri Lévy, André Glucksmann, Jean-Marie Benoist and others, made successful use of the media to propagate their views against what they call the dogmatism of Marx, of Marx's logos.

But before I give an exposition of the views of the 'new philosophers', let me enumerate briefly a few of the more common arguments—about the limits and limitations of Marxism—on which their ideas are based. The writings of Marx and Engels clearly express the idea that the economy is determinant in the final instance and that therefore the superstructures are in some sense determined. However, the superstructures are not simply reducible to the economy, they have relative autonomy. One of the most serious consequences of the lack of any precise mechanism connecting these two propositions—economic determination and the relative autonomy of the superstructures—is the absence of a theory of the political level. Additionally, the formal, abstract categories of 'base' and 'superstructure' have become an obstruction to analysis since they have displaced real human activities and historical processes as objects of study.

Moreover, Marx did not produce any coherent or comparative analysis of the political structures of bourgeois class power. There is no developed analysis in his work of the capitalist state.[12] Marx neglected changes in the international state system and did not appreciate the importance of nationalism and national cultures. And what is more, he was a positivist. The positivist conception of science within his works has had harmful consequences for the articulation of a Marxist politics. Indeed, a preoccupation with the scientificity of Marxism is said to be the source of the neglect of the centrality of human agency, experience and consciousness.[13]

There are also problems in Lenin's theory and practice. We are often told that there was a contradiction between his conceptions of workers' councils as a necessary revolutionary form of proletarian power and the subsequent reality of party authoritarianism and the development of a monolithic bureaucratic apparatus.[14] To put it simply, Lenin failed to integrate his doctrine of the party with his account of the soviets.

After Leninism, Stalinism. If it was possible for a single individual to create a personality cult around himself, there must be something wrong with the theory of historical materialism (which denies the role of 'the great individual' in history). On the other hand, if the cult arose from the Soviet system (Lenin?), then socialist society itself must bear the responsibility for the inherent potential of Stalinism.

And then there is the question of socialism. Marxism has little of substance to offer on the nature of the transition from capitalism to socialism. The nature of that which is to emerge from the ruins of bourgeois society remains problematic and relatively unformulated. One of the problems is the difference between the classical vision of Marxism and the reality of actually existing socialism. Marx did not realize that the transitional period of socialism might produce an indissoluble monolithic state machine. It is now quite clear that the power and pervasiveness of the state machine has created a situation in which, even given the abolition of capitalist private property, the producers do not exercise control over the processes of production and distribution, but rather control is centralized, hierarchically organized, and exercised by an élite, ostensibly in the interest of the producers.

Western European countries have seen the apparent decline of a militant working class and the emergence of 'non-class' political–subject groups. During the events of May '68, for

example, there arose mass movements, composed of many
spontaneously organized 'groupuscles'. There were new
social groupings around specific issues such as education,
women's liberation, ecology and so forth. The hierarchically
organized Marxist parties tended to be conservative and
could not represent the interest and desires of the new
groups. There were struggles that could not be conceptualized
as class struggles. When are Marxists going to learn that
the 'political' consists of more than class politics?

Existing socialist societies no longer contribute a good
model. The party political organization has become synonymous with the bureaucratic machine. Moreover, powerful
and privileged ruling strata have come into being. The
various military interventions by the USSR should be
considered, as well as the regular violation of human rights
in the USSR and other Eastern European states. In short,
these societies testify to the limitations of Marxist theory.[15]

The 'new philosophers'' denunciation is largely based on
these criticisms. They are fond of comparing the dominance
of Marxism in post-war France with the dominance of
Aristotle's logic in medieval times. Highly critical of Sartre,
they contend that his notion of freedom is irreconcilable
with his Marxist views and lean towards the anti-Soviet
position adopted by Camus in the early 1950s. The leading
publicist of the group, Bernard-Henri Lévy, in his book *La
barbarie à visage humain* attacks the Marxist theory of
power in which power is seen as maintained by varying
combinations of ideological mystification and physical
repression.[16] Against this model Lévy deploys a vulgarized
fusion of ideas drawn from Foucault and Lacan in which
power is everywhere, and yet is 'nothing'. It is nothing since
it cannot be located in specific mechanisms of institutions.
Rather than being imposed from above it filters up from
below, permeating *every* social relation. Now, in Foucault
there are at least 'resistances' counterposed to power, but
for Lévy there is only the impossibility of liberation: the
idea of a good society is an absurd dream.

Besides power, the 'new philosophers' are critical of the
concepts of reason, theory and history. The idea that the
social formation is an analysable totality is rejected. They

seem to have a vision in which conflict is no longer a political conflict between social *classes* but an ethical struggle within the individual between the 'desire for submission' and the 'love of freedom'. In a way, we are all oppressors and we are all oppressed.

The 'new philosophers' see all ideologies which envisage an endpoint to history (historicism) as dangerous and wrong. In their view theories that promise an end to power relations convince people that they can justify present means by that future end and so rationalize labour camps and mass slaughter. Deeply rooted in the unconscious is the lust for power. The only ethical way to live is to take the goal of limiting power as the basis of one's actions without believing that power can ever be eliminated.

It is significant that when Lévy wanted to express this he chose to tell his story through Lacanian concepts. For Lévy a Freudian politics that understands constraint, contradiction and the inevitability of power is our only hope, and it is Lacan who suggests its form with his theory of knots, his new topographical image for the indissociability of the imaginary, symbolic, and real.[17] Power is tied to desire and the impossibility of final resolutions just as the symbolic is tied to the imaginary and the real. There is no escape to the imaginary except through psychosis, and for Lévy this is not a workable solution. There is no Utopia, no 'beach underneath the co:'. estones'.

The two writers highly regarded by the 'new philosophers' are Lacan and Foucault. Lacan has never claimed to be a Marxist and has explicitly mocked the idea of 'sexual liberation' in the name of traditional Freudian pessimism. Foucault's work, ever since the beginning, has contained an implicit and explicit critique of Marxist concepts. In many respects Foucault's early book *Madness and Civilization* is privileged above its successors, since it is in this book that the 'new philosophers' find inspiration for their belief in the inherent oppressiveness of reason.

Not only does the new philosophy claim inspiration from his work (as it does from Lacan's) but Foucault himself has in certain respects shared the same intellectual and political trajectory as the militants who have become the 'new philosophers'. On his own account it was the explosion of May '68 and after—the development of localized struggles in the school, the prison, the psychiatric hospital—which made it possible for him to take up explicitly the problem of the interrelation of power and knowledge.[18]

As I remarked earlier, Foucault rejects the traditional conception of power as invested in a central, organizing state from which it filters down to successive levels. To Foucault the state is merely one apparatus amongst many. Both in Foucault and in the 'new philosophers' one comes across the idea that global struggles are recuperative, leading from one domination to another, while only local and partial struggles are truly subversive. It is interesting that several writers have noticed a similarity between Foucault's concept of power, with its rejection of class analysis in favour of a vision of a complex of forces which continually disaggregate and coalesce, and the views of American functionalists.

For the 'new philosophers' socialism is the embodiment of technological rationality and tyranny. Much of their writing is about the concept of Gulag, a term denoting Soviet oppression, derived from Solzhenitsyn. One of their leading representatives, André Glucksmann, has said:

> I reproach Marx with having traced a certain number of intellectual routes: the cult of the total and final Revolution; of the State that terrorizes for the good of the collectivity, and of social science that permits the masses to be guided in spite of themselves. These paths do not lead directly to the Gulag but to non-resistance to the Gulag.[19]

According to the 'new philosophers' there is now a move from the 'scientific', value-free problematic of structuralism to the problematic of the person and human rights. What is being emphasized now is not human subjectivity but the philosophy of the person. Their argument goes like this:

Marxism is concerned with abstract categories like 'the masses'. We should concern ourselves not with abstractions but with respect for the individual. Besides a universal respect for the human person, 'the otherness of others', there must also be a new respect for other cultures and religions. Marxists do not have any respect for the singularity of the human person, they are tyrants who have only contempt for the individual. Their notion of world revolution is a dream, a dangerous fantasy; those who have this dream are terrorists, orphans of violence. Platonists, Leibnizians are not guilty of putting people into concentration camps—Marxists are. Marxism-Leninism leads to the justification of tyranny. The Helsinki Agreement, a legal text signed by East and West, is being broken by the Soviet Union, where many dissidents are being persecuted. We must name those—like Andrei Sakharov— that are incarcerated. The question of human rights has become vital and has made the work of Kant relevant again. His *Critique of Practical Reason* provides a framework within which we can seriously think of ethical problems. Kant insisted that we should treat people not as means but as ends in themselves: 'Always act on that maxim which you can at the same time will to become a universal law.' We must oppose Marxism-Leninism with an ethic of love—love addressed to a single person.[20]

What criticism can be made of such bitter enemies of Hegel, Marx and Lenin? I will be brief. One, the 'new philosophers' criticize only the Soviet Union, never the United States. Two, they never refer to the exploitation and violence of capitalism and its support of authoritarian regimes throughout the world. Three, they are so involved in their 'ethical' concerns that they do not make any attempt to make the world better through political action. In other words, they focus only on the individual and neglect the collective. From listening to some of them I get the impression that the imprisonment of dissidents is the crucial issue. They do not focus on questions such as the danger of nuclear war and the urgent need for a powerful peace movement. Most of the 'new philosophers', who draw heavily on Nietzsche's thought, now reject both science and politics. There is a revival of interest in plurality and difference, the singular and the subjective; and some of them are seeking solace in aesthetics, metaphysics and religion.[21]

CONCLUSION

In this chapter it has been argued that many of the fundamental beliefs of post-structuralism have their roots in Nietzscheanism. If one looks at the work of the post-structuralists, such as Deleuze and Guattari, Derrida, Foucault, Lyotard and others, one can see the influence of Nietzsche's philosophy. They share with him an antipathy to any 'system'. Secondly, they reject the Hegelian view of history as progress. Thirdly, they are aware of the increasing pressure towards conformity and are highly critical of this tendency. Fourthly, their obsession with the subjective and the 'small story' has led them to affirm the anti-political individual.

Post-structuralism is largely 'a product of 1968'. Unable to break the structures of state power, post-structuralism found it possible to subvert the structures of language: 'The student movement was flushed off the streets and driven underground into discourse.'[22] Its enemies became coherent belief-systems of any kind, in particular all forms of political theory and organization which sought to analyse and act upon the structures of society as a whole. All total, systematic thought was now suspect: conceptual meaning itself, as opposed to libidinal gesture and anarchist spontaneity, was feared as repressive.

After briefly introducing the leading post-structuralists I turned to the work of the 'new philosophers'. It was stated that the 'new philosophy' is not just an aberration of a few intellectuals but must be seen as mirroring a widespread mood of disorientation among the generation of '68. The 'new philosophers' believe that human society is permanently and inherently oppressive; but domination is no longer conceived of in class terms. They uphold various forms of romanticism and individualism. They denounce 'science' and any totalizing beliefs in the name of the spontaneous and the particular. Most of these philosophers hold the view that science always operates within and reinforces relations of power; that Marxism is in some way responsible for the terror of the Soviet camps; that the state is the central source of social and political oppression and that therefore any politics directed towards the seizure of state power is dangerous and vain. These ideologues combine an odd idealization of rebellion with an ultimately passive pessimism and an acquiescence in the status quo. This is not surprising, as they have no conception of historical advance or permanent transformation.

Most of the theorists I have mentioned in this chapter think of Marxism as the last systematic attempt to understand the world, to find an immanent order in it. As such, they argue, it is a metaphysics. Marxism, they assert, no longer connects with the present. Indeed, it is a belief system which cuts people off from reality. Lyotard, for example, now sees Marxism as a form of religious discourse: the suffering proletariat is supposed to bring about, some time in the future, the redemption of the world.

The attitude of many post-structuralists seems to be: 'If Marxism isn't true, then nothing is.' Many thinkers feel that we are at a stage of confusion ('we don't know where we are going') and that Nietzsche best expresses that confusion. The irony is that theorists like Lyotard and others need a general theory to support their assertion as to why there cannot be a general theory. As they cannot provide any grounds for their views, they think of their viewpoint as being provisional, 'ironic'. Why do these intellectuals focus only on the heterogeneous, the diverse, the subjective, the spontaneous, the relative and the fragmentary?

CHAPTER 5

Postmodernism

INTRODUCTION

In the first part of this chapter I will discuss the question of social change in contemporary societies by drawing on the recent work of the French thinker Jean-François Lyotard, whom I briefly introduced in the last chapter. I think that an examination of his thesis can help us to understand some of the main concerns of postmodernism.

I will focus on Lyotard's reflections on science, the changing nature of knowledge in computerized societies, the differences between narrative knowledge and scientific knowledge, the ways in which knowledge is legitimated and sold, and the social changes that may take place in the future.

EDUCATIONAL CHANGE IN COMPUTERIZED SOCIETIES

Many people are aware that Western societies since the Second World War have radically changed their nature in some way. To describe these changes social theorists have used various terms: media society, the society of the spectacle, consumer society, the bureaucratic society of controlled consumption, post-industrial society. A fashionable description of such societies is that they are postmodern. Lyotard is a post-structuralist who adopts a postmodernist stance.

Postmodernism is in part a description of a new type of society but also, in part, a new term for post-structuralism in the arts. (In this chapter I will use postmodernism and post-structuralism synonymously.)

In *The Postmodern Condition* Lyotard argues that during the last forty years the leading sciences and technologies have become increasingly concerned with language: theories of linguistics, problems of communication and cybernetics, computers and their languages, problems of translation, information storage, and data banks.[1]

The technological transformations are having a considerable impact on knowledge. The miniaturization and commercialization of machines is already changing the way in which learning is acquired, classified, made available, and exploited.

Lyotard believes that the nature of knowledge cannot survive unchanged within this context of general transformation. The status of knowledge is altered as societies enter what is known as the postmodern age. He predicts that anything in the constituted body of knowledge that is not translatable into quantities of information will be abandoned and the direction of new research will be dictated by the possibility of its eventual results being translatable into computer language. The old principle that the acquisition of knowledge is indissociable from the training of minds, or even of individuals, is becoming obsolete. Knowledge is already ceasing to be an end in itself. It is and will be produced in order to be sold.

It is widely accepted that computerized knowledge has become the principle *force of production* over the last few decades. This has already had a noticeable effect on the composition of the work-force of the most highly developed countries. (There is a decrease in the number of factory and agricultural workers and an increase in professional, technical and white-collar workers.)[2] Knowledge will be the major component in the world-wide competition for power and it is conceivable that nation-states will one day fight for control of information, just as they battled for control over territories in the past. In the postmodern age science will probably strengthen its pre-eminence in the arsenal of productive capacities of the nation-states and the gap between developed and developing countries will grow even wider.

But already in multinational corporations, which are really new forms of the circulation of capital, investment decisions have passed beyond the control of nation-states. Lyotard suggests that power and knowledge are simply two aspects of the same question: Who decides what knowledge is? Who knows what needs to be decided?[3]

In the computer age the question of knowledge is now more than ever a question of government. It is suggested that the functions of regulation, and therefore of reproduction, are being and will be further withdrawn from administrators and entrusted to machines. Increasingly the central question is: who will have access to the information these machines must have in storage to guarantee that the right decisions are made?

For Lyotard knowledge is a question of competence that goes beyond the simple determination and application of the criterion of truth, extending to the determination of criteria of efficiency (technical qualification), of justice and/ or happiness (ethical wisdom), of beauty (auditory or visual sensibility), etc. Knowledge is what makes someone capable of forming not only 'good' denotative utterances but also 'good' prescriptive and 'good' evaluative utterances. But how are they to be assessed? They are judged to be good if they conform to the relevant criteria (of justice, beauty, truth and efficiency) accepted in the social circle of the 'knower's' interlocutors.

It is important to mention here that Lyotard, who has been greatly influenced by Wittgenstein's notion of language games, makes the following observations.[4] Each of the various categories of utterance can be defined in terms of rules specifying their properties and the uses to which they can be put. The rules of language games do not carry within themselves their own legitimation, but are objects of a contract, explicit or not, between players; if there are no rules, there is no game. Every utterance is thought of as a 'move' in a game. Messages have quite different forms and effects depending on whether they are, for example, denotatives, prescriptions, evaluatives, performatives, etc.[5]

Lyotard believes that language games are incommensurable. He distinguishes the denotative game (in which what is relevant is the true/false distinction) from the prescriptive game (in which the just/unjust distinction pertains) and from the technical game (in which the criterion is the efficient/inefficient distinction). It seems to me that Lyotard sees language games as essentially embodying a conflictual relationship between tricksters. I said earlier that we always tend to act according to the way in which we conceive of things. One pervasive metaphor in our arguments is war. We say some positions are indefensible, we talk of attacking, demolishing, shooting down other people's arguments. We can win or lose arguments. I maintained in Chapter 4 that we could always use other metaphorical concepts than that of war. For Lyotard, however, to speak is to fight:

> In a discussion between two friends the interlocutors use any available ammunition ... questions, requests, assertions, and narratives are launched pell-mell into battle. The war is not without rules, but the rules allow and encourage the greatest possible flexibility of utterance.[6]

NARRATIVE KNOWLEDGE AND SCIENTIFIC KNOWLEDGE

Scientific knowledge does not represent the totality of knowledge; it has always existed in competition and conflict with another kind of knowledge which Lyotard calls narrative. In traditional societies there is a pre-eminence of the narrative form. Narratives (popular stories, myths, legends and tales) bestow legitimacy upon social institutions, or represent positive or negative models of integration into established institutions. Narratives determine criteria of competence and/or illustrate how they are to be applied. They thus define what has the right to be said and done in the culture in question.

In traditional societies a narrative tradition is also the tradition of the criterion defining a threefold com-

petence—'know-how', 'knowing how to speak' and 'knowing
how to hear'—through which the community's relationship
to itself and its environment is played out. In the narrative
form statements about truth, justice and beauty are often
woven together. What is transmitted through these narratives
is the set of rules that constitute the social bond.

Lyotard discusses the retreat of the claims of narrative or
story-telling knowledge in the face of those of the abstract,
denotative or logical and cognitive procedures generally
associated with science. In the science language game the
sender is supposed to be able to provide proof of what s/
he says, and on the other hand s/he is supposed to be
able to refute any opposing or contradictory statements
concerning the same referent. Scientific rules underlie what
nineteenth-century science calls verification, and twentieth-
century science falsification.[7] They allow a horizon of
consensus to be brought to the debate between partners (the
sender and the addressee). Not every consensus is a sign of
truth, but it is presumed that the truth of a statement
necessarily draws a consensus. Now, scientists need an
addressee, a partner who can verify their statements and in
turn become the sender. Equals are needed and must be
created.

Didactics is what ensures that this reproduction takes
place. Its first presupposition is that the student does not
know what the sender knows; obviously this is why s/he
has something to learn. Its second presupposition is that the
student can learn what the sender knows and become an
expert whose competence is equal to that of the teacher. As
the students improve their skills, experts can confide in them
what they do not know but are trying to learn. In this way
students are introduced to the game of producing scientific
knowledge. In scientific knowledge any already accepted
statement can always be challenged. Any new statement that
contradicts a previously approved statement regarding the
same referent can be accepted as valid only if it refutes the
previous statement.

The main difference between scientific knowledge and
narrative knowledge is that scientific knowledge requires
that one language game, denotation, be retained and all

others be excluded. Both science and non-scientific (narrative) knowledge are equally necessary. Both are composed of sets of statements; the statements are 'moves' made by the players within the framework of generally applicable rules. These rules are specific to each particular kind of knowledge, and the 'moves' judged to be 'good' in one cannot be the same as those judged 'good' in another (unless it happens that way by chance). It is therefore impossible to judge the existence or validity of narrative knowledge on the basis of scientific knowledge or vice versa: the relevant criteria are different.

Lyotaɪd argues that narrative knowledge certifies itself without having recourse to argumentation and proof. Scientists, however, question the validity of narrative statements and conclude that they are never subject to argumentation or prooɩ. Narratives are classified by the scientist as belonging to a different mentality: savage, primitive, underdeveloped, backward, alienated, composed of opinions, customs, authority, prejudice, ignorance, ideology. Narratives are fables, myths, legends fit only for women and children.

Here there is an interesting twist in Lyotard's argument. He says that scientific knowledge cannot know and make known that it is the true knowledge without resorting to the other, narrative kind of knowledge, which from its point of view is no knowledge at all. In short, there is a recurrence of the narrative in the scientific.[8]

The state spends large amounts of money to enable science to pass itself off as an epic. The state's own credibility is based on that epic, which it uses to obtain the public consent its decision-makers need. Science, in other words, is governed by the demand of legitimation. The two myths which have acted as justifications for institutional scientific research—that of the liberation of humanity and that of the speculative unity of all knowledge—are also national myths. The first, political, militant, activist, is the tradition of the French eighteenth century and the French Revolution. The second is the German Hegelian tradition organized around the concept of totality. Lyotard examines these two myths as versions of the narrative of legitimation of knowledge.

The subject of the first of these versions is humanity as the 'hero' of liberty. Lyotard writes: 'All peoples have a right to science. If the social subject is not already the subject of scientific knowledge, it is because that has been forbidden by priests and tyrants. The right to science must be reconquered.' The state resorts to the narrative of freedom every time it assumes direct control over the training of 'the people' under the name of the 'nation', in order to point the people down the path of progress.

Lyotard remarks:

> In Stalinism, the sciences only figure as citations from the metanarrative of the march towards socialism, which is the equivalent of the life of the spirit. But on the other hand Marxism can ... develop into a form of critical knowledge by declaring that socialism is nothing other than the constitution of the autonomous subject and that the only justification for the sciences is if they give the empirical subject (the proletariat) the means to emancipate itself from alienation and repression.[9]

According to Lyotard these (older) master narratives no longer function in contemporary society. He argues that the grand narrative has lost its credibility, regardless of whether it is a speculative narrative or a narrative of emancipation. The decline of the unifying and legitimating power of the grand narratives of speculation and emancipation can be seen as an effect of the blossoming of techniques and technologies since the Second World War, which has shifted emphasis from the *ends* of action to its *means*.

THE MERCANTILIZATION OF KNOWLEDGE

With the Industrial Revolution it was found that a technical apparatus requires an investment; but since it optimizes the efficiency with which the task to which it is applied is carried out, it also optimizes the surplus-value from this improved performance. It is at this moment that science becomes a force of production, a moment in the circulation of capital.

An important aspect of research is the production of

proof. Proof needs to be proven. A scientific observation depends on facts being registered by sense organs. But the range and powers of discrimination are limited. This is where technology comes in. Technical devices follow the principle of optimal performance, maximizing output and minimizing input. Technology is, therefore, a game pertaining not to the true, the just or the beautiful, but to efficiency. A technical 'move' is 'good' when it does better and/or expends less energy than another. Devices that optimize the performance of the human body for the purpose of producing proof require additional money. The game of science becomes the game of the rich, in which whoever is wealthiest has the best chance of being right.[10] It is thus that an equation between wealth, efficiency and truth is established.

To put it in another way, the goal in science is no longer truth, but performativity—that is, the best possible input/output equation. Scientists, technicians and instruments are bought not to find truth, but to augment power. Since performativity increases the ability to produce proof, it also increases the ability to be right; the technical criterion cannot fail to influence the truth criterion.

The shift of attention from ends of action to its means, from truth to performativity, is reflected in present-day educational policy. It has been clear for some time that educational institutions are becoming more functional; the emphasis is on skills rather than ideals. It is probable that in the near future knowledge will no longer be transmitted *en bloc* to young people, once and for all; rather it will be served 'à la carte' to adults as a part of their job retraining and continuing education.

To the extent that learning is translatable into computer language and the traditional teacher is replaceable by memory banks, didactics (teaching) will be entrusted to machines linking traditional memory banks (libraries etc.) and computer data banks to terminals placed at the students' disposal. Lyotard argues that pedagogy would not necessarily suffer. The students would have to learn to use the terminals and the new languages; they would have to be taught what is the relevant memory bank for what needs to be known. It is only in the context of the grand narratives of legitimation—the life of the spirit and/or the emancipation of humanity—that the partial replacement of teachers by machines may seem inadequate or even intolerable. Lyotard remarks that it is probable that these narratives are already no longer the principal driving force behind interest in acquiring knowledge. The question now being asked by the student, the state or the university is no longer 'Is it true?' but 'What use is it?' In the context of the mercantilization of knowledge, more often than not this question is equivalent to: 'Is it saleable?' And in the context of power-growth: 'Is it efficient?'

It is clear that education must provide not only for the reproduction of skills but also for their progress. Therefore training must be given in all the procedures that can increase one's ability to connect the fields jealously guarded from one another by the traditional organization of knowledge. What is vitally important for students to have is the capacity to actualize the relevant data for solving a problem here and now, and to organize that data into an efficient strategy. Data banks are the encyclopaedia of tomorrow; they are 'nature' for postmodern men and women. What is important is arranging the data in a new way. This capacity to articulate what used to be separate can be called imagination. It is imagination which allows one either to make a new move (a new argument) within the established rules or to invent new rules, that is to say, a new game.

Lyotard writes that countless scientists have seen their invention of new rules ignored or repressed, sometimes for decades, because that invention too abruptly destabilized the accepted positions, not only in the university and scientific hierarchy but also in the discipline. The more striking the invention, the more likely it is to be denied the minimum consensus, precisely because it changes the rules of the game upon which consensus had been based.[11] Lyotard argues that such behaviour is terrorist. By terror he means the efficiency gained by eliminating, or threatening to eliminate, a player from one's language game. He is silenced or consents, not because he has been refuted but because the other players' ability to participate has been threatened: 'Adapt your aspirations to our ends—or else . . .'

BOURGEOIS ART AND ITS FUNCTION IN SOCIETY

Having give an exposition of Lyotard's book, I want to place his thesis in the context of the controversy about modernism and postmodernism. But before I do that I want to contextualize the controversy. The debate about postmodernism is partly about the arts and so in this section I will say something about the institution of art in bourgeois society and the bitter struggle waged against it in the 1920s by the avant-garde.

The best way I can think of understanding the recent development of art is by a glance at Peter Bürger's *Theory of the Avant-Garde*.[12] Distinguishing between sacral, courtly and bourgeois art, Bürger suggests the following historical typology:

Sacral Art (for example, the art of the High Middle Ages) served as a cult object. It was wholly integrated into the social institution 'religion', and was produced collectively as a craft.

Courtly Art (for example, the art of the court of Louis XIV) served the glory of the prince. It was part of the life-praxis of courtly society, just as sacral art was part of the life-praxis of the faithful. Courtly art is different from sacral art in that the artist produced as an individual and developed a consciousness of the uniqueness of his individuality.

Bourgeois Art. Whereas in different ways both sacral and courtly art are integral to the life-praxis of the recipient, bourgeois art forms a sphere which lies outside the praxis of life.

The tension between art as an institution and the content of individual works tends to disappear in the second half of the nineteenth century. All that which is dissociated from the praxis of life now becomes the content of works of art. The terminal point is reached in aestheticism, a movement in which art becomes the content of art.

Aestheticism, Bürger writes, must be seen in connection with the tendency towards the division of labour in bourgeois society. Gradually the artist also turns into a specialist. As the social subsystem 'art' defines itself as a distinct sphere, the positive aspect is aesthetic experience. Its negative side is the artist's loss of any social function.

What, then, is the function of art in bourgeois society? Herbert Marcuse has argued that works of art are not received as single entities, but within institutional frameworks and conditions that largely determine the function of the works.[13] In his seminal essay 'The Affirmative Character of Culture' Marcuse has described art's function in bourgeois society as a contradictory one: on the one hand it shows 'forgotten truths' (thus it protests against a reality in which these truths have no validity), on the other, such truths are detached from reality. The term 'affirmative' therefore characterizes the contradictory function of a culture that retains 'remembrance of what could be', but is simultaneously a justification of the established form of existence. Through the enjoyment of art the atrophied bourgeois individual can experience the self as personality. But because art is detached from daily life, this experience remains without tangible effect—it cannot be integrated into that life.

Let me recapitulate Marcuse's argument. All those needs that cannot be satisfied in everyday life, because the principle of competition pervades all spheres, can find a home in art, because art is removed from the praxis of life. Values such as humanity, joy, truth, solidarity are excluded from life and preserved in art. In bourgeois society art has a contradictory role, it projects the image of a better life and to that extent protests against the bad order that prevails. But by realizing the image of a better order in *fiction*, which is semblance only, it neutralizes those forces that make for change. Marcuse demonstrates that bourgeois culture exiles humane values to the realm of the imagination and thus precludes their potential realization. Art thus stabilizes the very social conditions against which it protests.

As long as art interprets reality or provides satisfaction of residual needs only in the imagination it is, though detached from the praxis of life, still related to it. It is only in aestheticism that the tie to society, still existent up to this moment, is severed. The term 'the autonomy of art' is used to describe *the detachment of art* as a special sphere of human activity from the praxis of life. But somehow this concept blocks recognition of the social determinacy of the process. The idea of the relative dissociation of the work of art from the praxis of life in bourgeois society has become transformed into the erroneous idea that the work of art is totally independent of society. We should remember that this detachment of art from practical contexts is a historical process; it is socially conditioned. Perhaps the reason that the artist's product could acquire importance as something special, 'autonomous', lies in the continuation of the handicraft mode of production after the division of labour—and the separation of workers from their means of production—had become the norm.

THE MAIN FEATURES OF THE AVANT-GARDE

Only after art has detached itself completely from the praxis of life can two things be seen: the progressive separation of art from real life contexts and the crystallization of a distinctive sphere of experience—the aesthetic.

Let us now turn to the historic avant-garde and its attempt to negate the autonomy of art.[14] (There may be several avant-gardes; Bürger's term 'the historic avant-garde' refers to the uniqueness of the avant-garde movements of the 1920s such as Dadaism and Surrealism.) The production of the autonomous work of art is generally seen as the act of an individual—who is often a genius. The avant-garde's response to this is *the negation of the category of individual creation*. For example, Marcel Duchamp, by signing mass-produced objects, mocked a society in which the signature meant more than the quality of the work.

The avant-garde did not develop a style; there is no such thing as a Dadaist or Surrealist style. One of the characteristics of the avant-garde is the availability to it of and its mastery over artistic techniques of past epochs. It is through the efforts of the avant-garde that the historical *succession* of techniques and styles has been replaced by a *simultaneity* of the radically disparate. For the Surrealists a general openness to impressions is not enough. They attempt to bring the extraordinary about. In the avant-garde movements *shocking the recipient* becomes the dominant principle of artistic intent. Moreover, the Surrealists emphasize the role of *chance*. Starting from the experience that a society organized on the basis of a means–ends rationality increasingly restricts the individual's scope, the Surrealists attempted to discover elements of the unpredictable in daily life.

The avant-garde is totally opposed to society as it is. Bürger writes:

> Since the Surrealists do not see that a given degree of control over nature requires social organization, they run the risk of expressing their protest against bourgeois society at a level where it becomes protest against sociality as such. It is not the specific object, profit as the governing principle of bourgeois-capitalist society, that is being criticized but means-ends rationality as such. Paradoxically, chance, which subjects man to the totally heteronomous can thus seem a symbol of freedom.[15]

It is with the avant-garde movements that self-criticism begins. The main point is that they no longer criticized schools that preceded them, but criticized *art as an institution*. The avant-garde turns against both the distribution apparatus on which the work of art depends and the status of art in bourgeois society as defined by the concept of autonomy. This protest, whose aim it is to reintegrate art into the praxis of life, reveals the nexus between autonomy and the absence of any consequences—art's lack of social impact.

Of course, we now know that the attack of the historic avant-garde on art as an institution failed.[16] Art as an institution continues to survive. Ironically, the procedures invented by the avant-garde with anti-artistic intent are now being used for artistic ends by the postmodernists.

MODERNISM AND POSTMODERNISM

As I said at the beginning of the chapter, there is a general feeling among many thinkers that at some point after the

Second World War a new kind of society began to emerge. This society is labelled in various ways depending on the way it is analysed: consumer society, post-industrial society, society of the spectacle, postmodernist society, etc. Post-structuralists, on the whole, argue that this new society is post-Marxist. They assert that Marxist theory is now outmoded; it does not and cannot apply to the new social developments. This argument often overlaps with another one concerning modernism and postmodernism. The crucial question in these debates is: Has the Enlightenment project failed? Should we, like the post-structuralists and postmodernists, declare the entire project of modernity a lost cause? Or should we try to hold on to the intentions and aims of the Enlightenment and of cultural modernism?

The project of modernity formulated in the eighteenth century by the philosophers of the Enlightenment consisted in their efforts to develop objective science, universal morality and law and autonomous art. Philosophers like Condorcet wanted to use this accumulation of specialized culture for the enrichment of everyday life. They hoped that the arts and sciences would promote not only the control of natural forces but also understanding of the world and of the self, moral progress, the justice of institutions and even the happiness of human beings.

But what has happened is in marked contrast to the hopes and ideals of the Enlightenment. Gradually each domain has been institutionalized; science, morality and art have become autonomous domains separated from the life-world. The structures of cognitive–instrumental, of moral–practical and of aesthetic–expressive rationality have come under the control of special experts.[17]

In America, France and elsewhere, cultural modernism is now under attack from many different quarters. An American neo-conservative, Daniel Bell, made a powerful critique some years ago of modernity.[18] According to Bell modernist culture had infected the values of everyday life. Because of the forces of modernism the principle of unlimited self-realization, the demand for authentic self-experience and the subjectivism of a hyperstimulated sensitivity have come to be dominant. This unleases hedonistic motives irreconcilable with the discipline of professional life in society. Neo-conservatives like Bell see hedonism, the lack of social identification, the lack of obedience, narcissism, the with-drawal from status and achievement competiton as the result not of successful capitalist modernization of the economy but of cultural modernism.

More recently, the Enlightenment project has been denounced by the French 'new philosophers' and their contemporary English and American counterparts. It has also been attacked, less stridently but with more intellectual sharpness, by the post-structuralists. I believe that their work should be included among the manifestations of postmodernism.

The concept of postmodernism is ambiguous and is not yet widely understood. It has probably emerged as a specific reaction against the established forms of high modernism. For some thinkers postmodernism is a periodizing concept whose function is to correlate the emergence of new features in culture. The concept seems to be connected with the appearance, between the 1950s and the 1960s, of a new social and economic order. Sometimes a useful distinction is made between premodernists, those who want to withdraw to a position anterior to modernity, antimodernists and postmodernists. In my opinion post-structuralists like Fou-cault, Derrida and Lyotard are postmodernists. There are so many similarities between post-structuralist theories and postmodernist practices that it is difficult to make a clear distinction between them.

THE MAIN FEATURES OF POSTMODERNISM

We may be able to understand postmodernism better by returning to Lyotard and seeing what he means by 'modern'. Lyotard uses the term 'modern'

> to designate any science that legitimates itself with reference to a metadiscourse ... making an explicit appeal to some grand narrative, such as the dialectics of the Spirit, the hermeneutics of meaning, the emancipation of the rational or working subject or the creation of wealth.[19]

To put it another way:

> Societies which anchor the discourses of truth and justice in the great
> historical and scientific narratives (récits) can be called modern. The
> French Jacobins don't speak like Hegel but the just and the good are
> always found caught up in a great progressive odyssey.[20]

Postmodernists distrust metanarratives; there is a deep
suspicion of Hegel, Marx and any form of universal
philosophy.

For Lyotard, then, the postmodern condition is one in
which the *grands récits* of modernity—the dialectic of Spirit,
the emancipation of the worker, the accumulation of wealth,
the classless society—have all lost credibility.[21] He goes on
to define a discourse as modern when it appeals to one or
another of these *grands récits* for its legitimacy. The *grands
récits* are master narratives—narratives of mastery, of man
seeking his *telos* in the conquest of nature. The Marxist
master narrative ('the collective struggle to wrest a realm of
Freedom from a realm of Necessity') is only one version
among many of a modern narrative of mastery. The advent
of postmodernity signals a crisis in a narrative's legitimizing
function, its ability to compel consensus.

Lyotard is critical of Marxism because he holds that it
wishes to create a homogeneous society which can only be
brought about through the use of coercion. He believes that
the individualistic, fragmented society that we have today is
here to stay. Yet, oddly enough, he seems to be nostalgic
for a premodern (traditional) society. As I said earlier,
traditional societies stress narrative, that is to say, myth,
magic, folk wisdom and other attempts at explanation.[22]
Lyotard believes that there is a conflict between narrative
and science (theoretical knowledge). Narrative is disappear-
ing and there is nothing to replace it. He seems to want the
flexibility of narrative knowledge—in which the aesthetic,
cognitive and moral are interwoven—and yet want also to
retain the individualism which developed with capitalism.

Lyotard argues that art, morality and science (the beautiful,
the good and the true) have become separated and autonomous. A characteristic of our times is the fragmentation
of language games. There is no metalanguage. No one can

grasp what is going on in society as a whole. He seems to be saying that there is no one system of domination. There are parallels between these ideas and some right-wing theorists (like Hayek) who argue that society works much better in terms of micro-events; a society that is left to market forces is better than a consciously planned society.

In short, the argument of Lyotard (and some other post-structuralists) is this: big stories are bad, little stories are good. Instead of a truth/falsity distinction Lyotard adopts a small/grand narrative criterion. Narratives are bad when they become philosophies of history. Grand narratives have become associated with a political programme or party, while little narratives are associated with localized creativity. (The stress on the local has often been associated with the Conservative tradition, with the thinking of Edmund Burke and others.) These ideas are similar to those held by Foucault, who is also against grand narratives and supports the idea of local struggles. But what puzzles me is this: why are the post-structuralists so frightened of the universal? And why is Lyotard telling us yet another grand narrative at the end of grand narrative?

Two significant features of postmodernism, as described by the American critic Fredric Jameson, are 'pastiche' and 'schizophrenia'.[23] Jameson begins by explaining that the great modernisms were predicated on the invention of a personal, private style. The modernist aesthetic was organically linked to the conception of an authentic self and a private identity which can be expected to generate its own unique vision of the world and to forge its own unmistakable style. The post-structuralists argue against this; in their view the concept of the unique individual and the theoretical basis of individualism are ideological. Not only is the bourgeois individual subject a thing of the past, it is also a myth, it never really existed in the first place; it was just a mystification. And so, in a world in which stylistic innovation is no longer possible all that is left, Jameson suggests, is pastiche. The practice of pastiche, the imitation of dead styles, can be seen in the 'nostalgia film'. It seems that we are unable to focus on our present. We have lost our ability to locate ourselves historically. As a society we have become incapable of dealing with time.

Postmodernism has a peculiar notion of time. Jameson explains what he means in terms of Lacan's theory of schizophrenia. The originality of Lacan's thought in this area is to have considered schizophrenia as a language disorder. Schizophrenia emerges from the failure of the infant to enter fully into the realm of speech and language. For Lacan the experience of temporality, human time, past, present, memory, the persistence of personal identity is an effect of language. It is because language has a past and a future, because the sentence moves in time, that we can have what seems to us a concrete or lived experience of time. But since the schizophrenic does not know language articulation in that way, he or she does not have our experience of temporal continuity either, but is condemned to live in a perpetual present with which the various moments of his or her past have little connection and for which there is no future on the horizon. In other words, schizophrenic experience is an experience of isolated, disconnected material signifiers which fail to link up into a coherent sequence.

On the one hand, then, the schizophrenic does have a more intense experience of any given present of the world than we do, since our own present is always part of some larger set of projects which includes the past and the future. On the other hand, the schizophrenic is 'no one', has no personal identity. Moreover, he or she does nothing since to have a project means to be able to commit oneself to a certain continuity over time. The schizophrenic, in short, experiences a fragmentation of time, a series of perpetual presents. Jameson contends that experiences of temporal discontinuity, similar to those described above, are evoked in postmodernist works such as the compositions of John Cage and the texts of Samuel Beckett.

TOTALITY OR FRAGMENTATION

You may have noticed that I have made several references to totality and fragmentation. I have said that Lyotard repudiates the big stories, the metanarratives of Hegel and Marx; he believes that no one can grasp what is going on in a society as a *whole*. It seems fashionable nowadays to say that there is no single theoretical discourse which is going to offer an explanation for all forms of social relations or for every mode of political practice. Postmodernists and others are always making this point against Marxism: they insist that it has totalizing ambitions and resent its claim to provide explanations for all aspects of social experience.

Rejecting totality, Lyotard and other postmodernists stress fragmentation—of language games, of time, of the human subject, of society itself. One of the fascinating things about the rejection of organic unity and the espousal of the fragmentary is that this belief was also held by the historic avant-garde movements. They too wanted the dissolution of unity. In their activities the coherence and autonomy of the work was deliberately called into question or even methodically destroyed.

Walter Benjamin's concept of allegory has been used as an aid to understanding avant-gardiste (non-organic) works of art.[24] Benjamin described how the allegorist pulls an element out of the totality of the life context, isolating it, depriving it of its function. (Allegory is thus essentially a fragment, the opposite of the organic symbol.) Then the allegorist joins several isolated fragments and thereby creates meaning. This is posited meaning and does not derive from the original context of the fragments.

These elements of Benjamin's concept of allegory accord with what is called montage, the fundamental principle of avant-garde art. Montage presupposes fragmentation of reality; it breaks through the appearance of totality and calls attention to the fact that it is made up of reality fragments. The avant-gardiste work proclaims itself an artificial construct, an artefact. The opposite holds true for the organic work: it seeks to make unrecognizable the fact that it has been made. In the organic work of art the material is treated as a whole, while in the avant-gardiste work the material is torn out of the life totality and isolated. The aesthetic avant-gardist fragment *challenges* people to make it an integrated part of their reality and to relate it to their experience. The best example of this principle is probably the Brechtian play. A play by Brecht does not aim at organic unity but consists of interruptions and juxtapositions which disrupt conventional expectations and force the audience into critical speculation.

The question as to whether a work of art should be an organic unity or consist of fragments is perhaps best understood by having a look at the debate between Georg Lukács and Theodor Adorno.[25] The contrast between organic and non-organic work underlies both Lukács' and Adorno's theories of the avant-garde. Whereas Lukács holds onto the organic work of art ('realism') as an aesthetic norm and from that perspective rejects avant-gardiste works as decadent, Adorno elevates avant-gardiste, non-organic work to a historical norm and condemns all efforts to create a realistic art in our time.

While Lukács adopted Hegel's view that the organic work of art (for example, the realistic novels of Goethe, Balzac, Stendhal) constitutes a type of perfection, Adorno believed that the avant-garde work is the only possible authentic expression of the contemporary state of the world, the historically necessary expression of alienation in late capitalist society. Like Adorno, Lukács believed that the work of the avant-garde is the expression of alienation in capitalist society, but he was very scathing about the blindness of bourgeois intellectuals who could not see the real historical counterforces working towards a structural transformation of society.

Adorno, however, did not have this political perspective. He believed that instead of baring the contradictions of society in our time, the organic work promotes, by its very form, the illusion of a world that is whole.[26] For him avant-gardiste art is a radical protest that rejects all false reconciliation with what exists and is therefore the only art form that has historical legitimacy. Lukács, on the other hand, acknowledges its character as protest but condemns avant-gardiste art because that protest remains abstract, without historical perspective and blind to the real counter-forces that are striving to overcome capitalism. He rejects the idea that avant-gardiste work allows ruptures and 'gaps' of reality to show through the fragmentary nature of the work itself.

But an important similarity between Lukács and Adorno should be noted: they both argue within the institution of art and are unable to criticize it as an institution for that very reason. I hope that I have said enough to signal that the Lukács–Adorno debate really consists of two antagonistic theories of culture. Adorno not only sees late capitalism as definitely stabilized but also feels that historical experience has shown the hopes placed in socialism to be ill-founded. In this respect he is very much like most of the postmodernists.

It could be said that there are two main traditions or modes of understanding the avant-garde. The first mode of thought is associated with Adorno, Artaud, Barthes, Breton, and Derrida. (Many writers have pointed out that the philosophies of Derrida and Adorno display interesting similarities.) The other mode of thought is associated with Benjamin and Brecht.

It is largely from the work of Benjamin that we have learnt that the social effect of a work of art cannot simply be gauged by considering the work itself but that it is decisively determined by the institution within which the work functions. It is art as an institution which determines the measure of political effect avant-garde works can have and which determines that art in bourgeois society continues to be a realm distinct from the praxis of life. Art as an institution neutralizes the political content of the individual work. It prevents the contents of work that press for radical change in a society—the abolition of alienation—from having any practical effect. Received in the context of artefacts whose shared characteristic is their apartness from the praxis of life, 'organic' works of art tend to be perceived as 'mere' art products.

It should be remembered that had there never been any avant-garde movements, Brecht's and Benjamin's reflections regarding a restructuring of the production apparatus would not have been possible. Brecht never shared the intention of the historic avant-garde artists to destroy art as an institution. Though he despised the theatre of the educated bourgeoisie, he did not conclude that the theatre should be abolished altogether: instead he proposed to radically change it.[27]

I believe that there are so many difficulties with the positions of Lukács and Adorno that they are both unsatisfactory. I want to suggest that one possible way out of the situation may be through the use of the materialist theories inspired by Benjamin and Brecht. In the next section I will make some critical comments on the Lyotardian neo-conservative position and then move on to present a case for what he rejects, the 'grand narrative' of human emancipation.

SOME CRITICISMS OF LYOTARD'S WORK

Lyotard's book *The Postmodern Condition* is on one level about the status of science and technology, about technocracy and the control of information. But on another level it is a thinly veiled polemic against Jürgen Habermas, who stands for a 'totalizing' and dialectical tradition. Habermas thinks that the totality of life has become splintered and argues that the cognitive, ethical and political discourses should come closer together. He wants, in short, to defend modernity against the neo-conservative postmodernists.

In contrast, Lyotard's main target is the Hegelian-Marxist concept of totality. He is scornful of Habermas's vision of a transparent, fully communicational society and sees language situations as an unstable exchange between speakers, as the 'taking of tricks', the trumping of an adversary. He repudiates, in short, Habermas's notion of a consensus community. Lyotard's view of science and knowledge is that of a search not for consensus but for 'instabilities'; the point is not to reach agreement but to undermine from within the very framework in which the previous 'normal science' had been conducted.

Lyotard thinks that Habermas makes the assumption that it is possible for all speakers to come to agreement on which rules are universally valid for language games, when it is clear that language games are incommensurable, subject to heterogeneous sets of pragmatic rules. He argues that the principle of consensus as a criterion of validation, as elaborated by Habermas, is inadequate: it is a conception based on the validity of the narrative of emancipation.[28] Lyotard writes, 'We no longer have recourse to the grand narrative—we can resort neither to the dialectic of Spirit nor even to the emancipation of humanity as a validation for postmodern scientific discourse.'[29] In his view the little narrative (petit récit) remains the quintessential form of imaginative invention.

Influenced by Nietzsche, post-structuralists like Lyotard attack philosophy as an imposition of truth. (Nietzsche is famous for his attack on truth; all perspectives, he said, are illusory.) At one time Lyotard supported Marxism but he now sees it as one of the 'grand narratives' he is against. He writes about the force of language beyond truth and wants to develop a theory of philosophical fiction—a discourse that tries to persuade without the traditional notion of 'argument'. In Lyotard's work problems of power are put to one side, and his views have led him to a form of relativism.

There is an ambiguity throughout Lyotard's work and that of other post-structuralists who have been influenced by Nietzsche's critique of systems. Lyotard argues that all theoretical conceptualizations, such as history, are coercive; in his view any interpretation of history is dogmatic. He does not make a distinction between large-scale theories and dogmatism; it is taken for granted that any large-scale theory is dogmatic. Now, it could be argued that some Marxist theories are dogmatic but that, given time and effort, the dogmatism could be dissolved. However, the post-structuralists never consider this possibility.

Why is this? Richard Rorty has suggested an explanation. He has criticized writers like Foucault and Lyotard for their extraordinary *dryness*:

It is a dryness produced by a lack of identification with any social context, any communication. Foucault once said that he would like to write 'so as to have no face'. He forbids himself the tone of the liberal sort of thinker who says to his fellow citizens: 'We know that there must be a better way to do things than this; let us look for it together.' There is no 'we' to be found in Foucault's writing, nor in

> those of many of his French contemporaries .... It is as if thinkers like Foucault and Lyotard are so afraid of being caught up in one more metanarrative about the fortunes of 'the subject' that they cannot bring themselves to say 'we' long enough to identify with the culture of the generation to which they belong.[30]

Politically, it is clear that thinkers like Lyotard and Foucault are neo-conservatives. They take away the dynamic which liberal social thought has traditionally relied upon. They offer us no theoretical reason to move in one social direction rather than another. On the whole, post-structuralists think of rationality as a limiting framework. They are against what they call the imperialism of reason. Lyotard's intellectual trajectory has brought him to the position where he now wants to abstain from anything that is connected with the 'metanarrative of emancipation'.

Conclusion

TAKING HISTORY SERIOUSLY

Lyotard is only one of many post-structuralists, 'new philosophers' and others who attack Marxism for being a 'grand narrative' and mock its belief in the emancipation of humanity. As they assert that Marx's story under Hegel's inspiration clearly exhibits a providential plot, it is important to ask, 'What is "narrative"?' One of the insights of recent literary theory is that narrative or story is not specifically a literary form. Fredric Jameson believes that narrative is really not so much a literary form or structure as an epistemological category.[1] Like the Kantian concepts of space and time, narrative may be taken not as a feature of our experience but as one of the abstract or 'empty' co-ordinates within which we come to know the world, a contentless form that our perception imposes on the raw flux of reality. This is not to say that we make up stories about the world to understand it; Jameson is making the much more radical claim that the world comes to us in the shape of stories.

Jameson argues that it is hard to think of the world as it would exist outside narrative. Anything we try to substitute for a story is, on closer examination, likely to be another sort of story. Physicists, for example, 'tell stories' about subatomic particles. Anything that presents itself as existing outside the boundaries of some story (a structure, a form, a category) can only do so through a kind of fiction. In Jameson's view structures may be abundantly useful as conceptual fictions, but reality comes to us in the form of its stories. Narrative, just by being narrative, always demands interpretation, and so we must always be aware of the distinction between manifest meaning and latent content. Moreover, we should remember that every narrative simultaneously presents and represents a world, that is, simultaneously creates or makes up a reality and asserts that it stands independent of that same reality. In other words, narrative seems at once to reveal or illuminate a world and to hide or distort it.

Narrative, the contentless form of our most basic experience of reality, has a function: it is a specific mechanism through which the collective consciousness represses historical contradictions. This is what is meant by 'the political unconscious'. Ironically, it was Freud who actually discovered the political unconscious but who, imprisoned through ideological circumstance within such illusory categories as 'the individual psyche' and the like, was in no position to understand the consequences of his discovery.

It is obvious that Jameson has been much influenced by structuralist thinking: there is the idea, for example, that the notion of 'individual consciousness' is incoherent. (This notion, he would say, implies some idea of a 'collective consciousness' or total social system.) For Jameson Marxism is the story of a fall out of collective life and consciousness into a world of estrangement and alienation where 'individual identity' becomes a primary category within thought. He would say that separation or individuality at the level of consciousness is itself a symptom of estrangement from the life of the collective. To treat the 'I', the feeling or experience of individual identity, as the main ontological category is to repress history itself.

Jameson is antagonistic to those post-structuralists who reject the idea of a master code or master narrative. He finds the notion of master code a valuable one and uses it in his own work. He argues that formalism, whose claims are based on immanent interpretation, is really a form of transcendent interpretation in disguise. Formalist criticism simply rewrites literary works in terms of an ethical master code that is a product of its historical moment. Another example is structuralism, a form of transcendent interpretation that uses the master code language.

Jameson argues that the 'master code' of any interpretative method is the ideology it works to perpetuate. Ideology is the repression of those underlying contradictions that have their source in history. Jameson conceives of ideologies as strategies of containment, and of literature as an ideological production mirroring such strategies at the level of individual works.[2] He tries to subject literature to symptomatic analysis, a mode of interpretation that reveals the specific ways in which works deny or repress history. Symptomatic analysis is also able to show that critical approaches usually assumed to be in competition with one another (the Freudian, the formalist, the structuralist, etc.) share at the deep level an identical set of assumptions, they deny history in an identical way.[3] This method has some similarities with Foucaldian or Nietzschean 'genealogy', which elicits from the structure of a cultural text that unexpressed subtext or *hors texte* it cannot acknowledge. What Jameson tries to do is to find certain patterns which represent strategies of containment; he looks at gaps or absences as specific signs of the way the text denies or represses history.

In Jameson's view taking history seriously means accepting some story as the means of knowing anything at all. (Indeed, I would argue that the more people believe that history should be moving towards the establishment of a rational society, the more likely history will be moving towards it. By making this link between theory and practice we make history conform to our notion of it.) Jameson defends the concept of 'mode of production'; the 'story' of the successive modes of production is heuristic and the value of the concept lies in its use as an instrument of social analysis. What the concept 'mode of production' is really concerned with is not some story of successive economic stages but the possibility of seeing all the social phenomena within a given historical framework as related to one another as to a totality.

Jameson conceives the social totality as something always constituted by a class struggle between a dominant and a labouring class, and he wants us to think of the social order at the cultural level in the form of a dialogue between *antagonistic class discourses*. This dialogue is always made possible by what he calls the unity of a shared code. (It is easy to forget that disagreement is made possible only by a shared language and a common set of assumptions.) The example Jameson provides is that of England in the 1640s when religion operated as the shared code within which was fought out the antagonism between opposing discourses. Historically speaking, we 'hear' only one voice because a hegemonic ideology suppresses all antagonistic class voices, and yet the hegemonic discourse remains locked into a dialogue with the discourse it has suppressed.

TOWARDS A PEDAGOGICAL POLITICAL CULTURE

The controversy over postmodernism is one example of class struggle at the cultural and political level. On the political level postmodernism is an attack on Marxism. On the cultural level it is a repudiation of the modern movement: abstract expressionism in painting, the international style in architecture, existentialism in philosophy. Most postmodernists reject the following models: the existential model of authenticity and inauthenticity, the semiotic opposition between signifier and signified, the Freudian model of latent and manifest, and the Marxist one of appearance and essence (the view that the empirical world, 'appearance', is causally connected to deeper levels, the structures and processes of the real, 'the essence'). These 'depth' models have been replaced by a conception of practices, discourses and textual play.

Jameson suggests that with postmodernism there has emerged a new kind of flatness or depthlessness, a new kind of superficiality.[4] The shift from the period of modernism to the world of the postmodern can be characterized as one in which the alienation of the subject is displaced by *the fragmentation of the subject*. The disappearance of the individual subject and the unavailability of unique and personal style has brought about a new practice: pastiche.

To recapitulate, pastiche has become a ubiquitous mode (in film, especially) which suggests that we wish to be recalled to times less problematic than our own. There seems to be a refusal to engage with the present or to think historically, a refusal that Jameson regards as characteristic of the 'schizophrenia' of consumer society. He believes that there has been a disappearance of a sense of history. Our entire contemporary social system has little by little begun to lose its capacity to retain its own past; it has begun to live in a perpetual present.

There seems to be a random cannibalization of all the styles of the past. At the same time we seem increasingly incapable of fashioning representations of our current experiences. For Jameson postmodernism replicates, reinforces the logic of consumer capitalism. The emergence of postmodernism is closely related to the emergence of present-day multinational capitalism.

Jameson has usefully periodized the stages of realism, modernism and postmodernism by drawing on the work of the economist Ernest Mandel. Mandel, who argues that technology is the result of the development of capital rather than some primal cause in its own right, outlines three fundamental leaps in the evolution of machinery under capital: machine production of steam-driven motors since 1848, machine production of electric and combustion motors since the '90s of the nineteenth century, and machine production of electronic and nuclear-powered apparatuses since the '40s of the twentieth century. This periodization underlines the general thesis of Mandel's book *Late Capitalism*, namely that there have been three fundamental moments in capitalism: market capitalism, monopoly capitalism (or imperialism) and multinational capitalism.[5]

Among the theorists of the New Right the assertion is fashionable that we are living in a type of society that no longer obeys the laws of classical capitalism (namely the primacy of industrial production and the omnipresence of class struggle) and that therefore Marxism is outmoded. In contrast with this postmodernist/post-structuralist view Mandel argues that the contemporary form of capitalism represents the purest form of capitalism to have emerged.

There has been a prodigious expansion of capitalism into hitherto uncommodified areas: for example the penetration and colonization of Nature and the Unconscious, that is to say, the destruction of the pre-capitalist agriculture and the rise of the media and the advertising industry.

Jameson's main political concepts, inherited from Lukács and the Frankfurt School, are those of reification and commodification. He contends that aesthetic production has become integrated into commodity production:

> This whole global, yet American, postmodern culture is the internal and superstructural expression of a whole new wave of American military and economic domination throughout the world: in this sense, as throughout class history, the underside of culture is blood, death and horror.[6]

Jameson is deeply concerned about the incapacity of our minds (at least at present) to map the great global multinational and decentred communicational network in which we find ourselves caught as individual subjects. He describes how we all, in one way or another, dimly feel that not only local forms of cultural resistance but also even overtly political interventions are somehow secretly disarmed and reabsorbed by a system of which they themselves might well be considered a part, since they can achieve no distance from it.

While the high modernists were very interested in time and memory it seems that now our daily life, our cultural languages, are dominated by the category of space rather than time. Jameson uses the metaphor of an alienated city to refer to a space in which people are unable to map in their mind either their own positions or the urban totality in which they find themselves. He argues that we should map our individual social relationship to local, national and international class realities, a process that requires us to co-ordinate existential data, the empirical position of the subject, with theoretical conceptions of the totality. We need to develop an aesthetic of cognitive mapping, a pedagogical political culture which seeks to endow the individual subject with some new heightened sense of its place in the global system.

While reading this you may have been asking, 'What has all this to do with me?' I agree with Antonio Gramsci's remark that 'everything is political, even philosophy and philosophies'. Texts, philosophies and so forth acquire power through what Gramsci describes as diffusion, dissemination into and hegemony over the world of 'common sense': 'In the realm of culture and of thought each production exists not only to earn a place for itself but to displace, win out over, others.'[7] I suggest that the controversy about modernism and postmodernism should be seen in the context of ideological struggle. This debate is, implicitly, about the status, the validity of Marxism. The project of modernity is one with that of the Enlightenment. And Marxism is a child of the Enlightenment. But the postmodernists declare that progress is myth. Obviously each position on or within postmodernism is marked by our political interests and values.[8] How we conceive of postmodernism is central to how we re-present the past, the present, and the future to ourselves and others.

A characteristic of human beings is that they make a distinction between 'the real' and 'the ideal'. By the real I mean an awareness of the present situation, and by the ideal, some notion of what life, the world, could be like. Human beings have a sense of what is possible in the future and they have the hope that tomorrow will be better than today. Marxists not only have this hope, this orientation towards the future, but they try to understand the world, to develop a critical consciousness of it, and try to develop strategies for changing it. Of course, they realize that progress is uneven, not unilinear; because of the nature of contradiction there are inevitably negative aspects, sad reversals and painful losses. Marxists struggle for a better future for all, but they know that this does not mean that progress is guaranteed or that the processes of the dialectic will lead to the Perfect. I believe that it is important for people to support the Enlightenment project because education is closely connected with the notion of a change of consciousness; gaining a wider, deeper understanding of the world represents a change for the better. And this, in turn, implies some belief in a worthwhile future. Without this presupposition the education of people would be pointless.

RE-VISION

Before I conclude I would like to give a brief 'précis' of the ground covered in the foregoing chapters. Its main purpose is not to tell you 'to read the chapters in a certain way' but to encourage you to reflect—and comment—on the issues raised. I began by discussing the three most influential post-structuralists: Lacan, Derrida and Foucault. Chapter 1, a general introduction to Lacan and his theory of psychoanalysis, suggested that Lacanian theory offered a way of thinking about the social and the linguistic construction of the self. We urgently need a model that overcomes the opposition between the individual and the social, because no political revolution can be completed until the 'character structures' inherited from prerevolutionary society are transformed. I think that a (revised) Lacanian model of the subject could perhaps help us to conceive of a different signification, a different subjectivity, and a different symbolic order.

There was an account of Derrida's thought in Chapter 2. I outlined his arguments against Lacan and other thinkers and then described his views on Freud, who influenced Derrida's thinking on reading texts, and Nietzsche, who influenced his understanding of the nature and function of metaphor. I argued that metaphors determine to a large extent what we can think in any field and that they shape what we do. Finally, after situating metaphor in the context of political and ideological struggle, I discussed the relationship between deconstruction and Marxism.

Chapter 3 focused on Foucault, a writer whose works are based on a vision of history derived from Nietzsche. I gave an exposition of Foucault's work which is largely concerned with the growth of the modern sciences and the process of modernization. The relationship between knowledge and power, another Nietzschean theme, was also discussed. For Foucault knowledge is not neutral or objective but is a product of power relations. Power in modern times is productive, it operates through the construction of new capacities and modes of activity. After describing some of the similarities and differences between Foucault and Althusser, I presented Foucault's arguments against Marxism. I stressed the point that Foucault and his many followers, both in France and in this country, have been vigorously propagating the view that Marxism is authoritarian and outmoded. Nietzsche's thought has influenced Foucault so deeply that it is not surprising that he rejects Marx's view of economics, history, politics and method. For Foucault it is no longer feasible to conceptualize relations of power in terms of the state, class struggle, relations of production and capitalist exploitation.

In Chapter 4 I outlined some of the important differences between the philosophies of Nietzsche and Hegel and stressed the fact that Nietzsche's thought—his antipathy to any system, his rejection of the Hegelian view of history as progress, his preoccupation with the subjective—is central to the post-structuralist's anti-Marxist stance. I introduced some of the ideas of writers like Deleuze and Guattari (who see in Marxism an instrument of domination and who glorify spontaneity, subjectivity and intensity), Foucault, Lyotard and others who always emphasize the local, the heterogeneous and the fragmentary. I then discussed the 'new philosophers' who also draw heavily on Nietzsche's thought and combine certain elements and themes from the work of post-structuralist writers.

I began Chapter 5 with an exposition of Lyotard's thesis: as knowledge is now becoming the principal force of production, we should seriously consider the changing nature of knowledge as computerized societies enter what is known as the postmodern age. It was explained that the debate about modernism and postmodernism is (partly) about the arts, and so there was a discussion about the role of art in bourgeois society. Postmodernists/post-structuralists believe that the modern narratives of the emancipation of the working class, the classless society, have lost credibility. Marxism is outmoded.

Post-structuralists, I maintained, are antagonistic to the

concept of totality and in its stead emphasize fragmentation. Everything consists of fragments; and as they do not recognize a unity against which the fragments can be measured they tend towards relativism. The post-structuralists also emphasize the local and the contingent and have a hatred of all overarching theories. With some thinkers, such as Derrida and Foucault, this had led to a conceptual relativism so strong as to seem self-defeating. It is not surprising, then, that Lyotard believes that power is increasingly becoming the criterion of truth.

Derrida, Foucault and other post-structuralists challenge the idea that knowledge 'grows' or 'progresses' in any more than a purely quantitative sense. (One paradox of their work is that although they repudiate any notion of a general theory, their theory does express a general view about the nature of knowledge.) Not only do they give up humanism's belief in epistemological progress, they also give up its belief in social historical progress. Derrida, Foucault and other modern Nietzscheans see history as 'ending' in the sense of dying. Having lost faith in the progessive character of history, they are reacting against the thinkers of the Enlightenment. They assert that the Enlightenment project of modernity has failed. In opposition to this view it was argued that Marxism, a child of the eighteenth-century Enlightenment, is committed to education, rationality and progress.

Of course, I agree with Jameson's point that we need to recover a history of society which hitherto has been misrepresented or rendered invisible. We need to develop a pedagogical political culture which seeks to endow the individual subject with some new heightened sense of its place in local, national, and international realities. This is an extremely difficult project. In contemporary societies there is a struggle for interpretative power, and the prevailing ideologies limit the means by which individuals understand their material experiences. The modern culture-industry robs individuals of 'languages' for interpreting self and world by denying them the media for organizing their own experiences. We urgently need to provide individuals and social groups with public 'spaces', in which they can deal with subliminally felt experiences and learn to understand these experiences on a more conscious, critical level.[9] History, literature, story-telling, therefore, have important functions because they provide discourses and opportunities for dealing with experiences by discussing them. Only experiences confirmed and corroborated through discussion and coped with as collective experience can be said to be truly experienced. According to this view consciousness is the historically concrete production of meaning, and every historical situation contains ideological ruptures and offers possibilites for social transformation.

Notes

INTRODUCTION

1 For a good introduction to these debates see K. Soper, *Humanism and Anti-Humanism*, London, Hutchinson, 1986.
2 C. Lévi-Strauss, *The Savage Mind*, London, Weidenfeld & Nicolson, 1966. The attack, ch. 9 of the above book, is published as 'History and Dialectic' in R. and F. DeGeorge (eds), *The Structuralists from Marx to Lévi-Strauss*, New York, Anchor Books, 1972.
3 F. de Saussure, *Course in General Linguistics*, London, Fontana/Collins, 1974.
4 J. Lacan, *Écrits: A Selection*, London, Tavistock, 1977, p. 154.
5 See J. Culler, *Structuralist Poetics*, London, Routledge & Kegan Paul, 1975, p. 247.
6 It is important to differentiate clearly structuralism, structuralist Marxism and post-structuralism. By putting these three together as theories of structure (as opposed to action) many writers fail to underline the profoundly anti-Marxist nature of post-structuralism. See, for example, I. Craib, *Modern Social Theory: From Parsons to Habermas*, Brighton, Harvester Press, 1984.

CHAPTER 1   LACAN AND PSYCHOANALYSIS

1 S. Turkle, *Psychoanalytic Politics, Jacques Lacan and Freud's French Revolution*, London, Burnett Books, 1979, p. 67.
2 The article 'Freud and Lacan' is in L. Althusser, *Lenin and Philosophy and Other Essays*, London, New Left Books, 1971.
3 J. Lacan, *De la psychose paranoiaque dans ses rapports avec la personnalité*, Paris, Éditions du Seuil, 1975.
4 See J. Mitchell, *Psychoanalysis and Feminism*, London, Penguin Books, 1974.

5 S. Freud, *Beyond the Pleasure Principle*, Standard Edition, vol. 18, London, Hogarth Press, 1955.

6 J. Lacan, *Écrits: A Selection*, London, Tavistock, 1977, pp. 1–7.

7 A. Lemaire, *Jacques Lacan*, London, Routledge & Kegan Paul, 1977, p. 92.

8 Ibid., pp. 156–60.

9 Ibid., p. 166.

10 When the psychoanalytic session begins the analysand talks of himself or herself as an object. This is what Lacan calls 'empty speech'. In contrast, 'full speech' is when the subject coincides with the object, when *who* is talking coincides with *what* is being talked about.

11 See Laplanche and Leclair, 'The Unconscious: a Psychoanalytic Study', *Yale French Studies*, no. 48, pp. 118–75; also A. Lemaire, op. cit., ch. 9.

12 Lacan, *Écrits*, p. 12.

13 J. Gallop, *Feminism and Psychoanalysis: The Daughter's Seduction*, London, Macmillan, 1982, p. 12.

14 Lacan, *Écrits*, p. 134.

15 D.W. Winnicott, *Playing and Reality*, London, Penguin, 1974, pp. 130–8.

16 Lacan, *Écrits*, p. 2.

17 J.-P. Sartre, *Being and Nothingness*, London, Methuen, 1957.

18 Lacan, *Écrits*, p. 119.

19 D. Archard, *Consciousness and the Unconscious*, London, Hutchinson, 1984, p. 25. This useful book contains a brief outline of Freud's theory and Sartre's critique of it, a clear exposition of Lacan and, finally, Timpanaro's critique of the 'Freudian slip'.

20 Lacan, *Écrits*, p. 161.

21 Ibid., p. 281.

22 A. Kojève, *Introduction to the Reading of Hegel: Lectures on the Phenomenology of Spirit*, assembled by Raymond Queneau, New York, Basic Books, Inc., 1969. It should be noted that for Hegel human consciousness was an aspect of *Geist*. Kojève brings Hegel down to earth and stresses the elements of labour, language and struggle.

23 Ibid., p. 37.

24 Ibid., p. 228.

25 Ibid., p. 206.

26 Ibid., p. 220.

27 Ibid., p. 58.

28 Lacan makes a distinction between need (a purely organic energy) and desire, the active principle of the physical processes. Desire always lies both beyond and before demand. To say that desire is beyond demand means that it transcends it, that it is eternal because it is impossible to satisfy. It is forever insatiable since it refers back to the ineffable, to the unconscious desire and the absolute lack it conceals. Every human action, even the most altruistic, derives from a desire for recognition by the Other, from a wish for self-recognition in some

form or another. Desire is the desire for desire, the desire of the Other.

29 J. Lacan, *The Four Fundamental Concepts of Psycho-analysis*, London, Penguin, 1979, pp. 196–7, 205. A useful account of the myth is given by K. Silverman, *The Subject of Semiotics*, Oxford University Press, 1983, p. 151.

30 For a discussion of Lacan's phallocentrism and its implications see J. Mitchell and J. Rose, *Feminine Sexuality*, London, Macmillan, 1982.

31 Jameson believes that both psychoanalysis and Marxism depend fundamentally on history and story-telling. See F. Jameson, 'Imaginary and Symbolic in Lacan: Marxism, Psychoanalytic Criticism, and the Problem of the Subject', Yale French Studies, 1977, nos. 55–6, pp. 338–95.

32 Wilhelm Reich (1897–1957), a prophet of sexual revolution, asserted that mental health is dependent on the capacity to experience orgasm and that mental illness is the result of inhibition of the capacity to experience orgasm. See C. Rycroft, *Reich*, London, Fontana, 1971.

33 See 'Introduction to Irigaray', *Ideology and Consciousness*, May 1977, no. 1, pp. 57–76. A good introduction to French feminist theory is T. Moi's *Sexual/Textual Politics*, London, Methuen, 1985.

34 The family is usually regarded as the central mediatory institution between the individual and the social realm. See, for example, M. Poster, *Critical Theory of the Family*, London, Pluto Press, 1978, ch. 2. See also ch. 4 for an account of Lacan.

35 For an extended discussion of this point see B. Ollman, *Alienation*, Cambridge University Press, 1976 (2nd edition), pp. 245–50.

CHAPTER 2   DERRIDA AND DECONSTRUCTION

1 J. Derrida, *Of Grammatology*, Baltimore and London, Johns Hopkins University Press, 1976; *Speech and Phenomena, and Other Essays on Husserl's Theory of Signs*, Evanston, Northwestern University Press, 1973; *Writing and Difference*, London, Routledge & Kegan Paul, 1978.

2 See T. Eagleton, *Literary Theory: An Introduction*, Oxford, Basil Blackwell, 1983, pp. 127–34.

3 Derrida's arguments are largely based on the chapter 'A Writing Lesson' in Lévi-Strauss's *Tristes Tropiques*, London, Penguin, 1976, p. 385.

4 For critiques of Saussure, Rousseau, Lévi-Strauss see Derrida, *Of Grammatology*.

5 Derrida finds the same powerful metaphors at work in Husserl's meditations on language and thought; see Derrida's *Speech and Phenomena*.

6 See Derrida's 'Freud and the Scene of Writing' in *Writing and*

Difference, p. 196. Derrida traces the emergence of the metaphor of writing through three texts placed on a thirty-year span in Freud's career: 'Project for a Scientific Psychology' (1985), *The Interpretation of Dreams* (1899), and *Note on the Mystic Writing Pad* (1925).

7 J. Habermas, *Knowledge and Human Interests*, London, Heinemann Educational Books, 1972, chapters 10–12.

8 Readers should be reminded that proper names such as Nietzsche, Freud, Heidegger are a convenient fiction. For Derrida the names of authors indicate neither identities nor causes. Proper names are serviceable 'metonymic contractions' that refer to problems.

9 Nietzsche faces reflexive concerns that have parallels with modern relativism, but instead of stepping back, which he regards as impossible, he endorses paradox and incorporates reflexivity into his own writing. See H. Lawson, *Reflexivity: The Post-modern Predicament*, London, Hutchinson, 1985, p. 32.

10 Nietzsche, 'On Truth and Falsity in their Ultramoral Sense', in O. Levy (ed.), *The Complete Works of Friedrich Nietzsche*, New York, 1964.

11 G. Lakoff and M. Johnson, *Metaphors We Live By*, Chicago, University of Chicago Press, 1980.

12 C. Hill, *Reformation to Industrial Revolution*, London, Penguin, 1967; quoted by Lawton in Taylor, op. cit.

13 M. Foucault, *Power/Knowledge, Selected Interviews and Other Writings 1972–1977*, edited by C. Gordon, Brighton, Harvester Press, 1980, pp. 68–70.

14 Gayatri Chakravorty Spivak, 'Translator's Preface', Derrida, *Of Grammatology*, p. lxxv. I have found this preface lucid and most helpful.

15 Ibid., p. lxxvii.

16 But, as Rée has pointed out, Derrida is so preoccupied with metaphor that he fails to remember such literary processes as narrative, story and plot. See J. Rée, 'Metaphor and Metaphysics: The End of Philosophy and Derrida', *Radical Philosophy*, 38, Summer 1984, p. 33. For an introduction to Derrida see D.C. Woods in *Radical Philosophy*, 21, Spring 1979.

17 Eagleton, op. cit., p. 138.

18 Ibid., p. 147.

19 V. Leitch, *Deconstructive Criticism, An advanced introduction*, London, Hutchinson, 1983, p. 246.

20 Post-structuralists, generally, favour authors who shift the textuality of their production, the ambiguity and the plurality of meanings, to the foreground. They admire authors like Rimbaud, Lautréamont, Robbe-Grillet, Joyce.

21 E.W. Said, 'Opponents, Audiences, Constituencies and Community', in H. Foster (ed.), *Postmodern Culture*, London, Pluto Press, 1985, p. 143.

22 Eagleton, op. cit., p. 148.

23 Lawson, op. cit., p. 113–15.

24 F. Jameson, *Marxism and Form*, Princeton University Press, 1971. See the note on p. 409. See also M. Ryan, *Marxism and Deconstruction*, Baltimore, Johns Hopkins University Press, 1982.
25 C. Norris, *Deconstruction: Theory and Practice*, London, Methuen, 1982, p. 84.
26 T. Eagleton, *Walter Benjamin or Towards a Revolutionary Criticism*, London, New Left Books, 1981, p. 137. Eagleton may have since changed his mind. In *Literary Theory*, 1983, he writes: 'The widespread opinion that deconstruction denies the existence of anything but discourse, or affirms a realm of pure difference in which all meaning and identity dissolves, is a travesty of Derrida's own work and of *the most productive work which has followed from it*' (p. 148, my italics).

CHAPTER 3   FOUCAULT AND THE SOCIAL SCIENCES

1 M. Foucault, 'Nietzsche, Genealogy, History', in D.F. Bouchard (ed.), *Language, Counter-Memory, Practice: Selected Essays and Interviews*, Oxford, Blackwell, 1977.
2 M. Foucault, *Madness and Civilization*, London, Tavistock, 1967.
3 Ibid., p. 46.
4 Ibid., p. 48.
5 Ibid., p. 64.
6 Ibid., p. 247.
7 Ibid., p. 254.
8 Derrida has criticized Foucault for still being confined within the structuralist science of investigation through oppositions. See the essay entitled 'Cogito and the History of Madness' in J. Derrida, *Writing and Difference*, London, Routledge & Kegan Paul, 1978, p. 34.
9 M. Foucault, *The Birth of the Clinic*, London, Tavistock, 1973.
10 M. Foucault, *The Order of Things*, London, Tavistock, 1970; *The Archaeology of Knowledge*, London, Tavistock, 1972.
11 M. Foucault, *Power/Knowledge, Selected Interviews and Other Writings 1972–1977*, edited by C. Gordon, Brighton, Harvester Press, 1980, p. 115.
12 M. Foucault (ed.), *I, Pierre Rivière . . . A Case of Parricide in the 19th Century*, London, Penguin, 1978.
13 M. Foucault, *Discipline and Punish*, London, Penguin, 1977.
14 Foucault, *Power/Knowledge*, p. 47.
15 Instrumental reason separates fact and value; it is concerned with discovering *how* to do things, not with what should be done. And so public affairs come to be regarded not as areas of discussion and choice but as technical problems to be solved by experts employing an instrumental rationality. The concept is explored in T. Adorno and M. Horkheimer, *Dialectic of the Enlightenment*, New York,

Herder and Herder, 1972, and M. Horkheimer, *Eclipse of Reason*, New York, Seabury Press, 1974. The latter is a popularization of the former book.

16 M. Foucault, *The History of Sexuality; Volume One: An Introduction*, London, Allen Lane, 1979. The second volume is called *L'usage des plaisirs, The Use of Pleasure*, London, Allen Lane, 1986; the third volume is *Le souci de soi, The Concern for Self*. Foucault died in June 1984, aged 57.

17 Foucault, *Power/Knowledge*, p. 98.

18 F. Nietzsche, *On the Genealogy of Morals*, New York, Vintage Books, 1969.

19 P. Dews, 'Power and Subjectivity in Foucault', *New Left Review*, No. 144, March–April 1984, p. 72.

20 L. Althusser, 'Ideology and Ideological State Apparatuses', in *Lenin and Philosophy and Other Essays*, London, New Left Books, 1971, p. 167.

21 For an excellent introduction to this debate see K. Soper, *Humanism and Anti-Humanism*, London, Hutchinson, 1986.

22 L. Althusser, *For Marx*, London, Penguin, 1969; *Reading Capital*, London, New Left Books, 1970. The latter contains a useful glossary of Althusserian terms.

23 M. Cousins and A. Hussain, *Michel Foucault*, London, Macmillan, 1984.

24 T. Benton, *The Rise and Fall of Structural Marxism: Louis Althusser and his Influence*, London, Macmillan, 1984. Benton suggests that the cognitive claims of science and its culturally produced character can perhaps be reconciled by a realist view of science, currently being developed by Roy Bhaskar and others, a view which was unavailable to Althusser. See R. Bhaskar, *A Realist Theory of Science*, Brighton, Harvester Press, 1978; *The Possibility of Naturalism*, Brighton, Harverster Press, 1979.

25 Foucault, *The Order of Things*, pp. 261–2. And see *Power/Knowledge*, p. 76.

26 Foucault, *Power/Knowledge*, p. 142.

27 Ibid., p. 62.

28 Ibid., p. 65.

29 Ibid., p. 85.

30 See M. Philp, 'Michel Foucault', in Q. Skinner (ed.), *The Return of Grand Theory in the Human Sciences*, Cambridge University Press, 1985, p. 79.

31 For the view that Foucault does not interrogate, as Marx did, the conditions of his own thought see M. Poster, *Foucault, Marxism and History*, Cambridge, Polity Press, 1984, p. 155.

32 Foucault, *Power/Knowledge*, p. 62.

33 Ibid., p. 203.

34 Ibid., pp. 207–8.

35 Ibid., p. 138.

36 See B. Jessop, *Nicos Poulantzas: State, Class and Strategy*, London, Macmillan, 1985.

37 See M. Ignatieff, 'State, Civil Society and Total Institutions: A Critique of Recent Social Histories of Punishment', in S. Cohen and A. Scull (eds), *Social Control and the State*, Oxford, Basil Blackwell, 1983.
38 N. Poulantzas, *State, Power, Socialism*, London, New Left Books, 1978. It has been said that this book is possibly the best exploration to date of the implications of Foucault's work for Marxist theory and politics; see B. Smart, *Foucault, Marxism and Critique*, London, Routledge & Kegan Paul, 1984, pp. 96–107.
39 Foucault, *Power/Knowledge*, p. 193.
40 Ibid., pp. 143–4.

CHAPTER 4   SOME CURRENTS WITHIN POST-STRUCTURALISM

1 G. Deleuze and F. Guattari, *Anti-Oedipus: Capitalism and Schizophrenia*, New York, Viking Press, 1977. See also G. Deleuze, *Nietzsche and Philosophy*, London, Athlone Press, 1983.
2 Deleuze and Guattari, op. cit., p. 131.
3 J.-J. Lecercle, *Philosophy through the Looking-Glass: Language, Nonsense, Desire*, London, Hutchinson, 1985, p. 199.
4 V. Descombes, *Modern French Philosophy*, Cambridge University Press, p. 173.
5 We should note that both these modes of thought cut across the political divisions of left and right. See the remarkable book by M. Berman, *All That Is Solid Melts Into Air: The Experience of Modernity*, London, Verso, 1983, which is a brilliant study of modernization and modernism.
6 J. Habermas, 'The Entwinement of Myth and Enlightenment: Re-reading *Dialectic of Enlightenment*', *New German Critique*, 26, 1982, p. 28.
7 M. Foucault, *The History of Sexuality*, London, Penguin, pp. 92–102.
8 See D. Howard, *The Marxian Legacy*, London, Macmillan, 1977. Chapter 9 is on Lefort and chapter 10 is on Castoriadis.
9 J.-F. Lyotard, *Discours/figure*, Paris, Klincksieck, 1971.
10 G. Lukács, *History of Class Consciousness*, London, Merlin Press, 1971.
11 L. Althusser, *For Marx*, London, Penguin, 1969, pp. 230, 248.
12 See E. Laclau, The Specificity of the Political, in *Politics and Ideology in Marxist Theory*, London, Verso, p. 51.
13 E.P. Thompson, *The Poverty of Theory and other essays*, London, Merlin Press, 1978. For a critical assessment of Thompson's work see P. Anderson, *Arguments within English Marxism*, London, Verso, 1980.
14 C. Claudin-Urondo, *Lenin and the Cultural Revolution*, Brighton, Harvester Press, 1977, p. 76.

15 For an elaboration of the points in this section see Barry Smart, *Foucault, Marxism and Critique*, London, Routledge & Kegan Paul, 1983.

16 B.-H. Lévy, *La barbarie à visage humain*, Paris, Grasset, 1977.

17 These Borromean knots are made of interlocking circles; when one is cut, the whole chain of circles becomes undone. They are described and illustrated in S. Turkle, *Psychoanalytic Politics: Jacques Lacan and Freud's French Revolution*, London, Burnett Books, 1979, p. 235.

18 This section is indebted to Peter Dews, 'The *Nouvelle Philosophie* and Foucault', *Economy and Society*, vol. 8, No. 2, May 1979. See also P. Dews, 'The "New Philosophers" and the End of Leftism', *Radical Philosophy*, No. 24, Spring 1980.

19 A. Glucksmann, *Les Maîtres penseurs*, Paris, Grasset, 1977.

20 These are the views of Jean-Marie Benoist, the author of *Marx est mort; The Structural Revolution*, London, Weidenfeld & Nicolson, 1978, and other works.

21 Even among British Marxists there is an increasing interest in religion. For example, Gareth Stedman-Jones has recently argued that socialism was religious before it was secular. In a sense, socialism was a post-Christian religion. See the work of Fourier and Saint-Simon.

22 T. Eagleton, *Literary Theory*, Oxford, Basil Blackwell, 1983, p. 142.

CHAPTER 5   POSTMODERNISM

1 J.-F. Lyotard, *The Postmodern Condition: A Report on Knowledge*, Manchester, Manchester University Press, 1984.

2 The term 'white-collar' is perhaps no longer useful as it puts together the well-paid positions at the top of the hierarchy and the mass of proletarianized workers. See the interesting chapter on clerical workers in H. Braverman, *Labour and Monopoly Capital*, New York, Monthly Review Press, 1974.

3 The important questions are: What is transmitted? Who does the transmission and to whom? Through what medium and in what form? With what effect? Only a coherent set of answers to these questions can form a viable educational policy.

4 L. Wittgenstein, *Philosophical Investigations*, Oxford, Basil Blackwell, 1958. I have found the following books helpful: A. Janik and S. Toulmin, *Wittgenstein's Vienna*, New York, Simon and Schuster, 1973; H. Pitkin, *Wittgenstein and Justice*, Los Angeles, University of California Press, 1972.

5 Those utterances which do not describe but 'do' something, e.g. 'naming', 'betting', 'marrying', etc., J.L. Austin calls *performatives*. For a short and clear introduction to these concepts see D. Silverman and B. Torode, *The Material Word: Some theories of language and its limits*, London, Routledge & Kegan Paul, 1980, chapters 3 and 9.

6 Lyotard, op. cit., p. 17.

7 Introductions to the philosophy of science include A.F. Chalmers, *What is this thing called Science?*, Milton Keynes, The Open University Press, 1978; R. Harré, *The Philosophies of Science*, Oxford University Press, 1972.

8 Fredric Jameson has cogently observed that Lyotard is rather unwilling to posit the disappearance of the great master narratives – they could have passed underground, as it were, and may still be influencing our thinking and acting unconsciously. This persistence of buried master narratives is what Jameson calls 'the political unconscious'.

9 Lyotard, op. cit., p. 37.

10 Ibid., p. 45. About this statement Eagleton contentiously remarks: 'It is not difficult, then, to see a relation between the philosophy of J.L. Austin and IBM, or between the various neo-Nietzscheanisms of a post-structuralist epoch and Standard Oil.' See T. Eagleton, Capitalism, Modernism and Postmodernism', *New Left Review*, No. 152, July/August 1985, p. 63.

11 But resistance to change has a use. See T. Kuhn, *The Structure of Scientific Revolutions*, Chicago, University of Chicago Press, 1970, p. 65. For a discussion of Kuhn's views see I. Lakatos and A. Musgrave (eds), *Criticism and the Growth of Knowledge*, Cambridge University Press, 1970.

12 P. Bürger, *Theory of the Avant-Garde*, Manchester University Press, 1984. I would like to suggest that the 'Foreword' to this book be read after the text.

13 H. Marcuse, 'On the affirmative character of culture', in *Negations, Essays in Critical Theory*, London, Penguin Books, 1986.

14 There may be several avant-gardes. Bürger's term 'the historic avant-garde' refers to the historical uniqueness of the avant-garde movements of the 1920s such as Dadaism and Surrealism.

15 P. Bürger, op. cit., p. 66.

16 Bürger feels that the avant-gardistes' attempt to reintegrate art into the life process is itself a contradictory endeavour. An art no longer distinct from the praxis of life but wholly absorbed in it will lose the capacity to criticize it, along with its distance. Perhaps the distance between art and praxis of life is a necessary free space within which alternatives to what exists can become conceivable? See Bürger, op. cit., p. 54.

17 See J. Habermas, 'Modernity Versus Postmodernity', *New German Critique*, 22, Winter 1981.

18 D. Bell, *The Cultural Contradictions of Capitalism*, New York, Basic Books, 1976.

19 Lyotard, op. cit., p. xxiii.

20 Lyotard in an interview with Christian Descamps.

21 Lyotard, op. cit., p. 37.

22 See the work of the anthropologist Robin Horton, for example, 'African Traditional Thought and Western Science', in B. Wilson (ed.), *Rationality*, Oxford, Basil Blackwell, 1970.

23 F. Jameson, 'Postmodernism, or the Cultural Logic of Capital', *New Left Review*, No. 146, July/August 1984.
24 Bürger, op. cit., p. 69.
25 For debates between Ernst Bloch, Georg Lukács, Bertolt Brecht, Walter Benjamin and Theodor Adorno see *Aesthetics and Politics*, with an afterword by Fredric Jameson, London, New Left Books, 1977.
26 For a concise description of Adorno's position see G. Rose, *The Melancholy Science: An Introduction to the Thought of Theodor W. Adorno*, London, Macmillan, 1978. See particularly chapter 6, 'The Dispute over Modernism'.
27 See W. Benjamin, 'What is Epic Theatre?', in *Illuminations*, London, Fontana, 1973.
28 The rhetoric of liberation has been denounced with passionate ambivalence by M. Foucault in *History of Sexuality; Volume One: An Introduction*, London, Allen Lane, 1979. Totality and totalization have also been rejected by many contemporary theorists; see M. Jay, *Marxism and Totality: The Adventures of a Concept from Lukács to Habermas*, Oxford, Polity Press, 1984.
29 Lyotard, op. cit., p. 60.
30 R. Rorty, 'Habermas and Lyotard on Post-modernity', *Praxis International*, vol. 4, No. 1, April 1984, p. 40.

CONCLUSION

1 F. Jameson, *The Political Unconscious: Narrative as a Socially Symbolic Act*, London, Methuen, 1981. For a useful introduction to this book see W. Dowling, *Jameson, Althusser, Marx*, London, Methuen, 1984.
2 Jameson claims that political criticism is the absolute horizon of all interpretation. Literary works are to be grasped not primarily as objective structures but as *symbolic* practices.
3 It has been remarked that Jameson's typical intellectual habit is to consider two or more apparently incompatible theses, show how each is symptomatic of a real historical condition and thus try to dissolve the contradictions between them. See T. Eagleton, 'The Idealism of American Criticism', *New Left Review*, No. 127, May/June 1981, pp. 60–5.
4 Jameson, *New Left Review*, No. 146, p. 58.
5 E. Mandel, *Late Capitalism*, London, Verso, 1978, p. 184.
6 Jameson, *New Left Review*, No. 146, p. 57.
7 For a study of the genealogy of the concept of hegemony see E. Laclau and C. Mouffe, *Hegemony and Socialist Strategy: Towards a Radical Democratic Politics*, London, Verso, 1985.
8 See the articles by Habermas, Jameson and Said and others in the anthology edited by H. Foster, *Postmodern Culture*, London, Pluto Press, 1985.
9 O. Negt and A. Kluge, *Öffentlichkeit und Erfahrung*, Frankfurt-on-Main, 1972.

Notes on Further Reading

This book is intended as a starting point for further thought. If you want to explore a topic look up the references in the *Notes*, where I have mentioned all the texts I have used, quoted or discussed. There are, however, some additional books that I would like to mention.

LACAN AND PSYCHOANALYSIS

For a most useful exposition of Lacan's main writings see Bice Benvenuto and Roger Kennedy, *The Works of Jacques Lacan: An Introduction*, London, Free Association Books, 1986. The book discusses Lacan's texts from the early works to the works of the mid-1970s in chronological order. Also helpful is Juliet Flower MacCannell, *Figuring Lacan: Criticism and the Cultural Unconscious*, London, Croom Helm, 1986. An indispensable (but expensive) book is Jean Laplanche and Jean Baptiste Pontalis, *The Language of Psychoanalysis*, London, The Hogarth Press, 1973; this is a work of encyclopaedic scholarship, a dictionary of articles which discusses almost 300 Freudian concepts. The key theme of Elizabeth Wright, *Psychoanalytic Criticism: Theory in Practice*, London, Methuen, 1984, is the relationship between different psychoanalytic theories and theories of art and literature. It is an excellent introduction to Freud, Klein and Lacan.

Is it true that Lacan spent so much of his time on theory

that he lost touch with clinical practice? And is the theory so intellectual that it neglects emotion and affect? I found Stuart Schneiderman, *Jacques Lacan: the Death of an Intellectual Hero*, Harvard University Press, 1983, a valuable account on this and other matters. He writes sensitively about death and its symbolization, the relation of the dead and the living, and the importance of Sophocles' *Antigone* for our understanding of ethical conduct. The author describes the organization of the École Freudienne and justifies Lacan's practice of the short session.

While Lacan does not neglect the question of power I think it could be said that he does not seriously consider that there may be systems of meanings that promote or mask relations of force. Freud held the Enlightenment view that the conquest of the irrational by the rational, of compulsion by freedom was possible. Lacan, on the other hand, seems to think that any sort of autonomy or self-determination is not possible. Is he justified in thinking this?

DERRIDA AND DECONSTRUCTION

Throughout his work Derrida hints at a complicity between the fundamental assumptions of Western thought and the violences and repressions which have characterized Western history, but the nature of this link is never really made explicit. One major reason for this is the disanalogy between texts and institutions, and Derrida's consequent inability to give an appropriate account of the latter. On the one hand, Derrida recognizes that institutions are powerful forces but this view contradicts his contention that there is no 'outside of the text'. Surely deconstruction is concerned with logical contradictions, to which political antagonisms cannot be reduced?

For an opposing view see the lucid study by Christopher Norris, *Derrida*, London, Fontana, 1987. According to Norris, Derrida is against the idea that there is some realm of pure textuality beyond the claims of political or ethical life. Derrida demands that we try to think beyond such disabling assumptions as those which would treat 'the world' and 'the text' in binary, disjunctive terms. He tries to demonstrate that Derrida's readings of Nietzsche and Freud insist on the 'worldly' consequences that follow from the act of writing, and he goes on to claim that there is an ethical dimension to Derrida's writing. In his view, deconstruction may have had such a great impact in the United States because it possesses a written constitution whose principles are yet open to all manner of far-reaching judicial review (for example, racial equality, civil rights, etc.). This gives a political edge to questions of textual and interpretative theory that they do not have in the British cultural context. Norris is particularly clear on the differences between Derrida and Foucault. Foucault's extreme epistemological scepticism leads him to equate knowledge with power, and hence to regard all forms of enlightened progress (in psychiatry, sexual attitudes or penal reform) as signs of increasing social control. Derrida, by contrast, insists that there is no opting out of that post-Kantian enlightenment tradition. It is only by working persistently *within* that tradition, but *against* some of its ruling ideas, that thought can muster the resistance required for an effective critique of existing institutions.

FOUCAULT AND THE SOCIAL SCIENCES

Foucault's work is attracting increasing attention, and there are a number of helpful commentaries. I recommend the selection of writings in Paul Rabinow, ed., *The Foucault Reader*, Harmondsworth, Penguin, 1986. The book by Hubert Dreyfus and Paul Rabinow, *Michel Foucault: Beyond Structuralism and Hermeneutics*, Brighton, Harvester Press, 1982, is a clear exposition. Part II which deals with the shift in Foucault's work from discourse to power is particularly useful. The authors continually compare Foucault's thought with that of Heidegger, Wittgenstein and Kuhn. There is, indeed, a striking similarity between Kuhn's account of normal science and Foucault's account of normalizing society. However, the authors tend to be uncritical and completely ignore the political implications of Foucault's work. A well-known book is Mark Cousins and Athar Hussein, *Michael Foucault*, London, Macmillan, 1984. Peter Dew's scholarly book, *Logics of Disintegration: Post-structuralist Thought and the Claims of Critical Theory*, London Verso, 1987, contains an excellent account of Foucault's views on power, subjectivity, and knowledge. There is no doubt that Foucault's intention is to dissolve the philosophical link—inherited by the Marxist tradition from German idealism—between consciousness, self-reflection and freedom. He wants to deny that there remains any progressive political potential in the ideal of the autonomous subject. Foucault gives a positive account of power but if the concept is to have a critical, political edge, there must be some principle, force or entity which 'power' crushes or subdues, and whose release from this repression is considered desirable. He neglects to tell us that which modern power represses. As Foucault cannot define what power operates against, his theory of power loses all explanatory content.

The validity of Foucault's ideas and the coherence of his position are also the main themes of the book edited by David Hoy, *Foucault: A Critical Reader*, Oxford, Basil Blackwell, 1986. It contains essays by Dreyfus and Rabinow, Hacking, Jay, Rorty, Said, Habermas and others. The most critical book is by J.G. Merquior. Merquior calls Foucault a neo-anarchist, and accuses him of negativism and irrationalism. (See J.G. Merquior, *Foucault*, London, Fontana, 1985.) He argues that in Foucault's work the historical evidence is too selective and distorted and that his interpretations are too sweeping and biased. He is devoid of any vision of non-alienated social relations. And, of course, Foucault tries to demonstrate the radical discontinuity in history. But, if one denies any kind of continuity in history, then how is one to explain the possibility of writing history?

POST-STRUCTURALISM AND POSTMODERNISM

Richard Harland, *Superstructuralism*, London, Methuen, 1987, is a clear exposition of structuralism and post-structuralism but, like many other books on these topics, it ignores the fact that ideas have a *political* dimension, that they arise in certain contexts and have certain social and ideological effects.

For post-structuralists, unity and universality are inherently oppressive and any move which promotes their disintegration is to be approved. It is assumed that once the aspiration to universality is abandoned, what will be left is a harmonious plurality of unmediated perspectives. But this sort of Nietzschean pluralism or perpectivism is fundamentally inconsistent because, in fact, the right to difference can only be upheld by universal principles.

There is a useful discussion of Nietzsche, the chief forerunner of 'postmodern' reactions against the spirit of modern culture, in J.G. Merquior, *From Prague to Paris: A Critique of Structuralist and Post-Structuralist Thought*, London, Verso, 1986.

The book by Jean-François Lyotard and Jean Loup Thébaud, *Just Gaming*, Manchester University Press, 1986, is interesting because it represents a break with Lyotard's earlier Nietzscheanism. In the book Lyotard states that it is not true that the search for intensities or things of that type can ground politics because there is the problem of injustice. (Indeed, the book should be entitled 'Just about Justice'.) There is an excellent discussion of Lyotard's *early* work in the book I mentioned above, Peter Dews's *Logics of Disintegration*. Despite the distinction between the vocabulary of forces and power and that of libido and drives, the homology between the arguments of Lyotard and Foucault is unmistakable. They both stress that life cannot be grasped from any single, comprehensive perspective. In both cases, it is Nietzsche who provides the inspiration for a post-Hegelian and post-Marxist position.

For a useful overview of this area—from Sartre, through structuralism, to post-structuralism—see Vincent Descombes, *Modern French Philosophy*, Cambridge University Press, 1980.

For post-modernists it is the project of the Enlightenment that has to be deconstructed, the autonomous epistemological and moral subject that has to be decentred; the nostalgia for unity, totality and foundations that has to be overcome; and the tyranny of representational thought and universal truth that has to be defeated. As a result of this frontal attack there has been a breakup of any consensus as to what philosophy is. See, for example, Kenneth Baynes, James Bohman and Thomas McCarthy (eds), *After Philosophy: End or Transformation*, The MIT Press, 1987, which contains essays by Derrida, Foucault, Lyotard and others.

For both Lyotard and Foucault the fundamental object of attack is Hegelian Marxism. They are both implicitly but insistently against the Enlightenment tradition. Habermas, in contrast, is critical of the post-structuralists and defends the Enlightenment project. This fascinating debate can be followed in Richard J. Bernstein (ed.), *Habermas and Modernity*, Cambridge, Polity Press, 1985. Habermas sees himself as a rational progressivist and describes Foucault, Deleuze and Lyotard as 'neo-conservative'. While the post-structuralists see universalism as a mask of dogmatism, Habermas sees it as a rational guarantee of truth. There are critical analyses of Foucault, Derrida and Lyotard in Jürgen Habermas, *The Philosophical Discourse of Modernity*, Cambridge, Polity Press, 1988. Habermas argues that Foucault and others have replaced the repression/emancipation model founded by Marx and Freud with an analysis of a plurality of discursive and power formations which cannot be differentiated according to their validity. Habermas points out that demystifying culture only makes sense if we preserve a standard of truth capable of telling theory from ideology, knowledge from mystification. In short, while most of the post-structuralists systematically disparage the Enlightenment (and its heir Marxism), Habermas, wanting to 'complete' the Enlightenment project, stresses the possibility of human liberation.

Index

Adorno, Theodor, 77, 136–8,
  156, 161
allegory, 135
Althusser, Louis, 1, 2, 3, 6,
  55, 78, 83–5, 107, 157, 158
art, 126–9, 135, 137
avant-garde, 128–9, 135,
  136–7

Benjamin, Walter, 135
Bentham, Jeremy, 75
Benton, Ted, 85, 157
Berman, Marshall, 105, 158
binary oppositions, 41, 43, 50,
  56, 57, 59, 164
Brecht, Bertolt, 136, 137
Bürger, Peter, 126–9, 160

capitalism, 77, 114, 145, 146
class, 82, 87, 89, 93, 99, 100,
  104, 110, 111, 112, 113,
  143, 144
confession, 78, 79
confinement, 66–7

deconstruction, 34, 37, 40, 56,
  57, 58–9, 60, 61, 62, 163,
  164
Deleuze, Gilles, and Guattari,
  Félix, 96, 99–104, 158
demand (Lacan), 24, 25, 153

Derrida, Jacques, 2, 3, 12,
  34–62, 96, 104, 154, 163,
  164
Descartes, René, 1
desire (Lacan), 20, 21, 24, 25,
  28, 30, 100, 101, 102, 104,
  153, 154
Dews, Peter, 83, 157, 159,
  165
différance (Derrida), 48
discourse, 70, 73, 80, 87, 88,
  105, 144
dreams, 11, 18, 46, 47

Eagleton, Terry, 59, 61, 62,
  154, 156, 159
education, 23, 124–5, 147
ego, 8, 11, 15, 17, 47
Enlightenment, 130, 131, 147,
  163, 164, 167

fascism, 100
forte-da game, 9, 27, 28
Foucault, Michel, 2, 4, 54–5,
  60, 63–95, 96, 105, 106,
  111, 112, 133, 139, 140,
  156, 157, 158, 164, 165,
  167
fragmentation, 103, 107, 108,
  132, 134, 144, 150

Freud, Sigmund, 6, 8, 9, 17, 18, 19, 20, 45, 46, 47, 49, 75, 78, 101, 105, 142, 153, 154, 155, 162, 163, 167

genealogy, 63–4, 88
Gramsci, Antonio, 147

Habermas, Jürgen, 105, 138, 155, 158, 167
Hegel, Georg W. F., 4, 6, 7, 16, 20, 22, 56, 63, 96–9, 132, 136, 153
Heidegger, Martin, 35, 49, 164
Hill, Christopher, 54
history, 2, 32, 63, 64, 81, 90, 93, 98–9, 106, 115, 141–3, 145, 150, 165
Husserl, Edmund, 4, 37, 38, 39, 49, 154

ideology, 40, 41, 83, 84, 85, 87, 88, 143, 144, 150
imaginary (Lacan), 27, 29, 30, 102, 112
intellectuals, 88, 105, 106, 109, 136
interpretation, 60, 101, 142, 143
intertextuality, 58, 59
Irigaray, Luce, 32

Jameson, Fredric, 32, 133, 141–6, 154, 156, 160, 161

Kant, Immanuel, 114
Klein, Melanie, 30, 162
knowledge, 70, 71, 73, 76, 81, 82, 85, 94, 97, 117, 118–25, 138, 149–50
Kojève, Alexandre, 20, 23, 153

Lacan, Jacques, 2, 3, 6–33, 47, 48, 102, 103, 107, 111, 112, 134, 152, 153, 154, 162, 163
lack (Lacan), 25, 28
Language, 3, 4, 7, 9, 10, 11, 12, 13, 27, 28, 30, 31, 35, 36, 37, 47, 50, 51, 52, 54, 57, 59, 61, 107, 118, 119–20, 134, 144
Lévi-Strauss, Claude, 1, 2, 10, 31, 43, 44, 152
literature, 51, 59, 143
logocentrism, 39, 40, 41, 44, 45, 48, 60
love, 16, 24, 25, 26, 28, 33, 114
Lukács, Georg, 136–8, 146, 158
Lyotard, Jean-François, 5, 96, 106–8, 117–25, 131–3, 134, 138–40, 158, 159, 160, 166

madness, 8, 65, 66, 67, 68, 69, 72, 83, 102–3
Mandel, Ernest, 145, 161
Marcuse, Herbert, 127, 160
Marx, Karl, 3, 6, 54, 61, 78, 81, 86, 94–5, 96, 98, 99, 101, 105, 107, 109, 110, 113, 132, 141, 167
Marxism, 1, 2, 3, 33, 60, 61, 85, 86–8, 94, 99, 100, 101, 106, 107, 109, 110, 113, 115, 116, 123, 132, 135, 139, 141, 142, 144, 145, 147
master and slave, 16, 20, 21, 22, 24
master narratives, 100, 131, 132–3, 139, 141, 142
May '68, 6, 7, 106, 107, 110, 113, 115

metaphor and metonymy, 11, 13, 18, 46, 47, 50, 51, 52, 53, 54, 55, 57, 148, 155
mirror phase, 10, 15, 27, 29, 30
modernization, 70, 148
montage, 135

narratives, 120–1, 122–3, 132, 133, 141–2
nature–culture, 18, 41, 42, 44, 48
need, 24, 25
'new philosophers', 109, 111–16, 131
Nietzsche, Friedrich, 4, 5, 49, 50, 51, 58, 61, 63, 65, 73, 76, 81, 83, 93, 96–8, 108, 115, 116, 139, 149, 155, 166
Norris, Christopher, 61, 156, 163, 164

Oedipus complex, 10, 19, 27, 28, 30, 101
Panopticon, 75, 76, 83, 89
pastiche, 133, 144–5
phallus, 19, 28, 29, 30, 31, 32, 33
phenomenology, 7, 38, 48, 106
phonocentrism, 38, 40, 41, 44
Plato, 26, 51, 58
postmodernism, 117–40, 144
Poulantzas, Nicos, 91, 92, 157, 158
power, 71, 73, 74, 77, 78, 80–3, 86–7, 90–4, 101, 106, 111, 112, 113, 115, 118, 124, 149, 165

real (Lacan), 31
Rée, Jonathan, 155
Reich, Wilhelm, 79, 100, 154

Rousseau, Jean-Jacques, 42, 44

Sartre, Jean-Paul, 1, 2, 15, 16, ·111, 153
Saussure, Ferdinand de, 3, 8, 12, 35, 39, 44, 45, 152
schizophrenia, 99–100, 102, 103, 104, 134, 145
sexuality, 78–80, 157, 161
Soper, Kate, 157
sous-rature (Derrida), 35, 41, 49, 56
state, 69, 86–7, 91, 92, 93, 97, 100, 101, 109, 110, 113, 115, 116, 118, 122, 123
structuralism, 1, 2, 3, 7, 43, 80, 142, 143
supplement (Derrida), 42
Surrealists, 128–9
surveillance, 73, 74, 75, 80, 84
symbolic (Lacan), 27, 28, 29, 30, 102

technical rationality, 76, 92, 156
time, 53, 55, 133–4, 146
totality, 86, 111, 122, 134, 138, 143, 161
trace (Derrida), 36

unconscious, the, 9, 11, 13, 17, 18, 31, 47, 48, 51, 100, 101, 142, 146

Weber, Max, 76–7
will to power, 51, 96, 98, 101, 104
Winnicott, D. W., 14, 153
Wittgenstein, Ludwig, 119, 159, 164
writing, 38, 39, 41, 42, 43, 44, 45, 46, 48, 49, 58, 155